A Brit Among the Hawkeyes

A
Brit
Among the Hawkeyes

Richard, Lord Acton

IOWA STATE UNIVERSITY PRESS / AMES

RICHARD, LORD ACTON holds B.A. and M.A. degrees from Trinity College, Oxford, and qualified as a barrister at the Inns of Court School of Law in London. He has lived and worked in England, Africa, and America. Over the last ten years his writing has appeared in numerous Iowan, American, and British publications. Acton and his wife, Patricia, are coauthors of the award-winning book *To Go Free: A Treasury of Iowa's Legal Heritage* published by the ISU Press in 1995.

Designed by Kathy J. Walker

GRATEFUL ACKNOWLEDGMENT IS MADE FOR THE FOLLOWING PERMISSIONS:
"The Magic of Undiscouraged Effort: The Death Penalty in Early Iowa, 1838–1878,"
©1991 State Historical Society of Iowa;
"'Hawkeye': What's in a Name?" ©1989 State Historical Society of Iowa;
"The Grandeur of Westminster Hall," © 1998 Cowles Magazine, Inc.;
"A Rip Van Winkle at Trinity College, Oxford," ©1998 Cowles Magazine, Inc.;
"London's Ancient Inns of Court," ©1995 Cowles Magazine, Inc.;
"A Curtsy for the Queen,"© 1994 Cowles Magazine, Inc.

♾ Printed on acid-free paper in the United States of America

First edition, 1998

International Standard Book Number: 0-8138-2190-8

IOWA STATE UNIVERSITY PRESS
2121 South State Avenue, Ames, Iowa 50014
Orders: 1-800-862-6657
Office: 1-515-292-0140
Fax: 1-515-292-3348
Web site: www.isupress.edu

LIBRARY OF CONGRESS CATALOGING-IN-PUBLICATION DATA
Acton, Richard, Lord
A Brit among the Hawkeyes / Richard, Lord Acton. — 1st ed.
p.   cm
ISBN 0-8138-2190-8 (acid-free paper)
1. Iowa—Social life and customs—Anecdotes.
2. London (England)—Social life and customs—Anecdotes.
3. Acton, Richard, Lord—Anecdotes. I. Title.
F625.A28 1998   98-3666
977.7—dc21

The last digit is the print number: 9 8 7 6 5 4 3 2

For Patricia

Contents

Lost Youth

Lords, Commons, and Crown

America, America

Bits and Pieces

Fragments of Iowa's Past

Foreword

MAY I INTRODUCE A FRIEND?

RICHARD GERALD LYON-DALBERG-ACTON, Fourth Baron Acton, is known to Iowans as that British lord who has written whimsical features about his observations on Iowa life for *The Des Moines Register* and *The Christian Science Monitor*'s radio broadcasts. In 1988, Richard married Patricia Nassif, a professor of law at the University of Iowa, and began spending half the year in Cedar Rapids and the other half in London while Parliament was in session. I first became acquainted with Richard when my secretary buzzed and informed me, "The Lord is on line two. Do you want to take the call now, or shall I put him on hold?" Nurtured through Baptist Sunday school as I had been, I took the call.

Acton often presents himself as a somewhat befuddled visitor to the Hawkeye State, doing battle with an ATM machine, struggling to understand a baseball game, or finding splendor in Iowa staples like pumpkin pie, Halloween, and supermarkets. Why, he asks, are you Iowans so obsessed with the weather? The Lord Acton we meet in the morning paper is the well-mannered guest who astutely keeps the conversation on topics that interest and delight his hosts.

Were these features all that we knew about Richard Acton, we might dismiss him as a literary lightweight, an author with a short shelf life though good for an occasional chuckle. But if we did dismiss him, it would be a mistake. The articles in this collection—from a variety of American and British publications—reveal a man with a keen intellect and a passion for history. We see in these chapters a Richard Acton who struggles with the legacy of decades of racial injustice. Read his moving account of the end of apartheid written by a white man who spent his childhood in a racially divided society. When he discovered that the first case to come before the Iowa Territorial Supreme Court concerned the status of a former slave who claimed freedom when he came to Iowa, he tracked down new evidence on the parties involved and wrote a lively account of the episode for an Iowa history journal. He and Patricia are currently writing a chapter on the legal history of black Iowans for a forthcoming anthology.

Trained in history and the law, Acton understands that tradition and past experience can provide a valuable perspective from which to view contemporary problems. What these writings also reveal is a man who promotes a fundamental code of civility in human conduct. The subject screams at us in his writings about Iowa, but we may have dismissed it on the assumption that he was "just being nice." Iowa is a civil society, Acton tells us; appreciate it! There is a fundamental decency in the state, which Iowans take for granted but which is a precious commodity in a world growing increasingly crowded and impersonal.

Richard was born in England in 1941, the third child and first son of Lord and Lady Acton. In 1948, the family moved to a farm in Southern Rhodesia, then a British colony but since 1980 the independent nation of Zimbabwe. By 1954 there were ten children in the Acton family happily romping around "M'bebi," the name given to the farm. By coincidence the corn-hogs agriculture that today surrounds Richard in Cedar Rapids reflects what he knew as a child on M'bebi. Acton ascribes his analytical approach to situations in part to his academic training by Jesuits in the private Catholic academy he attended in Salisbury, Rhodesia. Returning to England for college, Acton received BA and MA degrees in modern history at Oxford University's Trinity College and would later qualify as a barrister.

In 1964, Acton returned to Rhodesia to work in private business. After subsequent careers in banking and law in London, he offered his services as a senior law officer for the civil service of the newly independent Zimbabwe. In doing so, Richard became one of the very few whites who volunteered to work for the new black government. As he put it simply, "I felt I owed something." In his government position, he toured the United States on an official visitor program and committed the one sin for which Iowans find it difficult to forgive him. When he was in Nebraska studying this nation's only unicameral legislature, that body voted to make him an Honorary Citizen of Nebraska—and he accepted!

In 1989, Richard's father died, and Richard assumed his family's hereditary seat in the House of Lords. Tradition is an important part of who Richard is, and he enjoys explaining the intricate details of parliamentary customs and history or tracing the Dalberg branch of his family back to the eleventh century. Richard's great-grandfather, the first Lord Acton, made the family name famous by the astute observation that became known as Acton's Law: "Power tends to corrupt, and absolute power corrupts absolutely." (After they got to know him, his college friends at Oxford adapted it slightly: "Power tends to corrupt, but Richard Acton is absolutely corrupt.") But he also regards his seat in the House of Lords as a serious responsibility. He makes it his business to study and question legislation and policy on juvenile offenders, the probation service, mental health, and unemployment as well as the Commonwealth and South Africa.

His respect for tradition also inspired him as a historian. In 1995, Iowa State University Press published *To Go Free: A Treasury of Iowa's Legal Heritage* that he and Patricia coauthored, a carefully researched and very readable survey of milestones that have shaped Iowa law. The book won the State Historical Society's Shambaugh Award as the best book of the year on Iowa history. When nobody could tell him for sure why Iowa came to be known as the Hawkeye State, Richard took up residence in the Iowa City library of the State Historical Society. The result is a well-crafted account of the efforts of a Burlington lawyer to establish a positive nickname before Iowans suffered the fate of the citizens of Illinois and Missouri who had become known respectively as Suckers and Pukes. A hallmark of Richard's historical writings is their orientation toward people, both as his subjects and his readers. Richard Acton is a master storyteller, and his accounts come alive as he probes the details of people and events.

A gift that so few adults retain from childhood, Acton takes pure delight in exploring whatever is new to him. Whether it is the Iowa State Fair or the Tower of London, Richard loves to explore. For Richard, a trip to the local Hy-Vee is an adventure. He writes with that same childlike enthusiasm. He is not writing to convince you that what he says is interesting. Like a child, he takes that for granted.

These essays reflect his joy in exploring the worlds around him. They are enriched by the extraordinary diversity of Richard's experiences. He is a fascinating tour guide to topics about which most Iowans know little, like parliamentary tradition or southern African childhood and family life. But he also points out new perspectives on the familiar, on Iowa scenes or customs so commonplace to us that we are astounded when anyone finds them worthy of comment. A man with keen powers of observation and gentle wit, Richard Acton is indeed Iowans' answer to the supplication of poet Robert Burns, another Brit, who begged: "O wad some Power the giftie gie us To see oursels as ithers see us!"

Tom Morain
ADMINISTRATOR, STATE HISTORICAL SOCIETY OF IOWA

A Brit Among the Hawkeyes

Finding Myself in Iowa

I FIRST VISITED IOWA IN 1987. The following year, I married a University of Iowa law professor in Cedar Rapids and lived happily ever after. Since then, I've spent a part of each year in Iowa, mainly engaged in writing. This book is composed of essays, articles, reviews, and radio scripts, all written under the influence of Iowa and my Hawkeye bride, and nearly all written in Cedar Rapids, with the rest in London.

During the decade since my first journey to Iowa from England, I invariably have been treated with friendliness and warmth by the people of the Hawkeye state (as Iowa is so quaintly nicknamed). My accent reveals my origins to my hosts, and hence this book finds itself with the title: A Brit Among the Hawkeyes.

The introductory essay in this first chapter is written as a series of letters to my brother Edward, who is a history professor at the University of East Anglia in the English city of Norwich. He came to Cedar Rapids for our wedding, but was on a very tight schedule, as he had to get back to his university to teach. He crossed the Atlantic on Friday and recrossed it on Saturday night—his stay in Iowa was a grand total of twenty hours. The letters to him are intended to show aspects of what he missed by staying for such an absurdly short time.

The other articles in this chapter are on a medley of Iowa subjects. Some are about particularly attractive places and events, like Prairie Lights bookshop in Iowa City, the State Fair in Des Moines, and the Dvořák centenary in Spillville. Others are on subjects which, although not unusual in themselves, made a particular impression on me, like my first baseball game, investigating the inner workings of the post office at Christmas, and my happy encounters with the Iowa police.

Taken as a whole, this chapter is meant to record a small part of one Britisher's impression of the jigsaw puzzle that is Iowa.

A BRIT AMONG THE HAWKEYES

Dear Edward,

Well, here I am in Iowa ... safe, sound, and married. You asked me to write from time to time and describe my reactions to Patricia's state, and I will do my best—but you know what a hopeless correspondent I am.

Before leaving England, I surveyed everybody on the subject of Iowa. Ignorance predominated; most people just looked blank. A few muttered about Iowa potatoes. In fact, only two had anything concrete to say—a journalist mentioned the Iowa presidential caucuses, and Uncle Guy praised the Iowa Writers' Workshop.

Soon after arriving here, I was made to realise my own hopeless ignorance. I was reading about the Black Hawk War, which led to the dispossession of the Sauk and Meskwaki Indians and the settlement of Iowa. The book said of the great Sauk war chief: "Black Hawk crossed the river."

I had no idea *what* river. I asked a university professor, who collapsed with laughter and said: "The *Mississippi*, of course." Only the river of my schoolboy dreams—and I hadn't the faintest notion Iowa was within a thousand miles of it!

Your ignorant brother,
Richard

Dear Edward,

I must explode a myth: Iowa is not flat. *Kansas* is flat. Kansas is the scene of *The Wizard of Oz;* Iowa is the scene of *The Music Man*—and is decidedly *un*-flat.

Our house sits on top of a very real hill. We look across rolling bluffs and corn fields. Our lane is extremely steep—I puff up it like an ancient steam engine when I walk to collect the post.

Do you remember Felix Salten's *Bambi?* Well, I'm actually living in Bambi land. Cotton-tailed deer wander across the lawn in the morning and evening. A flock of wild turkeys scatters as we go down the drive. We have raccoons and possums and woodchucks. To Patricia and other

Reprinted from *Family Reunion: Essays on Iowa* (Iowa State University Press, 1995).

Iowans, these don't seem in the least exotic. To me, they represent so much that I imagined of America when I was a child.

Love from the hills of Iowa,
Richard

DEAR EDWARD,

Everything in Iowa seems to be called "Hawkeye"—the state itself, masses of shops, endless sports teams, and all of their fervent fans. I was driven quite mad because nobody—including my Iowa-born wife—knew *why* it was nicknamed the Hawkeye State. So I spent weeks investigating this weighty historical matter, and am now ready to make a pronouncement.

Just before Iowa became a territory in 1838, a Burlington lawyer called David Rorer coined the name. He wanted to block a horrid nickname like the "Suckers" of Illinois or, still worse, the "Pukes" of Missouri. He chose "Hawkeye"—the name of the hero in *The Last of the Mohicans*, the best-selling novel of the era. The "Hawk" part also had a ring of the great Black Hawk (of Mississippi River-crossing fame).

Rorer was a clever fellow. During 1839, he wrote wildly popular letters to newspapers in Dubuque and Davenport, eulogising Iowa and referring to its people as "Hawkeyes." He pretended to be a traveller from Michigan (a Wolverine) and signed himself, "A Wolverine Among the Hawkeyes." And Hawkeyes they have been ever since.

Now I'm thoroughly hooked on Iowa history. Obviously you must write to me by my new nom de plume ...

A Brit Among the Hawkeyes

DEAR EDWARD,

Do you remember how full Uncle Douglas was of wise sayings? One of his best was: "If you sent a telegram to every man in London that said, 'All is discovered, flee at once!'—at least half would start packing."

The Iowans I have met simply don't give one that feeling. Of course, Iowa has its share of problems. All of the modern nasties exist in its cities, though probably to a lesser extent than in many parts of America.

But in the sheltered life I lead, people seem much steadier than in London. My theory is that America is like an airplane with its wingtips in New York and Los Angeles. Those extremes plunge and soar, but the body in the middle stays relatively stable, and Iowa is the middle of the middle.

As you know all too well, in England church-going is a relatively rare occupation. In Iowa, a lot of people still do go to church. Every city has a host of churches and the whole gamut of religions. There's no established church like the Church of England, but far more people in Iowa seem to believe and practice their many religions, and maybe this adds to the stability one feels here.

Another reason could be age. Iowans have a high average age, and I suppose that the older people get, the steadier they get, although I've never really noticed that happening to me.

Anyway, for whatever reason, if Uncle Douglas had sent his telegram to the people *I've* met in Iowa, he would have been disappointed how few rushed for their suitcases.

Perhaps I am wrong. Perhaps Iowa secretly is a seething cauldron of depravity—but somehow I doubt it. I can't imagine *ever* wanting to flee.

Love, *Richard*

DEAR EDWARD,

I have just finished a week's course on essay writing at the Iowa Summer Writing Festival, and I'm high as a kite. Our group included people from Pennsylvania and California. We had a librarian from Van Horne in eastern Iowa and a playwright from Waukee in western Iowa. The ages ranged from the twenties to the sixties.

Our teacher was an Iowan essayist and poet. In fifteen minutes, she had brilliantly turned us into a unit, roaring with laughter together. We spent our time writing and talking about our writing. Then we wandered off to Iowa City restaurants and bookshops.

This is a wonderful place for writing. Apart from the Writers' Workshop, Iowa is the home of several first-class literary reviews. The state is littered with best-selling authors, fine poets, Pulitzer Prize winners and, above all, hordes of enthusiastic would-be writers.

I've come away from my class stimulated to read hundreds of books in the next year. Goodness knows there is opportunity enough. Cedar Rapids has a splendid public library, which puts the English equivalents to shame. The University of Iowa library is superb, but I'm at my happiest in the State Historical libraries in Iowa City and Des Moines.

Nothing equals the bliss of losing yourself in historical research.

I even feel inspired to write to you more often.

Love, *Richard*

DEAR EDWARD,

Today is a day of dark despair. It is the Fourth of July. Iowans are thinking about marathons, picnics, and fireworks. They are thinking about Independence from Britain and the birth of their nation.

I, on the other hand, feel more intensely English than ever. I feel totally alien, and spend as much of the day as possible with a pillow over my head, and the rest *wishing* I had a pillow over my head.

Nobody wants to begrudge these happy people their celebration. Yet my heightened sense of patriotism makes this a day I can't wait to end.

Yours from under the pillow,
Richard

DEAR EDWARD,

One of the things about life in Iowa is that you do more or less everything by motor car. For example, you drive up to a bank-teller machine to draw some cash, then you drive to one of the innumerable fast food places to buy your breakfast/lunch/dinner. If you want to go to the cinema, you just drive across town and park immediately outside. Think of London and the effort in actually getting to the cinema!

My car has become an extension of my feet. I've never once travelled by bus or train here, and I walk so little that I've grown into a fine figure of a man.

You know what a neurotic driver I am in London. Well, I'm slightly less nervous in Iowa. The state is nearly the same size as England, with only a fifteenth of the people and hence a fraction of the cars. I always maintain that two cars in Iowa is a traffic jam, which isn't quite true— but when you think of the hell of London on a Friday evening, driving is wondrously easy here. The only problem is that Iowans *will* drive on the wrong side of the road.

Iowans think nothing of driving vast distances in one go. We have been to Council Bluffs on the western border and back again to Cedar Rapids in a single day—we did 550 miles in eleven hours, but lived to tell the tale. Such a journey from London would land you somewhere in the north of Scotland and take the rest of your life.

That's enough for now. I'll just drive over to the post office and drop this letter in the drive-up post box.

Love, *Richard*

DEAR EDWARD,

Iowa life is full of mysteries. For example, the word "Iowa" has at least a dozen possible meanings. Undoubtedly the state is called after the Ioway Indians, and one translation of their name is "dusty noses." But a popular meaning is "beautiful place," and I am happy to settle for that—because it is.

Equally puzzling is the name "Des Moines"—the state's capital city. The town was preceded by the Des Moines River, which gets us nowhere. Somewhere I read that "Moines" is/are connected with monks, who are said to have lived in huts near the mouth of the river. But the general guess seems to be that "Moines" is a French abbreviation of an Indian place called Moingona.

The pronunciation is also shrouded in mystery. The French would say "Day Mwa." The English would pronounce it all out: "Dez Moinz." The Iowans end the first word something between an *e* and an *i*: "Deh" and the second word, "Moin."

I love going to "Deh Moin." It is our big city, and I get nearly the same lift when I see its State Capitol building and insurance towers rising in the distance as I do when the train pulls into London.

From Deh Moin with love,
Richard

DEAR EDWARD,

I have decided that Americans in general—and Iowans in particular—are obsessed by temperature.

When I first visited America in 1966, I was straight from colonial Rhodesia. Everybody wanted to know: "What is the mean temperature in Rhodesia?" I had *no* idea, but would gamely volunteer an answer. I would say: "23 degrees," or "... 123 degrees." People looked slightly puzzled, but relieved to have the information.

I put their questions down to the American thirst for statistics (oh, how Americans love statistics!). But Iowans are genuinely and wildly overstimulated by the daily temperature.

The winters are very cold (but not as damp as in England), and the summers are very hot (something like our summers in Africa). That seems to me to be all that one needs to know.

But no, life is not like that here. You rise in the morning and the local "meteorologist" dominates the television. The meteorologist—who carries star billing—reads the runes and pronounces on the day's weather.

With this infallible prediction ringing in your ears, you dress accordingly. Then you set out for the day, stopping for petrol or a doughnut. Everybody you meet says: "It's going to be a hot/cold one today." You agree and drive on.

As you drive, the radio meteorologist tells you endlessly what the temperature is all over Iowa. By now you pine for a fresh topic, but all you get on other radio stations is yet another meteorologist telling you yet another set of temperatures.

When you arrive at your destination, you park and walk down the street. Outside every bank a sign displays the current temperature. I can't think why—it's far too late to change your clothes.

I once saw a man muttering outside a bank. I couldn't hear what he was saying, but suspect it was: "66 degrees, and the meteorologist forecast 67 degrees!"

Have a hot/cold one.
Love, *Richard*

Dear Edward,

One of the discoveries I have made here is the joy of the supermarket. A chain of supermarkets called "Hy-Vee" is strung across the state. Our local one seemed to spring up overnight. I returned from London and a huge white temple of consumerism rose from a vast tarmac car park.

We duly attended the grand opening, and the first person we met was Miss Teen Iowa. Like most Iowans, she was friendly and open and had nothing about her that said, "I am a star."

Our supermarket is roughly the size of Alaska. Endless shelves in endless aisles groan with every sort of food and household convenience, an astonishing contrast to the bare shelves in Zimbabwe. I assumed that to get about I would need one of those little electric trolleys that cart elderly people around airports.

But you soon get used to the size and profusion, and our Hy-Vee has become a home from home. You run into masses of people you know, and you stop and chat and nosily eye their shopping. I've decided that Hy-Vee is the modern equivalent of the medieval village.

Hy-Vee has a cafeteria legendary for its 99-cent breakfasts. You give your first name to order breakfast, so everybody greets me with "Hello, Richard." When Cedar Rapids had an ice storm and my car slithered to a terrifying halt on the hill nearby, I took refuge in that cafeteria for *nine* hours—possibly a world record.

I wheel my trolley from the cafeteria to the bakery. When I was writing an article about the Dvořák centenary in the Iowa Czech town of Spillville, the key problem was the spelling of the greatest Czech pastry. The consensus at the Hy-Vee bakery at 6:00 A.M. one Sunday morning was that strictly speaking "kolach" was more accurate than "kolache."

The manager is a staunch ally. He has rescued my bank card when swallowed by the nefarious banking machine, and my car when the stupid owner left the lights on and flattened the battery. "Hello, Lord," he always says.

The greatest miracle is the check-out counter. Unlike England, you don't have to pack up your own purchases or carry them to the car—everything is done for you. And best of all, the cashiers are enthralled by my accent. "*Please* go on talking," they say. "We just *love* your accent." After a lifetime of people trying to silence me, I oblige with gusto.

Love from your garrulous brother,
Richard

DEAR EDWARD,

You ask me how I like my double life in England and Iowa, and what it is that makes me want to spend so much of the year here.

Well, the worst thing about dividing your time between two worlds is the awful jet lag. The great advantage is that you're constantly getting two different points of view.

What is it that makes me so happy in this far-away place? Obviously, Patricia is the reason that I'm here at all—and you don't need a panegyric on marriage. But the people of Iowa are also a great draw-card. They are straightforward and they are kind. Long ago I concluded that "kind" is the most important word in the English language.

In my youth, I craved excitement. But when I found it, really it was most disappointing. Now, deep in middle age, peace is what I want—peace tinged with stimulus. That is precisely what I find in Iowa.

If you are happily married, enjoy the people, and at last find peace, what more can you possibly hope for?

From Iowa with love,
Richard

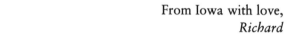

YOUR IOWA POLICE ARE WONDERFUL!

My father patriotically maintained that foreigners always said: "Your British police are wonderful!" As a barrister in the London courts, I was not so sure. Most of the police were fair. Others would do anything for a conviction. Old-fashioned notions like truth and justice seemed to elude them.

My faith was partially restored when I got bolted out of my flat. Six policemen raced round, clambered up the building, pried open a window, and unfastened the door. Brought up on the best detective stories, I asked tentatively: "Of course, you can't drink on duty, can you?" Off came six helmets. "Not have a drink!" they exclaimed. Two bottles of whiskey later, they meandered into the night.

In 1981, I returned to Harare in Zimbabwe. Crime was rampant. A long civil war had just ended, and people had swarmed into the city. There was such poverty that anything was worth stealing. A British bur-

Des Moines Register, May 6, 1990.

glar takes televisions or tape players—a Zimbabwean burglar was happy with the curtains. I ought to know, as despite burglar bars, our curtains were stolen no less than three times. On another occasion, a child was put through a tiny window at the top of a walk-in closet and all the clothes were stolen. Each time I summoned the police. Overworked, they took ages to come, and nothing was ever recovered.

Zimbabwe's most remarkable policeman was a sergeant. There had been a particularly large rash of burglaries in his suburb. Eventually he was put on the case full-time, and the burglaries increased dramatically. It took eighteen months before his superiors realized that the sergeant had been dutifully investigating his own crimes.

After a police-free interlude in Britain, I found myself in Iowa. My wife explained that one button on the telephone connected us directly to the sheriff's office. She warned that it was *strictly* for emergencies. One day, meaning to telephone Patricia's mother, I pressed the wrong button. A woman's voice said: "Sheriff's office." Horrified, I put down the receiver.

Seconds later, the telephone rang. "Sheriff's office," said the policewoman. "Did you just call us?" Nervously I stammered out my mistake. "You are British," she said. "I *love* British accents. Next time please try not to press the wrong button."

I love you, too, Iowa policewoman.

One evening I was speeding to dinner in Davenport, when a policeman signaled me to pull over. "Stay in the car and keep calm," my Iowan lawyer wife advised.

The policeman was brusque: "You were eight miles over the limit. Driving license?" I produced my licenses. "Your international license has no number," he said accusingly. I could only admit it. "Your British license has no photograph." I nodded warily—two unsatisfactory licenses sounded grim.

"I am going to give you a ticket," he said. Deferentially I asked: "When do I have to appear in court?" "You don't," he said. "This is just a warning ticket—no court, no fine, no penalty, no nothing. Have a nice evening."

Oh blessed Iowa policeman.

The ultimate episode happened one night near a public swimming pool in Cedar Rapids. Late as usual, I left my wallet at home. I had my swim and then, unsure of my bearings, drove carefreely the wrong way down a one-way street. I noticed some flashing in my mirror—in a daze,

I thought that there must be evildoers about. It never occurred to me that the flashes had anything to do with me. A siren wailed, and I pulled up.

Lacking my wife's guidance, I got out of the car and said, "Good evening, Officer," to the vast blonde policeman. "Up against the car!" he said. "Identity. Driving license." I had none. I searched my pockets. All I could find was a comb. I clutched it like a drowning man.

Suspecting a gun, the policeman said: "Take your right hand out of your pocket VERY SLOWLY." I did so. He reached in and pulled out the comb.

Satisfied that I was not an armed robber, we moved on to the question of whether I was a car thief. "Who owns the car?" "My wife." "Where are the registration papers?" I flailed around in the car, but couldn't find them.

The officer radioed from his car. "The car is not reported stolen," he announced cheerfully. "Where do you live?" I gave my local and British addresses. "What do you do?" "I am a writer in Iowa and a member of the House of Lords in Britain." "Can you prove any of this?"

All I could find in the car by way of evidence was an ancient copy of the *Des Moines Register* and a wet bathing suit. I explained that I had been swimming. It all sounded so improbable. I felt foreign and lonely.

"Well," said the policeman. "I am going to believe you. *No one* could fake that British accent. *No one* could make up such an unlikely story."

Then he said helpfully: "As you are a foreigner, I'm going to give you some advice. Don't drive the wrong way down one-way streets. When you see a police car light flashing, stop at once. Always carry your driver's license and registration. Never get out of your car when you are stopped by an officer." Then he grinned. "Don't worry about it, drive home carefully."

I sat in the car shaking with relief. I was not going to be arrested; Patricia was not going to have to put up bail; the newspapers were not going to scream: "British Lord Arraigned!"

Your Iowa police are wonderful!

THE MAGIC OF THE FIELD OF DREAMS

I've always been hopeless at cricket, and baseball is completely beyond me. Yet I loved the film *Field of Dreams* and *Shoeless Joe*, the
book on which it is based.

The author, W.P. Kinsella, writes compellingly of an Iowan farmer
who hears a voice that persuades him to build a baseball field in the
midst of his corn. I was entranced by Shoeless Joe Jackson and the other
long-dead baseball legends who miraculously reappear to play on the
field. Despite all the baseball, the story is so complete that it can be rel-
ished even by those of us who are totally ignorant of the game.

Recently I was in a class of the Iowa Summer Writing Festival at the
University of Iowa. I discovered that as a feature of the festival, Kinsella
was going to lead a party of writers to the site of the movie baseball field
near Dyersville—the "Field of Dreams" itself. It was to be Kinsella's first
visit.

I thought the trip sounded too good to miss, and my wife and her
brother, both devotees of the film, decided to come along for the evening
excursion.

As our bus rolled out of Iowa City and through the cornfields,
Patricia re-read *Shoeless Joe* and my brother-in-law sat with a faraway
look in his eyes. I talked to our neighbors.

They were writers from every part of America. One of them had
come all the way from northern California by train and had deliberately
selected a class that week in order to go on the outing. Immediately behind me were seated a pair of essayists from Connecticut and Massa-
chusetts, who were equally enthusiastic about the trip. We were among
true fans.

In Dyersville, a Chamber of Commerce board proclaimed: "Official
Field of Dreams Souvenirs." Signposts along the road announced: "To
Field of Dreams." Excitement stirred as we wound along the back roads
towards our goal. Then we arrived.

The baseball diamond was there, surrounded by tall corn, but the
field was not deserted as in the movie. Local residents milled about, television crews were everywhere, and a horde of photographers and journalists marched on Kinsella.

The author was a splendid performer. He answered endless ques-

Des Moines Register, July 25, 1991.

tions, and then obligingly swung a baseball bat. Kinsella was no natural player, and he stopped after he had managed to hit the ball a few times.

Then out of the corn, as if out of the pages of *Shoeless Joe,* emerged eight baseball players dressed in old-fashioned Chicago White Sox uniforms. It transpired they were local players who materialized on the field each week.

My wife was everywhere. She asked Kinsella to sign her book, and he wrote, "Go the Distance," one of the messages of the mysterious voice in the corn field. Then she was off to the souvenir kiosk to buy a Field of Dreams T-shirt for my son in England. Next she got a Field of Dreams baseball for an Iowan friend who is mad about the game. The genial Kinsella signed the ball with his same slogan, "Go the Distance."

Peace descended, and we munched our picnic near the farmhouse. Then we wandered across the field, which is divided between two farms. After the movie had been made, the farmer who now sells the souvenirs had kept his part of the diamond in being.

The other farmer put his half back to corn. He told us how he had let people pick the corn and had set out a box marked "Donations." Visitors had given money and had slipped notes into the box: "*Please* put back the Field of Dreams." The farmer had relented, and the field was again complete, surrounded by baseball lights.

As the evening wore on, the players in White Sox uniforms waved and disappeared into the corn, never to return. Kinsella, who for two hours had been giving interviews and signing autographs, at last had time for his box supper. We left our donations for the second farmer and strolled back towards the wooden baseball stand.

Insatiable tourists, we had idiotically forgotten to bring a camera. Fortunately, a Californian friend from my earlier writing class came to the rescue. She photographed us against the farmhouse, against the baseball field, against the corn, and against Kinsella.

The light began to fade. The television crews, photographers, and journalists were long gone, and the local people had dispersed. As we left, the field looked quiet, as it had in the film.

While our bus trundled back towards Iowa City, I wondered about the reactions of the writers and poets around me. As people with imaginations, how many of them had hoped to hear a voice? How many had come away from the Field of Dreams with their own private message?

And what about me? My fiftieth birthday loomed, and I feared the shortening years. Had I not hoped to hear a heartening voice say: "There is a long distance yet to go."

I laughed out loud at my flight of fancy, because in real life you don't hear voices in Iowa cornfields.

But suddenly, fifty did not seem so very different from forty-nine.

DRIVING ON THE WRONG SIDE

When I first came to Iowa, I committed a very British sin. Once, and once only, I mistakenly drove on the left-hand side of the road. No other cars were approaching, and no police saw me. In fact, the only witness was a big black dog who, with a pained expression on its face, leapt for safety.

The incident taught me a lesson. However much I might drive on the right-hand side of the road, my instinct in a crisis would always be to swing to the left. So I resolved to drive five miles under the speed limit to give myself a margin in which to think.

Admirable though this plan may be for a British driver, it does not always go down well with Americans. The polite ones—like the big black dog—look at me with pained expressions on their faces. The less courteous drivers bare their teeth or shake their fists as they watch me amble along.

But driving in Iowa is not just a question of staying on the correct side of the road. Among the other hazards is the utterly alien practice of turning right at red lights. I still feel like a criminal whenever I perform this feat. Clenching the steering wheel and keeping an anxious lookout for the forces of law and order, I slip furtively through the light.

An even more formidable American convention is the four-way stop. I found myself daunted by the mathematics of judging which of four cars had stopped first. If I saw a car coming from any direction, I would sit tight at the stop until the car had gone, heedless of the line of

Des Moines Register, May 27, 1992.

furious traffic behind me. Nowadays I close my eyes, think of England, and go. To my amazement, the system works, and people really can be trusted not to crash into you.

However, I am less sure about the whole matter of Yield signs. In England, "Yield" means "yield"—you stop until there is no crossways traffic. A nerve-wracking experience left me wholly confused as to the meaning of Yield in this country.

One morning I was driving my wife to Iowa City. We turned off the freeway onto an exit road, at the end of which was a sign saying "Yield." A solid line of traffic was flowing from my left along the traverse road. Like a good Englishman, I stopped at the Yield sign.

From behind me came a terrible blaring noise. I looked around and saw a vast truck careening towards us with the driver pressing the horn full blast.

My wife said, "Drive!"

I said, "I can't. I must yield." The truck got closer. My wife said, "DRIVE!"

I drove.

Somehow I got onto the road and immediately pulled over on the shoulder. The traffic gave way to the truck, which sailed past me in triumph.

Trembling with fright, I turned to my wife and said, "What is this?"

She said, "The truck is King of the Road."

"But what about the law? What about the danger? What about the Yield sign? Doesn't Yield *mean* yield?"

She shrugged. "The truck is King of the Road."

I was dissatisfied with her view of the incident and, a few weeks later, told my story to a judge whom we met at a dinner. He listened gravely.

"Who was right?" I asked. "My wife or I?"

"Well," he said in a thoughtful voice. "In law, you were right. You should have yielded. But of course, if you had, the truck would have smashed into you. So as a matter of practicality, your wife was right."

Since that episode, I have treated trucks with the deepest respect. When driving on a freeway, I dodge from lane to lane to avoid all trucks. I drive my standard five miles under the speed limit, while everybody else seems to go ten miles over it. As snarling drivers pass me, I pray for a land without cars.

Recently my prayers were answered when I visited the island of Sark in the English Channel. The authorities there ban all motor vehicles, and people get about the island on bicycles or horses. I thought myself in heaven as I wobbled around the winding lanes on my bicycle.

But my idyllic vision was shattered by a sign prominently displayed outside the village church:

POLITE NOTICE

Residents are reminded of the requirement to have a front light on
their bicycles during the hours of darkness. Several reported accidents
have been noted and the constables hope that all cyclists will conform.

Clearly Sark was too dangerous a place for the likes of me. I returned to Iowa, relieved to find myself in a familiar world of careening trucks, four-way stops, and big black dogs.

WILL THE OLD CREAMERY LIGHTS KEEP BURNING?

From my first days in Iowa, I heard rumors about the glories of the Old Creamery Theatre. I was told how, twenty years ago, a group of enthusiasts had discovered an old dairy cooperative in the tiny town of Garrison and had transformed it into a professional theater. They organized a non-profit company and have been performing plays there ever since.

The idea of a theater in the countryside intrigued me, but I kept procrastinating. After all, I could always go next month, and somehow next month kept turning into next year. Then this June my wife—who takes birthdays seriously—announced that she wanted her birthday treat to be an evening at the Old Creamery Theatre.

It transpired that the company was performing a musical comedy called *First Ladies of the Stage.* I love musical theater, but it was the price of the tickets that made me smile into my shaving mirror.

Des Moines Register, July 21, 1992.

In London earlier this year, we had gone to *Carmen Jones* at the Old Vic Theatre. Each ticket had cost precisely four times the price of a seat at the Old Creamery. Indeed, allowing for tips, the taxi fares to and from the Old Vic were much the same as two Old Creamery tickets. Thankful at such a light let-off, I booked tickets for the play and dinner at the theater.

Garrison turned out to be less than an hour from Cedar Rapids. We drove there on a fine June evening, and parked outside the post office opposite the Old Creamery.

The huge red brick dairy is the least probable of settings for a theater. At the front was a courtyard where early theatergoers were picnicking at wooden tables. We lined up for pork chops cooked on an outdoor grill, and found ourselves a table. What is it about barbecued pork which makes it taste so delicious in the open air?

After dinner we strolled up a gravel street and soon came upon a cornfield. A sign outside a potter's house gave a hint of the other artists who live in Garrison. We didn't meet a single soul on our walk; the town is peace itself.

Back in the theater, our program said that members of the Old Creamery Company had written *First Ladies of the Stage,* a salute to the great women of vaudeville. Four actresses made up the cast—two were members of the company, and two were visiting performers. The great height of the old building enabled the First Ladies to clamber from dressing rooms on an upper level down long ladders to the stage.

The singing was a delight—I love old numbers like "Oh, You Beautiful Doll"—but it was the dialogue that really showed the cast's professionalism. Timing is everything in comedy, and the timing of the First Ladies was superb. The audience could often see the punch line coming, and roared with laughter when it duly arrived.

During the interval, we went out into the courtyard. Night had fallen, and a huge wood fire was burning in a raised brick hearth—so simple, and so striking.

The second act passed all too fast. The audience gave the actresses a happy ovation. As we streamed out of the theater, people seemed to glow with pleasure.

Near the embers of the fire, a man was bidding the audience goodnight. We realized he must be Thomas P. Johnson, the Producing Director of the company. Formerly on the drama faculty at Iowa State University, he has been the moving spirit behind the Old Creamery throughout its life. We went over to thank him for the magical evening.

Mr. Johnson was delightful, and managed to chat with us while cheerfully greeting other people in the audience, many of whom he knew by name. But when I asked him how the theater was doing, his tidings were grim.

Public and private support for the arts has suffered in the present economic climate. Ticket sales at the Old Creamery have declined, partly because of the recession, and partly because young people look to other forms of entertainment. Mr. Johnson said that 1991 had been a dismal year at the box office. This year will be make or break for the Old Creamery Theatre.

We promised that we would be back, and said good-night. At the Old Vic in London, we had raced hundreds of others for a taxi. In Garrison, we sauntered thirty yards to our car.

As we drove into the night, I wondered about Iowa's theater lovers. Surely many who had never got round to visiting the Old Creamery would make the effort if they knew its plight? Surely many who had already enjoyed a trip to Garrison would now return to help the Theatre survive?

I looked back and saw the lights of the Old Creamery. Surely they would still be burning this time next year?

[Author's note: The Old Creamery Theatre Company closed its Garrison theater permanently in 1996, but it continues to perform and thrive at its Amana theater.]

ALIVE IN PRAIRIE LIGHTS

Prairie Lights in Iowa City is my favorite bookshop in the whole world. All its customers seem devoted to it. Jane Smiley, one of America's leading novelists, spoke for many when she said: "I *love* Prairie Lights. Prairie Lights is [an] 'A', Number One, terrific, marvelous, first-class bookstore."

I became acquainted with Prairie Lights in 1988, soon after I got en-

Condensed from "He Brings Literary Light to the Prairie," *The Iowan* (Summer 1992).

gaged to an Iowan. My fiancée's mother parked on Dubuque Street in central Iowa City. We walked past an old-fashioned drugstore and came to an entrance painted blue. She said, "You must see this bookstore." Obediently I followed her, and was amazed at the vast array of books. I wandered about looking at titles and listening to the strains of Mozart. Eventually I decided to give my fiancée a tome called the *Metropolitan Museum of Art,* happily marked down in price.

My future mother-in-law pointed out a man sitting at a desk in the middle of the shop, constantly talking on the telephone. "That is the owner—Jim Harris," she said, and beamed. Jim Harris has a large personality, a red beard, an easy laugh, and a whirring brain. He is proud to come from the small town of Bloomfield, Iowa. Harris was born in 1946, and books were in his blood. His father, as a law student in Iowa City, had started a second-hand book business with some friends, and had infuriated the town's major bookshop by undercutting it. Jim Harris, like his father, loves books. He loves what is in them; he loves the physical objects; and he loves the transmission of ideas through them. So he abandoned his master's course in history and worked unpaid at a bookshop in Seattle.

Iowa City has a tradition of unconventional bookshops. In the late 1960s, The Paper Place attracted the allegiance of people in the Iowa Writers' Workshop. After it closed, they patronized a new bookshop called Epsteins'. Epsteins' closed in 1974, so when Jim Harris decided to enter the book trade in Iowa City in 1978, there was a natural gap and a natural clientele.

Harris opened his bookshop a few blocks from its present site. At first it was small, with comfortable chairs so customers could sit and read at their leisure. He called it Prairie Lights—"Prairie" because of Iowa, and "Lights" after "City Lights," a bookshop in San Francisco.

The shop thrived and grew. In 1983, Prairie Lights moved to its present location, and in 1990 expanded to a second floor. Today, it is a large concern which deals with 100,000 titles and has about 60,000 books on its shelves. The greatest strength of Prairie Lights is the vast choice of fiction. But there are many other fine sections—children's books, poetry, biography, women's studies, and baseball are particularly striking. (Harris is a baseball and basketball fanatic.)

Paul Ingram—one of the best-read people I have ever met—does the buying. I once watched him serve a customer who only knew one word in the title of an obscure novel she sought. Ingram identified the book, discussed it thoroughly with the customer, and then told her about all of the author's other books.

Ingram's knowledge is uncanny, but I've often been impressed to see other members of the staff go straight to a book without first checking it on the computer. You immediately sense their love of books and their genuine desire to help. Many of them are novelists, short-story writers, essayists, or poets; several are graduates of the Iowa Writers' Workshop.

The Writers' Workshop and other faculty and students in this university town form the bedrock of Prairie Lights' customers. But many townspeople also frequent the shop, and people from other cities make pilgrimages. A Louisiana student told me he had come from Baton Rouge specially to visit the shop again. Listening to Jim Harris, I am certain he knows the names and literary tastes of thousands of individual customers.

The shop has the atmosphere of a community center. Strangers smile at each other in the aisles, and acquaintances exchange greetings. I once moaned about the dearth of funny modern short stories. Jim Harris gestured towards a woman in the next aisle. "Meet Deborah Eisenberg," he said. "She writes funny and brilliant short stories." Deborah and I have been good friends ever since.

Music plays gently, and red leather arm chairs—a reminder of the original Prairie Lights—are scattered throughout the shop. Browsing is encouraged. Nobody feels guilty or rushed. I noticed one young man spend two hours reading an entire book of poetry.

The children's section is a joy. One morning I watched a little girl push her fingers into a book called *One Green Frog*. A somewhat older, bespectacled girl chose C.S. Lewis's classic *Chronicles of Narnia* and marched purposefully up to the desk to buy it. Across the aisle, a boy of about twelve went through the baseball section, book by book, looking at all the pictures.

Readings by authors from their books have always been a feature of Prairie Lights, and the tradition continues on Sundays for members of the Writers' Workshop. In addition, each Friday night since June 1990—with the aid of Dennis Reese and Julie Englander of WSUI radio—readings are broadcast from both Iowa City and Ames in a weekly program called "Live From Prairie Lights."

The Pulitzer Prize-winning poet, Galway Kinnell, and authors with an international flavor, like Calcutta-born writer Bharati Mukherjee and English novelist Julian Barnes, have read their works on "Live From

Prairie Lights." Jan Weismiller—the assistant manager of the shop and herself a fine poet—thinks the readings give a climax to the week. The anticipation, the arrival of the author, the performance, and the discussions afterwards, add to the hum of Prairie Lights.

I have attended several readings. All were theater, all were fun, all were stimulating. The reading by Donald Kaul, the *Des Moines Register* columnist, was especially enjoyable. Members of the staff cleared a space upstairs and put out chairs. People crowded in—they sat in the chairs, on the floor, and leaned against the bookcases. Kaul sat at a table reading into the radio microphone from his new book, *They're All In It Together.* He was straightforward, cynical, and funny. The audience asked questions, and the hour flashed by. People's faces shone, as they do after a good play.

As I left the bookshop that evening, I pondered what makes Prairie Lights so splendid. Perhaps the key is that Jim Harris brings to the world of the bookseller the attitudes of small-town Iowa. He and his staff treat people as if they expect to see them again the next day—and they frequently do.

I think I found the soul of Prairie Lights when I asked Jim Harris, "Are you a happy man?"

"A very happy man," he said. "And a very lucky one."

THE GREATEST FAIR ON EARTH

"You mean you have never been to the Iowa State Fair?" said the television producer in a shocked voice. The other people at that dinner table in Des Moines gave me looks of mingled surprise and pity.

"Well no," I said.

"Then you must go tomorrow," she said.

"I can't. I am doing some research at the State Historical Society tomorrow."

Des Moines Register, September 5, 1992.

"Finish it in the morning and spend the afternoon at the State Fair," the producer said decisively. She scrutinized me and then glanced around the table. "He will never find his way to the fairgrounds. Who is going to take him?"

One of our fellow guests, a woman journalist, volunteered to be my guide. My fate was sealed. I gave in with grace.

The following day I fortified myself with a hearty lunch at a Greek restaurant. That was a mistake. I had not realized that the principal purpose of visiting the State Fair was to eat as much as possible. My guide collected me after lunch, and off we drove to the fairgrounds.

Food was everywhere. Out of duty, I began with a corn dog. Out of pleasure, I moved on to other delicacies. A turkey farmer from Dike presented me with a vast drumstick; a baker from Pella pressed me with a Dutch pastry; a confectioner from Des Moines enticed me with a wonderful caramel apple.

The people at the State Fair were happy on that fine warm day. A young woman wearing a sash that said Iowa Beef Princess smiled at us. A young woman wearing a T-shirt that said PETA smiled at us. The whole world seemed to smile at us.

We wandered through growing corn that towered feet above our heads. Nearby the very latest information system for farmers was on show. Crop prices, weather forecasts, and every type of news could be displayed on screens in remote farmhouses. I had never seen anything like it.

Next we made for a cattle barn and saw splendid animals of many breeds. I noticed a group of children sitting in a cow stall, their sleeping bags close by. My mind went back to the agricultural shows of Salisbury, Rhodesia (today's Harare, Zimbabwe) in the 1950s.

For months before the Salisbury Show, my brother Robert, my sister Jill, and I would practice exhibiting the best Jersey cows and heifers on our Rhodesian farm. When show week arrived, we would haunt the cow pens, grooming our special favorites before we took them into the ring, our stomachs tight with excitement.

I grinned at the Iowa children. Some of the boys and girls had a gleam of triumph in their eyes that said: "We won a prize." Did those children realize they were grinning back at the school boy who had led Exquisite to victory in 1957 as Salisbury's Champion Young Jersey Cow?

On we went to the pig barn, which was dominated by a boar who weighed nearly 1,000 pounds. He lay on his side with his eyes closed. A small girl called, "Wake up, you lazy pig!" The boar majestically ignored her.

We never had a boar to equal that Iowa giant. But we did have Margery, the grand champion Large Black Sow of the Salisbury Show. Margery had accompanied us from England when we emigrated to Africa, and she was my father's favorite pig.

One year, when Margery farrowed, she had a litter of twenty-two piglets. That very day, my mother gave birth to her eighth child, my brother Peter. People who had heard of the baby's birth said to my father: "Congratulations, Lord Acton." My father, in an ecstasy of pride, said: "I know. Twenty-two! Isn't it wonderful?"

Leaving the colossal boar behind us, my State Fair guide and I sat down for a drink next to a farmer from Preston. He was large of body and deliberate of speech. Too polite to talk of crop prices for long, he displayed an uncanny knowledge of Second World War leaders. His comparison between Winston Churchill and General de Gaulle held us spellbound.

Refreshed, we went to inspect the agricultural implements. The range of machinery was amazing. The insides of the internal combustion engine have always mystified me, but I couldn't help but be impressed by what I saw.

With delight I came upon some green John Deere tractors. They were more elaborate than "the big tractor"—a green John Deere my father had bought at the Salisbury Show forty years ago. Nonetheless, those tractors at Des Moines clearly belonged to the same tribe as the one that gave so many years faithful service on our Rhodesian farm.

My intrepid guide saw that I was suffering from an acute case of Iowa State Fair sore feet. So she hailed a passing golf cart. The driver stopped and kindly took us on our way. He said he had been to the State Fair every year for thirty-five years, starting when he was nine months old.

Obviously I could not match such an admirable record. But when we alighted from the golf cart and waved good-bye, I looked to the future: "See you at the State Fair next year."

UNDER THE GOLDEN DOME

The British House of Lords labors mightily, and then rests for two weeks at Easter. The Iowa legislature, with the stamina characteristic of the state, works even on Easter Monday.

I chose that day to visit the state capitol. Primed with a booklet entitled *Under the Golden Dome,* I made for the Iowa Senate.

The senators warmly welcomed me on the floor of their chamber. Almost immediately a vote took place. It intrigued me that most senators cast their vote simply by pressing a buzzer at their desks. A green or red light appeared by each name on a scoreboard to signify "aye" or "nay."

Some individuals voted where they stood. Senatorial arms shot towards the heavens, and thumbs went up or down in the classic gestures of ancient Rome. The whole vote was over in a minute.

In the House of Lords, we take about eight minutes to march along the voting corridors. "March" is a relative word, as the average age is around seventy. Some peers use a walking stick, and a handful of venerable octogenarians have two sticks. Peers take a circuitous route through the chamber and wander along the outer lobbies, where tellers count the votes.

The Iowa voting system seems foolproof; ours is not. Recently no less eminent a person than Margaret, Baroness Thatcher—the former Prime Minister—succumbed to confusion and walked down the wrong corridor. She was about to vote for the opposition when a kindly peer saved her with a delicate geographic hint.

The Iowa Senate voted on various of the governor's nominees in rapid succession. Then the senators went into private party caucuses to consider a controversial nomination. As I was neither a Republican nor a Democrat—nor indeed an American—I made a strategic exit.

A friendly lobbyist shepherded me into the capitol rotunda. People were furiously puffing on cigarettes as if they would never have another. Then I remembered—the Senate had just voted to ban smoking in the rotunda. If the House of Representatives and the governor concurred, that would be the end for legislative smokers. No wonder their puffs were so desperate.

My feelings about smoking are mixed. For decades I was a cham-

Des Moines Register, April 28, 1993.

pion smoker, until three years ago the Iowa culture (and my wife) cured me. But at the House of Lords, I'm used to the library being blue with assorted pipe, cigar, and cigarette smoke. To ban smoking there would be like banning baseball in America.

I passed through the rotunda to the floor of the House of Representatives, where I received another hearty welcome. Several representatives told me that drama lay ahead.

A gambling amendment was due for debate. Among other things, the amendment would have raised the maximum individual loss from $200 to $1,000 on riverboat excursions. The Speaker of the House was expected to rule the amendment out of order. Nobody knew whether there were the fifty-one votes necessary to override him.

Various representatives alerted me to a proposed Amending Amendment where one clause wrought a miracle: " 'Excursion gambling boat' also means the grandstand of a dog or horse racetrack."

I lapsed into fantasy. If grandstands could be gambling boats, surely the rotunda could become a gambling boat, too? Couldn't smokers who enjoyed a bet alleviate their craving for nicotine by playing roulette in the rotunda?

Then it struck me that Iowa's legislators in turn would find British parliamentary language rather curious. For example, in debates the House of Commons and the House of Lords *never* call each other by name—they are always referred to obliquely as "Another Place."

Glancing around the Iowa House of Representatives, I coveted the members' amenities. The legislators each had a desk, books, newspapers and—if they liked—a cup of coffee. In Parliament, we crowd together on benches. We cannot even bring briefcases or books into the chamber. A cup of coffee would probably get us sent to the Tower of London.

In Iowa, I—a foreigner—could wander around the floor of the House cheerfully chatting to legislators, clerks, and pages. No outsider is allowed on the floor of the Houses of Parliament. In the House of Commons, the traditional cry would go up, "I spy Strangers!" Certainly the Iowa legislature is a more hospitable place for a visitor.

At long last the gambling amendment came before the Iowa House. As predicted, the Speaker disallowed it. The representatives began a vote to override him. I felt an almost irresistible impulse to raise my arm and test the glories of the voting system.

The very last representative to cast her vote gave the fifty-first vote needed to override. The Speaker looked philosophical.

Sadly, I could not stay to hear any debate on the amendment. I learned later that it was ultimately defeated. Grandstands won't be floating down the Mississippi River just yet.

Driving away from the Golden Dome, I remembered that on a fleeting visit to Lincoln in 1984, the legislature had given me a certificate making me an honorary citizen of Nebraska. After my day in Des Moines, I didn't need a certificate to make me feel like an honorary citizen of Iowa.

THE DAY SPILLVILLE RAN OUT OF KOLACHES

When the great Czech composer Antonín Dvořák sought to escape the noise of New York in the summer of 1893, he made for peace and the tiny Czech town of Spillville in northeast Iowa.

There Dvořák and his family passed an idyllic season. He found what he wanted—his own people, his own language, birds, woods, and St. Wenceslaus Catholic Church.

One hundred years later, my wife and I set out for the final day of the Dvořák centenary festival at Spillville. The composer had crossed the continent by train and ended with a buggy ride from Calmar, Iowa. We had only to drive for a couple of hours from Cedar Rapids to reach our goal.

Despite the easy journey, we arrived at St. Wenceslaus Church on Sunday, August 8, too late for the special Czech mass. Dvořák was never late. He would have been up since 4:00 A.M. listening to the birds and composing music before playing the organ at mass.

As we entered the church, the choir was singing and the Czech archbishop of Dubuque was proceeding down the aisle. The congregation burst into enthusiastic applause.

At the back of the church, two Czech-speaking women signed the visitors' book. One of them, originally from Prague, had lived for years

Des Moines Register, August 22, 1993.

in Illinois. Hearing a trumpet-trombone refrain of Dvořák's "New World Symphony," she exclaimed: "Listen! They played that at my wedding in Prague."

We left the church and wandered down to the town square. Many of the people thronging the streets were in multi-colored folk costume. Spillville's nearly 400 inhabitants all seemed to have red geraniums outside their houses.

On one of the lawns, two men were playing chess at a wooden table. On another lawn, a television showed a video about the art of baking that incomparable Czech pastry—the kolach.

Overcome by hunger, we made for the Old World Inn. Inside, two violinists produced music. Our young waitress told us she was Spillville Czech, but could not speak the language. She added helpfully, "I *do* know some Czech swear words, though."

As we attacked the dinner of roast pork and dumplings, our table companions enthused over the festival. A Minnesotan summed up Dvořák: "He is the warmest composer in the world."

After lunch my wife watched Czech folk dancers, while I visited the house where Dvořák spent his summer. Downstairs are the remarkable wooden clocks carved by two legendary Spillvillians—the Bily brothers.

Upstairs in the Dvořák exhibit, the composer's reflection on the town is prominently displayed: "The three months spent here in Spillville will remain a happy memory for the rest of our lives."

Near the exit was a guest book signed by visitors to the festival from all over America. There also were names from Spain, Germany, India, France, Belgium, Mexico and—proudly—the Czech Republic. I hastily added Britain.

Back with my wife, we suddenly realized a great gap in our lives. We had not eaten a single kolach. The man at the kolach stand by the kolach-making video was sorry—he was sold out. Not a kolach was to be had in the square. The Czech Historical Research Center sold delicacies—but no kolaches. They directed us to the school.

Outside the school, the tables groaned with food. But nothing resembled a kolach. Desperate, we went into the school kitchen. The manageress was apologetic. "We've wanted kolaches for the staff for the last hour. There is not one kolach left."

For the first time in the history of Spillville, the town had run out of kolaches.

Exhausted by the great kolach hunt, we went and sat on the grass.

From the church nearby came the sound of a piano; from the town square drifted the sound of a brass band.

The evening was the climax, with the closing concert in St. Wenceslaus. A dazzling string quartet from Prague played some of Dvořák's most beautiful works, including the "American" Quartet, Opus 96, composed in Spillville. The third movement twitters with the sounds of the scarlet tanager—a red bird with black wings that the composer had heard in the Iowa woods.

In the sunlight at intermission, a friendly Spillvillian pointed down the steep slope on which St. Wenceslaus stands. "My grandfather and the men brought limestone in wagons down there," he said. "My grandmother and the women carried the stones up this hill to build the church."

Back inside St. Wenceslaus, the soaring music made me think of Dvořák and the musicians and the incredible effort of Spillville in mounting the festival. The rapt faces of the audience brought to mind my music-loving father.

At a lunch party in his old age, my father discussed music with a rather arrogant conductor. Eventually the conductor asked: "Sir, to what part of the musical world do you belong?" My father squared his shoulders. "I belong to the most important part—I'm a member of the audience."

I think that is how everyone there will remember the Dvořák Centenary. We will say proudly: "We were at Spillville in 1993. We were members of the audience."

AMERICA'S ONLY PLUM PUDDING RIDES THE CHRISTMAS MAIL

If Scrooge had sent a Christmas present to the editorial writers of the *Des Moines Register*, he would have used a horse and sleigh. I chose the United States Mail. Longing to fathom the mysteries of the post

Des Moines Register, December 23, 1993.

office, I determined to track my parcel from Cedar Rapids to Des Moines.

The parcel—wrapped in shiny green paper—held something unique. Everybody knows the legend about the only fruitcake in America. Well, my parcel was even better—it contained the only English plum pudding in America.

A plum pudding has much the same gooey ingredients as a fruitcake. The whole sticky mass is glued together by beef kidney suet and then boiled in a cloth for eight hours. My plum pudding originally had come from Harrods in London, and for two years had lain in my mother-in-law's deep freeze, aging nicely.

Thus armed, I presented myself at the Cedar Rapids post office at 4:30 one dark December afternoon. Priority mail came to $2.90.

I had pictured mountains of parcels in the delivery area, but automation has changed all that. Machines were everywhere. The distribution manager located my green parcel on a conveyor. A clerk lobbed it into a high wheeler, which we pushed to the pouching area.

There my parcel disappeared into an orange priority mail sack. I left it, and rushed home for supper.

Back at the post office at 8:00 P.M., I met my truck driver. "Just follow this trailer—blue number 412259," he said.

The orange sack vanished into the truck. The driver sealed the door with an aluminum strip, and we were off.

I had no difficulty in keeping blue #412259 in sight. Soon we were on I-80 from Iowa City to Des Moines—surely the most boring stretch of road in the entire universe.

For those of us with voices like old crows, I-80 is ideal for singing purposes. Radio blaring, the great soprano Kathleen Battle and I sang a memorable duet of "O Come All Ye Faithful."

Our convoy stopped in Malcom to gulp a cup of coffee. After a few minutes, the driver looked at his watch: "Time to go. We will arrive at 10:55."

He was one minute wrong. We reached the main Des Moines post office at precisely 10:56 P.M. Solemnly, the driver broke the trailer's aluminum seal. There was my orange sack—the plum pudding had reached Des Moines.

A man wheeled a cage containing my sack along the post office floor, which was roughly the size of France. Letters on automatic machines were whizzing in every direction.

At the sorting area, a worker emptied the contents of the sack onto a conveyor. A row of clerks plucked parcels from the conveyor and checked their zip codes. With astonishing accuracy, they skimmed the parcels into a series of hoppers—one for each Des Moines postal area.

When its hopper was full, the green parcel was wheeled over to dispatch. A woman supervisor put it in a canvas bag, fastened it with wire, and wrote: "R.& T." on its label. "What's R.& T.?" I asked. "Register and Tribune," everybody chorused.

I went on a quick tour of France. At the most dramatic machine, several clerks were checking post codes on letters, which raced before their eyes at the rate of one per second.

Towards midnight, feeling a traitor, I slunk off to a hotel. Visions of blue #412259 danced in my head, while ghostly green parcels floated round the room. By 3:45 A.M., I was hurrying back to the post office through a lifeless Des Moines.

The postal workers grinned at me—they must have thought me ragingly eccentric. But being courteous Iowans, they gave no hint that it was peculiar for an Englishman to chase a parcel through Des Moines at 4:00 A.M.

A driver loaded the "R.& T." canvas sack onto his mail van. I bid farewell, and followed the van to the 15th and Grand Avenue delivery center—the Metro Annex.

The supervisor welcomed me and the canvas sack. He took out the green plum pudding and put it on a desk. Mail carriers appeared. They greeted me, punched the clock, and started sorting their day's delivery.

Towards 6:00 A.M., overcome by great gusts of hunger, I went downtown and ate a breakfast worthy of the occasion. By 8:00, I was back at the Metro Annex.

My heart stopped—the green parcel had vanished. But only, it transpired, into the safety of the supervisor's office.

The "R.& T." mail carrier put my green parcel in a blue sack. At 8:40, we drove in a procession to the *Des Moines Register*. On the fourth floor, the carrier delivered the parcel to the mail room. I nearly cheered.

The mail carrier and I went down to the street and shook hands. We'd done it.

Then cruel fate intervened. The *Des Moines Register* has a newsroom policy against accepting gifts.

Back the plum pudding will have to go. Back through three post offices, back in a blue sack, a canvas sack, and an orange sack. Back along I-80, past Malcom; back to Cedar Rapids.

Never mind. I'll just put the plum pudding back in my mother-in-law's deep freeze. It will be even riper next Christmas.

IOWA CELEBRATES THE QUEEN'S BIRTHDAY

What do you take as a gift to a tea party to celebrate the Queen's birthday? *Not* in England ... in Iowa City, Iowa.

I found the perfect answer at an antique market—a teaspoon from Queen Elizabeth II's coronation year engraved "E. II R. Coronation 1953." It was still in its original tissue paper and box.

The invitation to Iowa City's Fifth Annual Garden Party for the Queen's Birthday read: "Ladies—hats and gloves suggested." I wore a dark suit.

I drove through rolling midwestern cornfields and arrived at the park just on 3 o'clock. The guests—some in dresses, hats and gloves, some in jeans, shirt sleeves and sandals—crowded in a picnic pavilion next to a duck pond. A hundred tiny Union Jacks and strings of colored bunting streamed from the rafters.

A gilt-framed photograph of the Queen dominated the pavilion. A pair of corgis—naturally named Victoria and Albert—frisked at our feet. Outside, a bagpiper dressed in a red tartan kilt scattered the ducks with his wailing sounds.

I presented my teaspoon to the organizer of the party—a wonderfully dedicated Anglophile. Then I turned to join the other guests.

They had a variety of reasons for being there. One woman had fallen in love with the books of Sir Walter Scott when she was twelve. The corgi owners had a daughter who studied in England. A university professor taught English literature; a music teacher had trained in Scotland.

Radio Commentary, Weekend Edition, Monitor Radio, the broadcast edition of *The Christian Science Monitor*, June 17, 1994.

Then we sang for our tea. We started with some ancient sheet music of "God Save the King," substituting "Queen" where appropriate. We chorused "Land of Hope and Glory" and "Rule Britannia" to the strains of an electronic keyboard. Nobody in the world sings British patriotic songs with more fervor than Iowa City Anglophiles.

Then the ninety of us sipped cups of tea and partook of a feast fit for a Queen. Scones and clotted cream and strawberry jam; shortbread and lemon curd tarts; cucumber and egg sandwiches.

I bade good-bye as Gilbert and Sullivan's "For He Is an English Man" issued from a cassette player. "Yes," I thought. The party had made me feel more English than the Trooping the Colour in London.

I was filled with enthusiasm: Next year, the British ambassador should be invited to Iowa City for the Queen's birthday party. And then the following year ... who *knows*?

IOWA BY THE SEA

I freely admit that geography is not my strongest subject. But I remain wholly convinced that Iowa is in the *middle* of the United States.

So *why* is the governor of Iowa holding a celebration on the Saturday of Memorial Day weekend at Long Beach, California? Why is he anticipating Iowa's 150th birthday with a party on the Queen Mary, of all places??

The answer is an intriguing blend of bicycling, initiative, and history.

Every year, thousands of people take part in the *Des Moines Register*'s Annual Great Bike Ride Across Iowa—known as RAGBRAI. One of RAGBRAI's co-hosts is the *Register*'s popular columnist, Chuck Offenburger. He and his wife, Carla, are bicycling fanatics, and they dreamed a grand dream of cycling across the whole continent.

They decided to organize this once-in-a-lifetime event to launch Iowa's Sesquicentennial. One of their RAGBRAI friends is a former

Radio Commentary, Weekend Edition, Monitor Radio, the broadcast edition of *The Christian Science Monitor,* May 26, 1995.

Iowan, transplanted to Long Beach, California. When he heard of the great plan, he insisted, "You *must* start the bike ride in Long Beach."

For ages, Long Beach has been known as "Iowa by the Sea." Thousands of Iowans have moved there and, for many years, the Iowa Association of Long Beach sponsored vast reunion picnics. The guests recited the Pledge of Allegiance and sang the "Iowa Corn Song" and feasted, presumably, on Iowa sweet corn.

Chuck Offenburger leapt at the idea of "Iowa by the Sea." Then he added the Queen Mary as the "perfect fantastic touch." And after the governor's shipboard party, 308 cyclists will set off on a near 5,000 mile bicycle ride across America, promoting Iowa as they go.

The triumphant cyclists will finish at Washington, D.C., on Labor Day, where the renowned Iowa opera singer, Simon Estes, will sing their praises.

So my geography *is* wrong, and Iowa is, indeed, by the sea. There's only one problem left—I tend to fall off bicycles.

FIGHTING THE FULLER FIGURE IN IOWA

When I reached middle age, I swelled to the proportions of a small elephant. My father was too tactful to confront my new figure head-on. He described me as having an "Orson Welles look." Now Orson Welles had many fine qualities, but thinness was not one of them.

My sister Catherine, noticing that I was bulging out of my clothes, sent me to a special men's shop in London's Knightsbridge called High and Mighty. As the shop assistant reached for his tape measure, I said apologetically, "I'm afraid I'm rather fat."

A horrified look crossed his face. "We *never* use that word in here, sir," he said. "We speak only of 'girth.'"

My practical brother Robert eyed my girth thoughtfully. "You must go to a health farm," he announced. I went to Shrubland Hall Health

Des Moines Register, June 5, 1996

Clinic in Suffolk, and duly wasted away. We inmates made fast friends and thought of little but food. In two weeks, I managed to shed seventeen pounds.

Not long after—in 1987—I met a University of Iowa law professor, and soon marriage loomed. I went onto a regime of starvation rations, and a few months later, walked down the aisle of the Cedar Rapids church looking like a wraith. I had conquered my girth.

The American phase of my metabolic life began with a trip to Charleston, South Carolina—a place of great historic renown, but deserving still greater fame for its world-class fudge. I ate the fudge with ever-increasing enthusiasm.

Back we came to Iowa, and that hot summer I learned of potlucks and of picnics and of high school graduation parties. I found that there were many excellent reasons for living in Iowa, but the most excellent of all was the desserts—or "puddings" as we British call them. I, who had never tasted a brownie nor even heard of a chocolate-chip cookie, was a constant attender at the groaning dessert table.

Oh, the joys of those ethnic American desserts! Czech kolaches, Norwegian kringles, Lebanese baklawas, Dutch pastries, German cakes—the list just grew and grew, and so did my waistline. My wife had her own euphemism for my new look. She called it "the fuller figure."

Giving up smoking inspired me to eat in earnest. I liked to go to the shopping mall, where I would read the newspapers and enjoy a hearty cinnamon roll. I would watch idly as strange creatures with grim determination on their faces and tennis shoes on their feet puffed their way round the mall.

"How peculiar Americans are," I thought. "They even go for exercise walks in shopping malls." I added this eccentricity to the list of things never to do.

But of course I did take some remedial action. I would go for the occasional swim and substituted artificial sweetener for sugar in my tea. I usually managed to diet away a few pounds before departing for England. Then I would return with fresh resolve. But the superabundance of Iowa would overcome me, and back up would go my weight.

As a precautionary measure, I brought my bathroom scale from England to Cedar Rapids. I would set it a couple of pounds below zero, and then clamber on board. Whenever my figure reached its fuller stage, I would dance on the scale with one foot. It probably made the difference of only a half pound, but it did make me feel thinner.

I took up mall walking with a vengeance—after all, one does have to conform to local customs. And if Iowans could lose weight that way, doubtless I could, too.

This year, my Orson Welles look got out of hand. I danced once too often on my scale. With a whirr and a ping, it gave up the ghost. I bought a new scale—clearly the manufacturers had lied, as I weighed five pounds more than on my trusty old friend, and dancing made no difference.

Once again bursting out of my clothes, I was taken last week to a men's store in Cedar Rapids. The clerk examined me with a critical look. "I don't know what we will have to fit you, sir," he said doubtfully. Then his eyes lit up. "We will try the stout section."

The stout suit fitted, more or less. Then he produced some special trousers called Adjust-Ease, with an "extra-comfort waistband that expands and recovers for comfort and shape."

A new man in my adjustable trousers, now I must put on my tennis shoes and set off for a mall walk. But I just might stop at Donutland on the way ...

TAKE ME OUT TO THE BALL GAME

If you are married to an American, a time eventually comes when you are obliged to attend a baseball game.

I did play the gentle English game of cricket in my youth. At Trinity College, Oxford, we had a very amateur team called the Trinity Triflers. I achieved the singular distinction of being bowled out first ball in three successive matches. Without going into technicalities, that is *not* a praiseworthy accomplishment. So I decided to hang up my bat forever.

But baseball was something very different, very foreign, and utterly incomprehensible. My total knowledge of the game came from the film, *Field of Dreams*.

Recently, my wife announced that the fateful day had arrived. We were going to see the local minor league team, aptly called the Cedar

Rapids Kernels. As we parked our car, I was puzzled to find the field completely deserted. Had we come on the wrong evening? The explanation was much simpler—I was looking at the neighboring football field. Patricia firmly steered me to the correct entrance, where strange notices greeted us:

Be Alert for Objects of the Game
Leaving the Game and Entering the Seating Area

"What can that possibly mean?" I asked the program seller.

"Be careful you don't get hit by a ball," he replied. "Where are you sitting?" He looked at our tickets. "Watch out for left-handed batters," he warned.

Already unnerving, the news quickly deteriorated. Yet another notice read:

No Food or Drink or Containers
May Be Brought in Ballpark

This was most disappointing, as I had been faithfully promised by way of inducement that eating would be unlimited at the baseball game. But once inside, I was relieved to see an endless row of food vendors. One of them explained that the rogue sign merely meant you couldn't bring your own food. Who would want to, with all the delights that awaited me?

We bought hot dogs and bratwursts, iced tea and lemonade, the mandatory ballpark peanuts, and three different sorts of ice cream. I began to see the point of baseball.

As we munched contentedly in our seats, I glanced around and saw others eating with equal enthusiasm. Some particularly well-fed patrons even managed to make me feel comparatively thin. I celebrated with a slice of pizza.

The Kernels came onto the field to play the Clinton Lumberkings [hereafter referred to as "the enemy"]. A young woman in a black cocktail dress sang a jazz rendition of the Star-Spangled Banner. I don't think anybody has ever sung a jazz (or any other version) of God Save the Queen at a cricket match.

The game began. The umpire—a man of infinite courage—crouched behind the catcher. Periodically he sent mysterious semaphore messages to the pitcher. "What *can* that mean?" I wondered aloud.

The woman in front of me took up the challenge. "He is signaling the number of balls and strikes," she kindly explained.

I looked over at the scoreboard, which proclaimed: "Balls, Strikes, R, H, and E." "R is runs, H is hits, E is errors," my expert announced. I understood R and H, but E remained a mystery.

An enemy batter was caught in mid-field. The inning was over. The scoreboard announced a Kernels player, "Hutchins, 227." His shirt said "15." Could 227 be his weight? "No," said my friendly expert. "It's his batting average."

Between innings, strange Disneyesque mascots wandered around. Children vied for prizes on the field. Little girls twirled themselves dizzy and then raced; a little boy caught tennis balls in a fishing net.

The crowd was frequently exhorted to join in a mysterious ritual, the central motif of which was: "STOMP, STOMP, CLAP. STOMP, STOMP, CLAP." I felt obliged to join in with the odd stomp and one or two languid claps.

Billboard advertisements at the edge of the field caught my eye. Supermarkets competed with car dealers and the Marlboro Man. I glanced back at the game to find that the Kernels were one run ahead. Then, gloriously, a Kernel batter hit the ball over the Marlboro Man and towards the moon. Home run! The crowd and its emotion swept me to my feet.

In the seventh inning, the crowd rose as one and burst into a song new to my repertoire. "Take me out to the ball game ... " As we sat down again, my wife asked: "Is baseball more exciting than cricket?" I pondered a moment. "Well, it's certainly a lot noisier."

Towards the end of the eighth inning, the enemy stole home, and now the score was tied at four runs apiece. When the Kernels went to bat, the atmosphere was like a frenzied soccer match. A Kernel stole to second base. Then his teammate hit the ball hard, and the second base was home. The stadium erupted.

Ninth inning. The Kernels lead, five to four. The enemy comes to bat. Number one batter is caught out. Number two batter is caught in the foul zone. The third batter hits high and long, and the outfielder catches.

Peanuts forgotten, cricket forgotten, merged in a sea of baseball fans, I leap to my feet and shout in a thoroughly un-British way: "Yea, yea, yea, yea!"

I turned to my wife: "So when's the next game?"

London Bridges

THIRTY-ODD YEARS AGO *in Salisbury, Rhodesia (today's Harare, Zimbabwe), my father made a speech. The occasion was the premiere of the film* My Fair Lady, *which was being shown for the Red Cross, of which he was the national chairman. His voice shaking with emotion, my father started his speech: "This film is about London, the greatest city in the world."*

I've often pondered those words. Washington, D.C., is more powerful, Paris is more beautiful, Rome is more ancient, and yet ... and yet—London is London. Dr. Johnson hit the nail on the head in 1777 with the famous words: "When a man is tired of London, he is tired of life; for there is in London all that life can afford."

Most of the articles in this chapter were written in London for publication in America. This spanning of the Atlantic led to the title, "London Bridges." The pieces are about various features of my London life. Big Ben, for example, is known all over the world—I was lucky enough and just fit enough to climb it. McDonald's in Knightsbridge is a less famous landmark, but it holds a particularly happy memory for me.

Another article is devoted to London's fleet of black taxis. This may seem an unusual topic, but many Americans who come to London as tourists or on business find themselves rhapsodizing about London cabs. A London cabbie who congratulated my wife on her American accent inspired the writing of this article.

Some of the pieces are about obvious tourist havens. Buckingham Palace is one of them. Londoners on the whole take the palace for granted, but watching my wife's excitement when royal cars came out of the gates made me want to write about our own stint as tourists outside the palace. Another landmark is Westminster Hall next to the Houses of Parliament, and I've written about President Nelson Mandela's visit to that venerable edifice. And having been a barrister myself, I couldn't resist including something about my own Inn of Court, the Inner Temple.

I hope these few articles will result in the occasional start of recognition in those who have already visited London, and that they will encourage others to visit that city for the first time, because I love London. I am not tired of life, Dr. Johnson, and yes, Daddy, you were right. London is the greatest city in the world.

LONDON'S BLACK TAXIS DRIVE LIKE JEHU

This weary traveller between Cedar Rapids and London's Gatwick Airport feels truly home when he arrives at Victoria Station and climbs into a familiar, black London taxicab.

London's taxis are the nearest thing to heaven on wheels. They can thread their way through impenetrable traffic and catch an uncatchable train. If you have a mountain of luggage, no matter, there is always ample room.

After a long flight, the thing you want to do above all else is to stretch. London taxis are ideal for this purpose—however long your legs, you can stretch them out in comfort.

If you have an obscure destination, a London taxi driver will invariably find it. To get a license, cabbies spend three years studying the streets of London. Would-be taxi drivers go about the city on mopeds, with maps propped in front of them, learning every conceivable route around London. Cabbies call this ordeal "doing the knowledge."

Finally the trainee driver takes a strenuous test and, with luck, obtains a license. After renting or purchasing the traditional black cab (which costs over $30,000), the cabbie embarks on a new career.

Sadly, in the current British recession cab driving has become a precarious living. Rows of taxis cruise the streets with their "FOR HIRE" signs lit. Taxi drivers complain that tourism has plunged dramatically since the Gulf War. Patricia's Iowan accent is greeted with delight when she enters a cab—American passengers, and in fact all tourists, are a prized commodity.

Apart from economic hard times, black-cab drivers feel threatened by competition from "mini-cabs." Currently, the latter are permitted only to obtain passengers by telephone bookings, and cannot stop for customers in the street. A mini-cab driver with any sort of car can get a license immediately—without "doing the knowledge."

Black-cab drivers gloomily speculate that the government may change the law to permit mini-cabs to "ply for hire"—or pick up passengers on the streets of London. They fear all their years of training will go for naught, and that red Fiestas and blue Corollas will supplant the traditional fleet of large black taxis.

Des Moines Register, March 19, 1993.

Let us hope they are wrong. Black taxis are as much a part of London as Big Ben, and have played an essential role in my own London life.

As a young man I worked for a London bank that owned a taxi known as "Jehu." The name came from the Second Book of Kings, chapter 9, verse 20: "The driving is like the driving of Jehu the son of Nimshi; for he driveth furiously." The chairman of the bank was immensely proud of Jehu. He would boast to customers that Jehu went like the wind and turned on a sixpence.

London cabs also figured in my next career as a barrister. I spent endless hours defending taxi drivers—who were wonderfully enthusiastic clients—from charges under the Hackney Carriage Acts passed in Queen Victoria's reign. Together we did battle in courts all over London.

Now, at the House of Lords, I find the very method of summoning taxis recalls the gaslit Victorian era. At the flick of a switch, a lamp in the courtyard flashes the presence of a customer to prowling taxis in nearby Parliament Square. When one of them emerges from the night, I half expect Sherlock Holmes and Dr. Watson to step out.

Taxis also play an enormous part in social life. As a boy on our African farm, I heard my mother give my eighteen-year-old sister—who was leaving for London—some sage Victorian advice. "If a man tries to kiss you in a taxi," my mother warned, "open both doors, and a policeman will come at once!"

Quite how my sister was supposed to perform this feat has never been explained. A sense of delicacy has prevented my asking her whether she ever tried it, and whether a faithful police officer did indeed appear.

When I in turn got to London and began my own social life, I incurred a special debt to a cabbie. After a merry late-night party, I took a taxi and gave my address near Victoria Station. As we bowled along, I realized to my horror that I only had one shilling, and the taxi meter already showed two shillings.

Apologizing profusely, I explained my predicament to the driver. He said, "don't worry," switched off his meter, and drove to Victoria Station. The cabbie refused my shilling, pressed sixpence into my hand, and said: "Go and get a cup of tea to clear the fumes from your brain."

No one else has ever tipped me. Small wonder that I love London taxis!

THE AMERICANIZATION OF LONDON

L iving partly in Iowa and partly in London, I'm often asked whether shifting between the two worlds isn't a great culture shock. The answer is "less and less so"—because London has become so thoroughly Americanized.

Buckingham Palace, Westminster Abbey and Big Ben are definitely still there, but Pizza Huts, Kentucky Fried Chickens, and Burger Kings have sprouted all over London.

Oprah Winfrey, Roseanne, and some dreadful characters called Beavis and Butthead chase each other across British television screens. If you stroll to a newsagent, you inevitably find *USA Today* and the *Wall Street Journal* selling alongside the London *Times* and the *Daily Telegraph*.

During the Gulf War in 1991, my wife seemed to be the only American in London. Now when you walk down the street, every third person sounds as if he or she is from New York or Chicago.

Desiring a quintessentially English experience, we recently purchased tickets for the ballet *Romeo and Juliet* at the Royal Opera House in Covent Garden. Did we spot any of the royal family? Did we bump into any of my old British cronies? No, of course not. However, within minutes of arriving, we did fall unexpectedly into the arms of two friends—from Cedar Rapids.

In fact, Iowa seems omnipresent in London these days—even in the underground railway, known as the "tube." Ascending and descending the tube escalators during a trip from Leicester Square to St. John's Wood, I counted no less than 20 posters that read: "Where Can You Go After *Madison County*? Robert James Waller's *Cedar Bend*." Stiff-upper-lipped Brits have been sighted on the tube, lost in *The Bridges of Madison County*, tears starting in their eyes.

So much social life in London now revolves around things American. A terribly English couple invited us out for what we assumed would be a strictly British cultural evening. They assured us that the restaurant was the height of London fashion; we were faint with anticipation. They led us to a door guarded by a seven-foot cigar-store Indian, and into a restaurant with the impeccable Cockney name, "Texas Lone Star Cafe."

Cow horns and posters of Sam Houston adorned the walls; red

neon-lit advertisements extolled the virtues of Budweiser and Miller beers. French's mustard and Heinz ketchup dominated the table. We consumed taco salads, washed down with mammoth glasses of Southern iced tea, as we listened to the strains of country-western music.

After our Texan dinner, our friends decided to bypass the great English film *Remains of the Day*, and whisked us off instead to Stephen Spielberg's *Schindler's List*. The whole evening could have taken place in any city in the United States.

But perhaps the ultimate experience of Americanized London came on our wedding anniversary. Should we have breakfast at the Ritz Hotel in Piccadilly, with its fabled dining room—pink marble walls, pink curtains, frescoed ceiling, chandeliers reflected a thousand times in sparkling mirrors—and be served by endless waiters dressed in dinner jackets? Should we go instead to Simpsons-in-the-Strand, which for 150 years has specialized in hot joints on silver carving wagons, and now serves a vast traditional English breakfast—porridge, streaky and back bacon, black pudding, kidneys and eggs, fried bread, bubble and squeak, baked beans, fried mushrooms and tomatoes?

We did neither.

My wife's idea of heaven is to wander around Harrods, the legendary department store in London's exclusive Knightsbridge district. My idea of heaven is to avoid all shopping, especially at Harrods, and to linger over the breakfast table sipping tea and reading endless newspapers.

So we didn't go to the Ritz, and we didn't go to Simpsons-in-the-Strand. We had our anniversary breakfast one block from Harrods—at the local McDonald's. We celebrated with Egg McMuffins and toasted each other with orange juice in plastic cups.

Perhaps I should face the ghastly truth. I am in grave danger of becoming just as Americanized as London.

GUARDING BUCKINGHAM PALACE

There is a young girl in Iowa City who collects water from oceans, lakes, and rivers. It is manifestly a duty to help foster this remarkable hobby. Thus one evening recently I found myself squatting by the pond in London's St. James's Park trying to will water into the narrow neck of a shampoo bottle.

My Iowan wife started gesticulating wildly—something unusual was happening at nearby Buckingham Palace. She had seen a gate opening in the railings at the front of the palace. We were to investigate *forthwith*. Clutching my bottle in my hand I guided my wife through the traffic in the Mall. (This is always essential in England because, unaccustomed to left-hand traffic, she invariably courts death by looking in the wrong direction.)

We came to rest among the knot of American tourists and British passers-by at the palace gate. In addition to the red-coated sentries outside the palace proper, several policemen were on duty at the gate. After a few minutes a radio crackled, and one of the police officers called to us: "The Duchess of York's car is just coming out." A flash of red hair, a smiling young woman, a wave, and she was gone. My wife, an inveterate reader of *Royalty Magazine,* exclaimed: "I can't believe it—I have just seen Fergie!"

One of the policemen, entertained by her fervor, kindly said: "If you wait five minutes, you'll see something even more exciting." "Do you mean *the* Queen is coming through?" she asked incredulously. The policeman just smiled.

While we waited I occupied myself by peeling the label off my precious bottle. Two Californian women walked by, and in the interests of international relations, I told them that the Queen was just going to come out of the palace. They were as excited as my wife—like her, they had never seen the Queen.

Security visibly tightened. A tension came into the policemen at the gate. A senior police officer with red hair materialized on the pavement. A man with "plain clothes detective" stamped all over him came out of the palace and leaned against the railings near us. When word came through that the royal car was expected, we were courteously escorted behind a small barrier. I put away my bottle and waited.

Des Moines Register, June 16, 1990.

At last the car appeared. The Queen was partly obscured in the back seat by her husband, Prince Philip. But her smile, her pink dress and pill box hat were clearly visible. The British among us reacted in a very restrained, very British way—we watched respectfully as our sovereign's car sped away. My wife and the Californians were less inhibited. They did a decorous dance and whooped with delight.

We walked round the palace towards our dinner and fell into conversation with the red-haired senior police officer. He was tired but friendly, explaining that now he could go off duty. He said that people thought the Queen's whole life was official engagements: "But she manages to have some private life as well. For example, this evening she has gone out to a quiet dinner with some friends."

We asked him about security at the palace and about the intruder who had got into the Queen's bedroom eight years ago. The officer gave the background. For one hundred and thirty years, since Queen Victoria's time, there had never been any real security problem at Buckingham Palace. Everybody had just assumed that the system was infallible. Then unbelievably one night a young man had managed to enter the Queen's own bedroom. Her Majesty had talked to him and succeeded in calming him down. Inevitably there had been a huge Home Office Inquiry. Security had been tightened in every respect.

My wife wondered if there were ever any problems now. "Well," the officer said, "Every week there are people at the gate who think they are long-lost cousins of the Queen. Sometimes people claim to be members of the Austrian imperial family or other foreign royalty. We just listen to them when they demand to be let into the palace. After we have talked to them politely, they usually move on. But every few weeks somebody tries to climb the palace walls. Then we grab them."

"It must be a very responsible job," I said. "You must get nuts outside the palace constantly."

"Yes we do," said the officer. Then he smiled. "You will forgive my saying so, Sir, but you were playing with a bottle outside the palace earlier this evening."

I was astonished. "It was only water from St. James's Park for a young friend in Iowa!"

"Well," said the officer, "there was a plain clothes detective behind you. If you had taken that bottle out just before Her Majesty came through the gate, he would have had you flat on your back."

"You mean that *I* was tonight's nut?" I asked. "Did the police think I had nitroglycerine in my bottle?"

"Well, Sir, we do have to look after the Queen, don't we?"

REVISITING AN ANCIENT INN OF COURT

Every English barrister must belong to one of London's four ancient Inns of Court—Inner Temple, Middle Temple, Lincoln's Inn, or Gray's Inn. My Inn, where I practiced law from 1977 to 1981, is the Inner Temple, whose grounds slope down from Fleet Street to the Thames Embankment.

The Temple was founded in 1161 by the crusading order of the Knights Templars. The order was destroyed in 1312, and the Temple passed to the Knights of St. John.

During the fourteenth century, lawyers began to reside in the Temple. The date of the evolution of the two separate Inns of Court—the Inner Temple and the Middle Temple—is unknown. What is known is that by 1388, lawyers were practicing in those two societies, which continue to this day.

The Inner Temple is rather like a historic village. Scattered about its grounds are massive stone and brick buildings with quaint names like Pump Court and Paper Buildings. There barristers have their offices, known as "chambers."

At the center of the village is the law library and the dining hall. Sadly, the old library and hall fell victim to German bombs during World War II and had to be rebuilt.

The library evokes memories for me of endless hours spent studying for the examination, called Bar Finals. You were expected not only to master the principles of law in many subjects, but also to learn the names of vast numbers of legal cases. At the time it seemed like torture—now it is a happy memory.

"London's Ancient Inns of Court," *British Heritage* (October/November 1995).

The Inner Temple hall is built on the site where the refectory of the Knights Templars stood. In my day, to qualify as a barrister you were obliged to "keep" twelve terms—a remnant of the collegiality when students actually lived in their Inn of Court. This you did by eating dinners in hall three times each term, sitting with your fellow students on benches at long wooden tables.

When you had successfully passed the exams and eaten your dinners, you were formally Called to the Bar at a ceremony in the hall of your Inn. Then you became a pupil—a practicing barrister took you on as an ignorant assistant and instilled in you the ways and ethics of the bar.

My pupil master—the kindest of men and now a judge—periodically would take me to lunch in hall. Rows of barristers, relaxing after the morning in court, would talk and laugh and, inevitably, argue.

I practiced as a barrister in chambers at No. 12 King's Bench Walk. Recently I took my American wife there to show her the names of the current barristers listed at the bottom of the stone staircase. Only three of the sixteen barristers from my time still remained. Inquiry of the clerks who run the chambers (all new since my era) revealed that my three old friends were all in court.

The most ancient feature of the Inner Temple grounds is the Temple Church, and we took ourselves there the following Sunday morning. The circular nave—known as the Round—was completed by the Knights Templars in 1185, and they added the chancel in 1240. During Morning Prayers, the choir, in white surplices and red cassocks, justified its international reputation with its soaring Te Deum Laudamus and Jubilate Deo.

After an organ voluntary triumphantly ended the Anglican service, we wandered among the tombs in the Round, where the medieval effigies of nine illustrious associates of the Knights Templars slumber. There is the effigy of Geoffrey de Mandeville, First Earl of Essex, who died in 1144. Set in the floor nearby, are the words: "Remember in Your Prayers Those Who Died in the Second World War 1939-1945." Eight hundred years in a few feet.

The Church is the oldest part of the Inner Temple, but the garden, with its vast lawn, is my favorite. The story goes that an American visitor asked how to produce such a splendid lawn. "Well," said the old gardener. "You want to put down some manure and roll the lawn a bit." "Is that all?" asked the visitor. The old man considered. "Well, it helps if you do it for a few hundred years."

Shakespeare set the scene of the quarrel that ultimately led to the Wars of the Roses in the Temple Garden. He had aristocratic law students—future leaders of the Yorkist and Lancastrian factions—take sides by plucking white and red roses. The Middle Temple claims the scene for its garden. I loyally ascribe it to the Inner Temple garden, but nobody actually knows which garden Shakespeare meant.

The great essayist Charles Lamb was born and lived for his first seven years opposite the Inner Temple garden at No. 2 Crown Office Row. In 1821, in a famous essay called "The Old Benchers of the Inner Temple," Lamb gave vent to his fury at the lawyers of neighboring Lincoln's Inn for dismantling the fountain he had cherished since childhood. The fountain had consisted of four little marble boys, and Lamb wrote:

> They are gone, and the spring choked up. The fashion, they tell me, is gone by, and these things are esteemed childish. Why not then gratify children by letting them stand?
>
> Lawyers, I suppose, were children once.

If you walk through the wrought-iron gates and cross the lawn, you can see how the lawyers of my Inn appeased the wrath of Charles Lamb's spirit. In 1928, they built a fountain in the Inner Temple garden facing Crown Office Row. At the edge of the fountain's basin is the leaden figure of a beautiful boy. He holds an open book at his knee, his head is raised, and he stands gazing towards the place of Charles Lamb's birth.

The words in the young boy's book show that the lawyers had hearkened to Lamb's pointed message. And, as they are wont to do, the lawyers had the last word. Etched on the book is the simple phrase:

"Lawyers, I suppose, were children once."

WHITE CURLY WIGS
AND BLACK STUFF GOWNS

Sometimes in America my English customs make me feel gloriously anachronistic. One such occasion was the first Barristers Ball given by the University of Iowa law students. Their president kindly invited me to attend, and explained that they wanted me to come as a barrister—an English trial lawyer—dressed in my wig and gown.

My white wig with its curls and pigtail presented no problem, because I kept it in Iowa. My long black stuff gown unfortunately was in England. I improvised and borrowed an academic robe which, if a trifle short, was at least pitch black. Anticipating that a speech was called for, I prepared a lofty peroration on the origins and history of the wig and gown.

Wigs evolved in seventeenth-century France to keep men's hair clean. After King Charles II was restored to the throne of England in 1660, he made wigs fashionable in that country. By the end of the eighteenth century, the fashion had died out. But, despite the invention of shampoo, judges and barristers have continued wearing wigs to this day.

When King Charles II died in 1685, barristers marked the nation's loss by dressing in funereal black robes. Three centuries later (such is the conservatism of the law) modern barristers are still mourning King Charles by wearing long black gowns in court.

On the great day of the Barristers Ball, all of this oratory was forgotten. For when I stood before the throng of law students and carefully placed the wig on my head, I was greeted with gales of laughter. So I hastily donned the gown, executed an elephantine pirouette, and left the dance floor to a storm of applause.

Iowa law students are not the only people intrigued by wigs and gowns. This year the whole matter has been widely discussed in English newspapers and legal circles. The culmination was a recent debate in the House of Lords.

Most speakers wanted to keep both wigs and gowns. Lord Campbell of Alloway, a senior barrister and Second World War hero, represented the views of the majority: "I am basically a retentionist. We ought to retain an air of dignity, anonymity and authority which the uniform of this type of public service commands."

Des Moines Register, September 1, 1992.

An eminent retired judge, Lord Brightman, had taken an informal poll of non-legal friends and acquaintances, who overwhelmingly favored wigs. The reasons given were "tradition and the importance of maintaining the solemnity of court proceedings."

Lord Renton, a leading lawyer whose daughter is also a barrister, thought that wigs had a great levelling effect among barristers—men and women, young and old. Lord Harmar-Nicholls, a non-lawyer, urged that some barristers needed a good disguise: "There are many whimpish-looking, weak-kneed people practicing in our courts who are not whimps and who are not weak-kneed but they *look* as though they are."

Lady Faithfull, a staunch fighter for youth, championed the accused's point of view. She related how once she had stood in the dock to support a young girl defendant. The latter, pointing at the judge in his wig, asked: "Why are you wearing that funny hat?" He replied, "I'm the judge." She said, "Thank goodness for that. You're different from other men and I might get justice."

Those peers who spoke for abolition concentrated their fire on the wig. Lord Richard, a former rugby player with a fine portly figure, complained: "I have always disliked wigs. I do not believe they add any dignity to the proceedings and I do not believe they add any dignity to me. I believe that I look ridiculous wearing a wig." Based on his thirty-seven years at the bar, Lord Richard concluded that wigs were "insanitary, scratchy, and extremely hot."

Lord Redesdale summarized popular opposition to wigs: "I believe that wigs are a relic of the past. They give the impression that the law is remote, inaccessible and lend an air of mysticism to the general public."

At the end of the debate the Lord Chancellor, who administers the courts, announced he would publish a detailed consultation paper. The final decision will lie with the Queen, on the advice of her senior judges.

I await the Lord Chancellor's report with some anxiety. Personally, I favor wigs and gowns. I like the tradition; I like the quaintness; I like the pageantry. However, I believe that in the end those who view barristers' court dress as archaic will triumph. First wigs, and ultimately gowns, will vanish.

If wigs and gowns are indeed abolished, I shall have to find a suitable home for mine. Perhaps I shall bequeath them to the University of Iowa law school.

I can imagine the scene at some Barristers Ball in the distant future. An Iowa law student—overcome by a great wave of loyalty to King

Charles II—will dress up and cavort in my wig and gown. Doubtless the crowd will react as it did to my own pose in barristers' garb—with howls of incredulous laughter.

CONQUERING BIG BEN

I stood staring up at the tower of Big Ben, and my heart sank.

I am fat, fifty-ish, and my feet hurt. Why on *earth* was I planning to climb the 334 steps of Big Ben?

The answer lay with a fellow peer. He haunts the Houses of Parliament and knows every nook, cranny, and subterranean tunnel. I think of him as the Phantom of the House of Lords.

The Phantom is a superbly fit fellow. He bicycles to Parliament every day, and to him, a quick sprint up Big Ben is a pleasant jaunt.

Feebly, I gave in to the Phantom's enthusiasm. Thus I find myself at the base of Big Ben, and with wild optimism hope to manage the climb and hear the midday chimes.

I've taken one essential precaution. I've brought a bar of chocolate to give myself inspiration in moments of stress.

So here we go.

[Sound of footsteps ascending steps of Big Ben.]

Well, after thirty-four steps I decide to have a little rest. The Phantom bounds on ahead, while I fortify myself with chocolate for the remaining 300 steps.

[Sounds of breathing, unwrapping chocolate bar, and munching.]

I set off again. Soon I pass the tiny cell where miscreant peers and Members of Parliament can be imprisoned. The cell hasn't been used for a hundred years—but you never know. The thought puts temporary wings on my heels.

Somehow I struggle up. The oxygen seems to thin, and I imagine myself Sir Edmund Hillary climbing Mt. Everest. This is the south approach, the south knoll of Everest—the last rest before assaulting the

Radio Commentary, Weekend Edition, Monitor Radio, the broadcast edition of *The Christian Science Monitor,* January 28, 1994.

summit, and I feel every hour of fifty-one-years-old and every pound over 200 that I actually weigh. I think I need more chocolate."

[Sounds of candy wrapper rustling.]

At last I reach the belfry, where the Phantom awaits me. The view over London is breathtaking.

And here is Big Ben—a colossal bell, over nine feet in diameter, weighing thirteen and one-half tons. It's one minute to midday, and we are going to hear Big Ben make its wonderful and eternal ring.

[Radio fades out as Big Ben strikes twelve noon.]

THE GRANDEUR OF WESTMINSTER HALL

Westminster Hall is the oldest and most majestic part of the Palace of Westminster, where the Houses of Parliament are situated. Between 1097 and 1099, King William II built the vast stone hall, which is an astonishing 240 feet long and 68 feet wide. The oak hammer-beam roof—an architectural masterpiece—was added by the year 1400.

For hundreds of years the royal courts of justice conducted their proceedings in Westminster Hall, and it has been the site of the most notable state trials in English history. In 1305, the valiant Scottish patriot, William Wallace of *Braveheart* fame, was put on trial there for treason to Edward I. "I cannot be a traitor to Edward," he said, "for I owe him no allegiance. He is not my god; he never received my homage and whilst life is in this persecuted body, he never shall receive it." Wallace was sentenced to be hanged, drawn, and quartered.

In 1535, Sir Thomas More, Henry VIII's saintly Lord Chancellor and a hero of a very different stamp from Wallace, was also tried in the great hall. He had refused to accept the king as supreme head of the Church of England, and for this he was charged with treason. Upon hearing the verdict of guilty, he declared: "I verily trust and shall therefore right heartily pray, though your Lordships have now here in earth

Condensed from "The Grandeur of Westminster Hall," to be published in *British Heritage,* 1998.

been judges to my condemnation, we may yet hereafter in Heaven merrily all meet together, to our everlasting salvation."

The greatest of all trials held in Westminster Hall was the trial of the king himself—Charles I in 1649. Having lost the Civil War against Oliver Cromwell and the parliamentarians, he was brought to the hall to be tried by parliamentary commissioners, including Cromwell. It was here that the king heard the awful sentence against him: "For all which treasons and crimes this Court doth adjudge that the said Charles Stuart, as a tyrant, traytor, murtherer and publique enimy to the good people of this nation, shall be put to death by the severing of his heade from his body."

However, many of the royal scenes in Westminster Hall have been ones of rejoicing. For centuries kings and queens held magnificent coronation feasts there. The first one recorded was for Henry II's son, Henry, in 1170. Uniquely, he had been crowned during his father's lifetime, and hence is known as the "Young King." Trumpets sounded, the boar's head was carried into the hall, and Henry II himself—on bended knee—served the Young King.

Coronation feasts in Westminster Hall continued down the centuries, and the final one in 1821 was a particularly lavish affair in honor of George IV. The guests ate thousands of pounds of beef, veal, mutton, and lamb off silver plates. There was a profusion of venison, chickens, geese, fish, shellfish, soup, eggs, vegetables, pastries, creams, and jellies. The nobles drank champagne, claret, burgundy, moselle, hock, madeira, port, sherry, ale, and iced punch. The bill for the coronation came to an astounding 243,390 English pounds.

During the nineteenth century, Westminster Hall ceased to be the site of lavish coronation feasts and of the royal law courts. But at the end of the century—in 1898—the hall was put to a new purpose. The body of the eminent Liberal prime minister, William Ewart Gladstone, lay in state in Westminster Hall while thousands of people paid their last respects. This precedent was followed on the deaths of Edward VII in 1910, George V in 1936, and George VI in 1952.

Then, in 1965, Britain's legendary Second World War prime minister, Sir Winston Churchill, died. His body lay on a catafalque, while for three days and nights 321,360 people quietly filed past. Five thousand people had to be turned away when the body of Sir Winston was moved to St. Paul's Cathedral for the funeral service.

Only rarely has a foreign head of state addressed members of both houses of Parliament in Westminster Hall. In 1960, the towering figure

of French President Charles de Gaulle—Sir Winston's wartime colleague—delivered a speech entirely in French to the assembled members
of the House of Commons and the House of Lords.

On July 11, 1996, Nelson Mandela, President of South Africa since
1994 and a political prisoner there for twenty-seven years, followed in
de Gaulle's footsteps. On this splendid occasion—at which I was privileged to be present—peers and their guests sat on one side of the vast
hall and members of the House of Commons on the other, eagerly awaiting President Mandela.

The band of the Grenadier Guards played as we watched the
Yeomen of the Guard and the Gentlemen at Arms enter, resplendent in
their scarlet costumes. They took their places at the top of the stone
steps.

Prime Minister John Major, the Leader of the Opposition, Tony
Blair, and other parliamentary dignitaries were present. The Speaker of
the House of Commons, Betty Boothroyd, and the Lord Chancellor
(who presides over the House of Lords), both robed in black and gold,
left to escort President Mandela into the hall.

At two minutes past 11:00 A.M., the yellow-clad State Trumpeters
sounded a fanfare, and 2,000 of us stood for Nelson Mandela. He
walked down the red carpet covering the steps, holding hands with
Madam Speaker. This hand-holding doubtless resulted from his natural
warmth. It also gave him support, for at seventy-seven, Mandela had
difficulty descending the steps to the stone platform.

The band played South Africa's new national anthem, *Nkosi
Sikelel'i Afrika* (God Bless Africa). Looking at that lined and dignified
face, I felt the tears pricking in my eyes—how much he and how much
that tune had meant to so many people during the hopeless years of
apartheid.

The Lord Chancellor read a speech of welcome. Then President
Mandela walked to the lectern, raised his spectacles, and gave his
speech. He talked of the tortuous history of Britain's relations with
South Africa, starting with colonialism in 1795. He spoke of the "founding stones" of the new South Africa—unity, democracy, race and gender
equality, and economic rebuilding. He ended by promising "a glorious
summer of a partnership for freedom, peace, prosperity and friendship."

The entire hall rose as one, and applauded and applauded and applauded. At last the South African President brought the ovation to a
close.

In thanking him, the Speaker described Mandela and the new South

Africa as one of the greatest triumphs of the century. I think a lot of people cried during her speech. Next to me, my sister Mary-Ann, a hardier soul than I, had tears on her cheeks.

The Speaker caught the moment with simple, splendid words. "Mr. President, as a result of your determination to end apartheid you spent more than a third of your life in prison, though your spirit was freer than that of your captors outside."

Then the South African President, holding hands with Madam Speaker, walked down the aisle. He stopped near us to shake hands with some peers in wheelchairs. Then he was out of my sight ... and he was gone. The band ceased to play. Reluctantly, we left the great chamber.

Thus, on that glorious July day, Nelson Mandela took his place in the cavalcade of giants who have passed through the nine-hundred-year history of Westminster Hall.

MIRACLE CHUNNEL TRAIN LINKS LONDON AND PARIS

Trains were the height of glamour during my boyhood in the 1950s. We lived in landlocked colonial Rhodesia, and every year or so, we would go by train to the seaside near Durban, South Africa. The journey took four days as we trundled along behind a puffing steam engine.

Nowadays, so much of long-distance travel seems to be by airplane. I am an air curmudgeon. When the pilot says, "We hope you have had an enjoyable flight," I long to rise to my feet and demand: "How could anybody actually *enjoy* a flight?"

So when the glad tidings arrived that one could go by train all the way from London to Paris, I jumped with joy. At the first opportunity, I booked tickets to Paris on the Eurostar, as the passenger train which goes through the Channel Tunnel—or "Chunnel"—is called.

The first attempt to bore a tunnel under the English Channel was

Des Moines Register, March 21, 1995.

made in 1880, but was abandoned after a mile. The successful attempt began a century later, with a joint Anglo-French statement of intent. After huge sums had been raised, tunneling began in December 1987. The terminals were sited at Folkestone in England and Calais in France.

On December 1, 1990, the undersea service tunnel broke through, allowing people to cross dry-shod between England and France for the first time since Britain broke off from continental Europe some 12,000 years ago.

The tunnel was officially opened in May 1994 by Queen Elizabeth of England and President François Mitterand of France. Later in the year, regular train services began. My wife and I were to be in the Class of 1995—hardly pioneers, but relatively early travellers nonetheless.

The Eurostar train leaves from London's Waterloo station, named after the battle in Belgium where the British and Prussian forces crushed Napoleon and the French army in 1815. At the station that Friday evening, I wondered if the British had deliberately chosen Waterloo just to irritate the French.

Boarding the train lacked the tension and strain one feels at airports. Smiling staff looked at our tickets and pushed our luggage through security checks. They escorted us to our carriage, which was clean, comfortable—and only one-third full.

The train was due to leave at 5:45 P.M. As the time approached, the train manager announced on the intercom that there would be a delay. At an airport, the hair would have stood up on the nape of my neck, but at Waterloo station, I remained astonishingly calm.

Gradually, it transpired that one of the automatic doors on the train would not shut. The manager explained that we would have to move to another train, and we all trudged across the platform, where still-smiling staff showed us to our new carriage. We glided away, one hour late.

Our fellow passengers were mostly French and English. An American man from Boston sat near us, constantly talking on a portable telephone to contacts in the oil business. Nearby, his Spanish wife looked after a year-old baby called Nick, who had the decency not to cry once during the entire journey.

As we raced through the night, we passed a station called Petts Wood. There, incredibly, *French* immigration officers examined our passports. To this Englishman, the experience was as improbable as if a Canadian or Mexican immigration officer had boarded a Greyhound bus outside Des Moines to examine an Iowan's passport.

We ate English sandwiches and drank French Perrier water. Then came the announcement we had been waiting for: "In ten minutes we shall be entering the Channel Tunnel. Transit time is twenty minutes. Please adjust your watches; French time is now 9:00 P.M."

Suddenly, with no feeling of descent, we were in the Chunnel. The sound got slightly hollow. Our ears popped. The wall of the narrow tunnel flashed green light, green light, green light, green light, white light—repeated again and again.

The baby Nick ate placidly. He was not interested in the thousands of years the island of Britain had been separated from France. He was unmoved by the millions of tons of water of the English Channel above us. He was quite right—we felt no sensation of claustrophobia.

In no time, we were out of the Chunnel and seeing the lights of Calais. After a brief stop, we hurtled towards Paris, reaching the train's maximum speed of 184 miles per hour.

My last train journey came to mind. A few months earlier, we had taken my mother-in-law for her birthday on the Iowa Star Clipper dinner train at Waverly (near Iowa's version of Waterloo). That splendid train had proceeded at a sedate eight miles per hour.

People in our Eurostar carriage talked together like old friends. The Bostonian began to telephone his oil contacts in France. Baby Nick closed his eyes and went to sleep.

Soon we were approaching the Gare du Nord station in Paris. Then came the best news of all. The train manager announced: "As we will arrive more than one-half hour late, you will be fully refunded for your London to Paris tickets."

That's what I call a civilized response to delay. Maybe somebody ought to tell the airlines.

THE BRITS: COLD, BRAVE, AND OBSTINATE

It was cold in London on February 7, very cold. It does not snow in London like it does in Iowa, but on that day it made a valiant try. The cold is different from Iowa—it is wetter and damper, and somehow penetrates deeper. It was far too cold to go out unless one had to, which I did, as I had to go to Parliament.

Before leaving, I switched on the radio in case there was any dramatic news about the Gulf War. The commentator was just saying that three missiles had been fired from a van in Whitehall at Number 10 Downing Street. The prime minister and war cabinet had been sitting, but none had been hurt. They had adjourned to another room where they continued their meeting.

My first reaction was a jumble of IRA and Iraq. Libya had connections with the IRA—did Iraq as well? The next news report made fairly clear the police thought it was the IRA.

A window overlooking the garden at Downing Street had been broken, and one person had been cut by flying glass.

I adjourned to a pub for a good hot pie; then it was time to go to Parliament. I stopped a taxi and asked for the House of Lords. "That's impossible," said the driver. "They have cordoned off the whole area because of the missiles at Downing Street."

"Can one get through by underground train?" I asked.

"I think so," he said. "You will just have to try." So I set out by underground.

There were few people about when I got to Westminster. The policeman at the door smiled and nodded at me, saying: "Good to see a familiar face." I went up to a weekly meeting of independent peers. The baroness who chairs the meeting told me to sit at the front—she did not expect much of an attendance, what with the frightful weather and the bombs.

When later the full House assembled, the Leader of the House of Lords made a statement about the morning's events: A white transit van had been parked in Whitehall, from which the attempt had been made. Fortunately only one person was injured. Two men had been seen running from the van. Our democracy would not be disrupted by such a cowardly attack.

Des Moines Register, February 16, 1991.

The leaders of the Labour and Liberal Democrat parties endorsed all that was said. Tributes were paid to the police, then the House proceeded with its business.

I had arranged a meeting with a friend to discuss my maiden speech. Afterwards we went into tea at the long table where peers congregate. I was complimented and teased about my planned speech. Nobody mentioned the attack on Downing Street.

That evening I tried again for a taxi. The House of Lords has its own method. "We have had the summons light on for half an hour," said the policeman apologetically.

Then miraculously a taxi appeared. An immensely distinguished silver-haired peer and I agreed to join forces—I was to drop him off first. I told him my name and was delighted to learn he had been at Cambridge University with my father.

Then he told me who he was—Lord De L'Isle. He had had an outstanding career in public life. But above all, he holds the Victoria Cross. The "V.C." is easily Britain's most important military honor. Few have been awarded since World War II, and not many V.C.s survive from that war. Certainly Lord De L'Isle is the only V.C. in Parliament.

I asked him what it was like to receive the medal. "Well," he said, "I was overwhelmed, and of course, I did not deserve it—it was just an astonishing honor."

Then he laughed. "My wife told all the newspapers I got the V.C. for being so obstinate!"

After I dropped off my companion, the taxi battled through the snow towards my flat, and I reflected on the day. Missiles had been fired on Downing Street. What would Dan Rather and Tom Brokaw and Peter Jennings have made of a similar attack on the White House?

Yet nobody I had met had really mentioned the incident. There had been the official remarks in Parliament, but otherwise silence reigned—and the prime minister had nearly been killed.

I groped for an answer. Were the British cold like the climate? Were they brave like Lord De L'Isle? Or were they perhaps just obstinate, as Lady De L'Isle had said of her gallant husband?

Lost Youth

I COME FROM AN OLD ENGLISH FAMILY *who for centuries owned an estate called Aldenham Park in the county of Shropshire, but my branch of the family are nomads. My four-greats-grandfather, Edward Acton, who was born in 1709, became a doctor, emigrated to France, and married a French woman. His eldest son was born in France; his eldest son in Sicily; his only son in Naples, Italy; his eldest son in Bavaria, Germany; and his eldest son—my father—in northern Italy. Twice during the centuries, our family have been made British by act of Parliament, because it had become so vague what nationality we were.*

In 1941, I became the first Acton eldest son to be born in England since Dr. Edward Acton in 1709. My father's nomadic instincts came to the fore after World War II, and in 1947 he sold Aldenham and the following year brought my mother and the six of us children out to the British colony of Southern Rhodesia (today's Zimbabwe). There we children—who had become ten by 1954—were brought up and lived very happily.

The first piece in this chapter contains vignettes of our childhood on our farm, M'bebi. When I originally came to Iowa, I would accompany my wife Patricia every day to the law school in Iowa City where she worked, and she would say, "Write me a story about your childhood." I started with a story called, "Fire." It and the other childhood stories in this chapter are the ones that the editor of the North American Review *thrilled me by publishing.*

We children adored M'bebi. I have begun the story called "M'bebi" with a description of it by the famous British writer, Evelyn Waugh. Like my mother, he was a Roman Catholic convert, and they were friends of long-standing. Regarded by many critics as one of the greatest of twentieth-century British novelists, Waugh is probably best known in the United States for his novel, Brideshead Revisited, *and the fine television series based on it. The second piece in this chapter is about Waugh and his visits to M'bebi, but although Waugh is the figure around whom we all danced, really the article is about my family.*

This chapter is called "Lost Youth," and I'm not sure when youth ends, but it certainly embraces university. I spent three happy years at Trinity College, Oxford, devoting rather more of my time to social life than to history books. Recently I went back to Trinity, accompanied by my niece Natalie, who is now an undergraduate at New College, Oxford. The resultant article, "A Rip Van Winkle at Oxford," gives a glimmer of what life was like there in the early 1960s.

Looking back at these descriptions of my youth, they do not adequately convey the closeness of us brothers and sisters, which continues to this day. However, I think the last line of the story called "M'bebi" manages to capture the feeling we all had for our childhood home:

"When I die, I want to go to M'bebi."

M'BEBI STORIES:
A COLONIAL AFRICAN CHILDHOOD

Emigration

Aldenham Park had been in our family for centuries. My father came back from the Second World War determined to farm the remaining acres, but he felt himself hedged in by the post-war restrictions of the Labour Government, and even more hedged in by lack of profits. A large old house costs a fortune in maintenance—especially when our great-great-grandmother had roofed in the vast saloon hall, and there was not the money to stop the roof leaking.

Our father had gone to Canada as a young man and had dreamed dreams of being a Mountie. Impetuously, he bought a farm unseen in Africa, and rushed out to occupy it. "We are going to live in Rhodesia," my mother announced. "Southern or Northern?" asked my uncle. "Goodness, I don't know," said my mother.

There were six children in our family then, and three cousins accompanying us. The good times were coming, and we were wildly excited. Rhodesia was so mysterious, so far away. Our father wrote that one of his workers was called "Telephone." One of my cousins burst into our bedroom and announced, her face blackened with burnt cork, that she was Telephone. We were filled with curiosity. Could there really be people who were black? I had never seen one, and the burnt cork was my image. Could there really be people called Telephone?

There was a round of parties to say goodbye to my mother. One of our uncles kindly took Charlie and me down to the railway line and told us to put the big old pennies of the day on the track. When a train had roared over them, we went to examine our pennies and recovered them squashed and distended. This was living.

Eventually we embarked on our ship. Violent sea sickness in the Bay of Biscay was followed by measles off the port of Dar es Salaam. We lay sweltering and sick. At last we recovered. Charlie, aged five, gave lessons to old men on how to play chess.

The last night before we reached our destination of Beira in Mozambique, Charlie and I, aged six, decided we must give a cocktail party for our friends. We had heard some grown-ups talking of parties, and pre-

---

"A Colonial Childhood: Coming of Age in Rhodesia," *The North American Review* (June 1990).

sumably impelled by the succession of parties given for our mother before leaving, thought it the conventional thing to do. So we went round the ship issuing invitations to our friends.

Then we told the news to our mother. "What do you mean you are giving a cocktail party?" "Well, everybody's coming—the Chief Engineer and the Captain have promised." Our mother was pained, but paid up with good grace. It was a roaring success.

It was strange to realise that the red-faced man with the big hat who came out in the little boat to the ship was our father. Stranger still to be at last on dry land, and to find waves of black people.

Had we but realised it, there was a premonition of things to come. When we at last fetched up at old Meikles Hotel in Salisbury, the black waiters were on strike for higher wages. But the politics of it were beyond us. We just wanted to see our farm and the house, which we had been told was a bungalow. We could not conceive of a house with no stairs. We had never seen one, and thought this a symbol of colonial splendour.

Our father drove us along the old Mazoe Road to M'bebi. There was no tarmac, and whenever we got behind a big lorry, clouds of dust invaded our noses and throats. We went past Mount Hampden, the site chosen for the white pioneers' capital city. But they had got lost and stopped at Salisbury instead.

On our right was a range of hills which we promptly christened mountains. We passed black families walking on the road, the man walking ahead and the woman carrying bundles on her head. Then we turned off where a ploughshare said *M'bebi*.

Up the steep back drive we went, with the thatched huts of our compound on the left. Little black children waved shyly at us and we waved back.

When we reached the top we saw a long white house surrounded by a veranda with arches filled with mosquito netting.

"Here we are," said my father.

M'bebi

The writer Evelyn Waugh, who was a friend of my parents, wrote several descriptions of his stay at M'bebi. The most dramatic was to Ann Fleming on 10 March 1958:

Children were everywhere, no semblance of a nursery or a nanny, the spectacle at meals gruesome, a party-line telephone ringing all day, dreadful food, an ever present tremendously boring ex-naval chaplain, broken aluminium cutlery, plastic crockery, ants in the beds, totally untrained black servants (all converted by Daphne to Christianity, taught to serve Mass but not to empty ash trays). In fact everything that normally makes Hell but Daphne's serene sanctity radiating supernatural peace. She is the most remarkable woman I know.

A briefer version was in his letter to his wife of February 9, 1958: "The house hideous surrounded by the roughest rough grass you could want with a few gaudy flowers emerging. Tin roofs, concrete walls, large bare rooms, everything painted white and awfully dirty."

Waugh was a brilliant writer and has caught some of the essence of M'bebi. And yet, and yet.

Take the house. The architecturally minded might find it hideous. But to us the wide veranda known as the *stoep* was glorious. Surrounding the main house, it was a place to run races, ride tricycles and play endless games. The fridge marked its starting point. The fridge had been bought with the house in 1947 and was old when it was bought. Since then it had done service for a family which had grown to twelve. Not surprisingly, as it was rarely defrosted, it would object to keeping anything cold. Suddenly it would wake up, give three hoots like the Queen Mary and start up again.

At the other end of the stoep was the "chicken lavatory," christened by Charlie and his favourite place. It was near the back door—which did not shut, so the chickens would wander in and out. Charlie would spend happy hours in it, reading and locked away from the annoyances of his brothers and sisters.

Tin roofs do not impress aesthetes. But there is nothing to beat the cosiness of lying in a warm bed in the rainy season, when the heavens opened and a noise like thunder on the roof went on for hours until one drifted off to sleep.

Charlie and Golly and I shared a room in the New Wing. It had the merit of being large, so that we could run steeplechases in it quite comfortably after we had supposedly gone to sleep. It had the dubious advantage of being near to the Milk Recorder's Bathroom. Near but not near enough, as it was necessary to go down the passage to get to the bathroom. A section of the ceiling of the passage had been removed to reveal the boiler and, unwittingly, to provide a nest for bats. As one walked down the passage, the bats would dive-bomb one's hair. I always ran.

The water in the bath ran red with rich earth. This might have been a barrier to a fastidious Englishman like Waugh, but was no bar to us. What *was* a problem was that if one put a foot in the bath, one's foot on the concrete floor somehow completed an electric circuit and gave a frightful shock. The wise balanced with both feet and hands on the edge of the bath like a monkey and jumped in. The resulting scalding or freezing was nothing compared to the electric shocks.

Our gramophone in the drawing room also gave electric shocks. It was prudent to wear rubber boots to put on music—but the joy of the operas and musicals and hit tunes was a wonder. The red sofa in the drawing room was the most comfortable sofa in the world; it was a race to be first to it. Catherine was particularly keen, and thirty years later arguments still break out as to who should get the red sofa.

We frequently watched films in the drawing room. We must be the only people on earth who saw the test film for our projector, *The Lady Vanishes,* ten times in four days. The first showing of any film would be for our family, the second on the stoep where the black families from the farm came to join us.

My sister Mary-Ann would endorse Evelyn Waugh's view of the food. She found the minced meat in the cottage pie so disgusting that even with the aid of so-called water sauce she could not get it down. This may have been the basis of Waugh's "gruesome spectacle at meals." But it has done Mary-Ann no harm—she is today a happy vegetarian prudently exempting smoked salmon.

Breakfast was delicious. Eggs, bacon, mushrooms, tomatoes, toast, cold ham and tongue, fig jam—that was a real breakfast. And tea. Where else could one eat condensed milk or tinned shrimps in such profusion? And then after either meal sit lazily talking and smoking cigarette after cigarette. Today's health fanatics will shudder, but to us it was bliss.

Our mother got hold of some white South African wine which cost two shillings a bottle. It was both delicious and had a kick like a mule. Our mother bought it in bulk, and we would reel out of dinner. It was christened "Mummy's white thunder." There has never been a vintage like it.

We may have had no nanny, but the elder girls ran the children and perhaps learned motherhood. The "roughest, rough grass" parted to show the Flamboyant tree—the red tree—when in full bloom the most glorious of sights. And there was the joy of tennis at the bottom of the garden. (Perhaps the grass on the croquet lawn was so long that year that Waugh could not see the tennis court from the stoep.) The tennis tournaments with their handicaps were tremendous fun.

But perhaps Evelyn Waugh has caught something of the spirit of M'bebi when he talks of our mother's personality. "Serene sanctity radiating supernatural peace."

When I die, I want to go to M'bebi.

Fire

During the course of the long, hot Rhodesian dry season, fire would come over the range of hills opposite our home—mountains to us children—and slowly burn the undergrowth on the hills and burn itself out.

One year the rains were poor and so the undergrowth was sparse. There was no fire that year and the crops were disappointing. But then in November the rains came with a vengeance and everything was lush and green and, not surprisingly, the maize crop was outstanding. The following September there were two years of undergrowth.

It is a long time since I was sixteen, but I still remember watching the fire coming over M'bebi Mountain. Unlike previous years, it was burning briskly. We realised that it was likely to come down into the valley, and then the precious stooked maize in our highest yielding field would be at risk.

Tony was our short, jolly, pipe-smoking farm manager. He took D'soka, the old Number One Foreman with his lined face and the perpetual handkerchief knotted under his cap, down to the valley to assess the situation. Tony and D'soka decided that the fire would reach the valley, and that all we could do was to try to contain it and keep it from the maize.

By the time Daniel, the one-armed Number Two Foreman, and the other workers arrived in the red lorry, the fire was roaring in the valley. There was a strong wind which stoked and speeded it.

We stood on the edge of the maize field beating at the fire with green-leaved branches. It was exhausting work. The blacks' faces were shiny with sweat and specked with soot, whilst Tony's white face was streaked with black. My mother came down in her bus with cold water, which we all gulped greedily.

I did not really realise how dangerous the fire was, not only to the maize, but to life itself, until Tony said "Thank God" as he saw Daniel and his gang reappear from where they had been battling out of our sight.

Tony dispatched me to the next-door farm to explain we needed help. The tradition among Rhodesian farmers, farmers everywhere, and perhaps all human beings, is to help in a crisis. So I rushed over to the neighbouring farmhouse in the Land Rover.

When I explained the position to the neighbour's wife, she said that it was impossible to do anything to help because they were giving the Gwebi Agricultural College students tea. I tried to impress on her the danger to our maize and the potential danger to their farm, but my entreaties were in vain. The tea party was her priority. I returned and reported to Tony, who cursed quietly, raised his eyes to the heavens and then shrugged.

The fire was gathering force, but we were lucky. Thanks to the Herculean efforts of D'soka, Daniel, and the other men, we only lost a few stooks of maize on the edge of the field.

As we reached the boundary of the farm, with the fire raging ahead, we heard screams. We decided that a family of wild pigs had been trapped up the neighbours' mountain and had reached an untimely death.

We were wrong.

When our neighbours saw that the fire was getting near their land, they sent their manager and a gang of thirteen men to stop it. The manager told the men to burn a firebreak to stop the fire in its tracks. This would have been sensible a month before, but the fire was approaching too fast, and there was no time to burn a big enough break.

The manager then told his gang to line the firebreak and meet the fire head-on with green branches—foot soldiers with spears resisting a wall of tanks. The black workers obeyed and lined the firebreak. The fire, roaring along the hill and down the valley, jumped the firebreak. The men ran up the hill, but they could run no further. The hill became so steep it was impassable. Eleven men were burned to death. (The manager climbed a tree and was not even singed.)

My mother, who twice a day acted as the nurse on our farm, was sent for, and the two other survivors were brought to the bus. I was deputed to accompany her to the hospital. The first black victim had terrible burns on his body. The second was burned almost white.

My mother did her duty as she saw it. She baptised the two men. I can still hear their moans as the christening water touched their poor burned bodies. Both men died that night in the hospital.

The fire was the main news in Rhodesia that day. I wanted to tell the newspaper the full story of our neighbours and their manager, and the part they had played in the tragedy. My father asked me whether that would bring the dead back to life.

And in November the rains came again.

Going to the Races

Our first glimmer of interest in racing came from playing the new dice game Totopoly. We found it far more thrilling than Monopoly, and I can remember the best horses, Dark Warrior and Dorigen, haunting my dreams. Next came Escalado, a game where the horses were shaken mechanically across the Ping-Pong table. The result was truly open, and we learned all about odds and the thrill of backing a winner.

When our father went on business to Durban in South Africa, he would go to their race meetings. He would come back armed with *Duff's Guide to the Turf,* which had photographs of the field at various stages of each race. He would go through the races with us, and we would analyse them and discuss them for hours.

After a great deal of nagging we finally persuaded him to take us to the old Belvedere racecourse in Salisbury. From then on the whole family was hooked. We never missed a race meeting during the holidays.

But that was the problem. Only four months of the year were holidays, and every Saturday for the other eight months we were locked up at school. The frustration of messing about on the rugger field or cricket pitch when the horses were galloping at Belvedere or, later, Borrowdale was ghastly. It became even more so when our father's horses started winning races, and we had to wait till Sunday morning to get the results.

Finally I thought of a scheme to get to the races during term. We had no squash court at school, and if you were keen enough you could give up cricket and instead play squash in town. I became the keenest squash player in the school.

Every Saturday I would march off to the Salisbury Sports Club and do battle with my squash racquet. Often I played the Rhodesian Junior Champion. He would give me a five-point start and play left-handed and back-handed only. I still seldom took a point off him.

Then (breaking every rule) I would walk and run to the racecourse. I would arrive puffing and panting, boiling hot, red in the face, carrying my squash racquet and wearing tennis shoes and squash clothes. With luck I would see the last two races and then run two miles back to school. It was better than nothing.

When my brother Golly became a senior he took a tycoon's view of the situation. "Surely there must be some way of bribing these priests to let us go racing," he said to our father. Our father, after reflection, went to the bishop. He would like to give a hundred pounds to the Church every time one of his horses won. The bishop's eyes glistened. The only stipulation was that his son should be allowed to go racing on Saturdays. The bishop saw no difficulty.

Every Saturday, waving goodbye to his schoolfellows, Golly would be whisked off to the races in our father's large green Chevrolet. Meanwhile priests all over Rhodesia would be on their knees praying for the success of our horses. My mother had a very good horse called Devil's Choice. When Golly returned from the races, Father Stockdale, the priest in charge of teaching religious doctrine, would say hopefully to him: "I pray Devil's Choice won?"

Thou Shalt Not Steal

The Ten Commandments seemed very dull to me when I was little. I had never wanted to murder anybody, not even my little brothers. I loathed sharing a bed with one of my brothers, so what was all this grown-up nonsense about men and women deliberately choosing to sleep together? And what would I want to steal? I had my own bicycle and toys. Catherine had hers, Charlie had his. The purpose of theft was beyond me.

I went to a Jesuit school called St. George's College when I was seven years old. In 1949 the philosophy of the school was based on the English public school of the 1890s. A bamboo cane played a huge part in discipline. I remember that in one term I was beaten fifty-five times in eighty-four days. My crimes were talking and cheek. Smoking was a grave crime, and theft was punishable with expulsion.

As boys, my brother Charlie and I used to wander in our red school blazers down the Manica Road to shop. It was in what was known as the "Cows Guts" section of Salisbury, and most of the customers were black. There was a wonderful store called Macklins. Charlie and I would go there and find Superman and Captain Marvel comics. We would buy them and walk to old Meikles Hotel. There we could lock ourselves into the Gentleman's and smoke and read our comics. It was bliss. As we grew older the comics gave way to *Boxing and Wrestling* and *Ring* magazines. The cigarettes continued, supplemented by chicken sandwiches when we could afford them.

One day when I was thirteen I went alone to another small store near Macklins. There was a coloured (mixed blood) lady serving, surrounded by black customers. I could not find a new boxing magazine, and my eye fell on a booklet called, "Diana Dors as Seen on T.V." I glanced through the magazine. Diana Dors was apparently Britain's answer to Marilyn Monroe, whom the boys at school sniggered about. She was a tall blonde lady. And then to my astonishment I came to a picture of Diana Dors sitting in a bath, with her blonde hair curling provocatively over one eye and naked breasts. I had never seen a woman's breasts before. I had to have that magazine.

I was wearing my school blazer; to have bought the magazine would have brought disgrace on the school. It had a picture of a half-naked lady in it. I would be found out. There was only one option. I tucked the magazine under my blazer and started to walk out. In a horrified voice the coloured lady said, "You should be ashamed of yourself. You are a white boy stealing a paper ... (gesticulating towards the black men) IN FRONT OF THESE PEOPLE."

My ears burned to the colour of my school uniform. I paid for the magazine and ran out of the store. When I was in the street, breathing deeply, I tore the magazine into a thousand pieces.

The Water Diviner

"The water diviner is coming tomorrow," our father announced one evening, sitting on the stoep. It was the best place to sit in the evenings as it was cool, and one could drink one's drink and look at the all too brief Rhodesian dusk and listen to the crickets.

We were full of questions which tried our poor father's patience severely. "What is a water diviner?" "How does he find the water?" "Can he smell it?" "Is it magic?" Our father, who did not know the answers, decided to answer all of the questions with the Italian words: "*E molto misterioso*—it's very mysterious." This meant: "I don't know, stop asking questions, and the whole thing is a complete mystery anyway."

The next day a dusty ramshackle old truck drove up, and a big white man got out. He wore standard Rhodesian "bush" clothes—a khaki shirt, khaki shorts (in his case very short shorts with the cuffs turned up to make them even shorter), and long khaki stockings. His ensemble was completed by a bush hat with a piece of brown snakeskin woven round the rim. He was very sunburned, and you got the feeling that he had never actually visited a city in his life. Two rather mangy dogs snapped at his heels.

"Hello," he said. "I'm Dave Harris. I have come to find you some water."

Our problem was that we needed to irrigate in the centre part of the farm, but there was no stream or pool to draw from there. We had to find underground water and tap it with a bore hole. Dave Harris's job was to find the underground water.

We set out for the right locality. A large rich field, which I always thought of as the potato field, would be the ideal place.

Dave Harris got out a tin box, slightly bashed in. I thought wonderful scientific instruments would appear, but all he took out was a piece of steel shaped like a capital "Y." It would have made an ideal catapult.

With a solemn look on his face, Dave grasped the metal by the two ends of the fork and pointed the longer strip towards the ground. Nothing happened. Then he started walking, pointing the long strip in front of him. The dogs and the rest of us followed respectfully.

After he had walked about a hundred yards, the long strip of metal quivered slightly. Dave said, "Here we go." The metal shook violently and then shot downwards. "Here is your water," he said. "I will just make quite sure." He approached the spot from the other end of the field. Exactly the same thing happened—the metal stick quivered, shook and pointed downwards.

He could see that I was enthralled. "Here, boy, you try," he said and passed me the stick.

I grasped it as he had and walked where he had walked. Absolutely nothing happened. The metal remained lifeless in my hands. Just a metal "Y"—which was, after all, all it was.

"Come on, I'll show you," he said. I held the metal "Y," and he held my hands with his big hands, so that we were both touching the metal. Then we walked over the spot where he had found the water. The stick spontaneously shook and quivered. When it shot down Dave said: "Try to hold it up." I put all my force into trying to make the metal point upwards, with no effect whatever.

"It's just a gift," Dave said modestly.

Three months later we had a splendid bore hole at precisely the place that Dave had marked with a pile of stones.

It was not just a gift. It was magic.

Big Cats and Broken Dogs

When my brother Peter was very little, he was with our father one day as he was discussing horse racing with a friend. Our father said something about the champion South African Jockey "Tiger" Wright. Later, various owners in Natal were discussed and mention made of a prominent owner named Mr. Lyons. Peter's eyes grew round with dismay. "What is the matter Peter?" our father asked. "I'm very frightened of the tiger and lions," said Peter.

He had no need to fear tigers at M'bebi. As far as I know, "Tiger" Wright was the only member of his species in Africa. But we did have one visit from a pride of lions at M'bebi. Six or seven of them came to the dairy and pigsties, which were only a couple of hundred yards from our house. Our father had embarked on a policy of calling heifers after our sisters, and so the lions attacked, killed, and ate "Catherine." Some pigs were also killed and eaten, and then, presumably having satisfied their hunger, the lions retreated.

It was thought that the taste of veal and pork would entice the lions back. So the next night our father and a group of his friends, described in our family legend as "men from Salisbury," sat up in haystacks near the Jersey cow pens. After some hours when nothing happened, our father saw something yellow move in the dark—and, quick-triggered, fired. It was only a cow. The lions never returned. In the same year our greatest cow, L'Etacq Rita, won the prize as the grand champion in Salisbury. Inevitably, the two stories got blended, and years later in London people said to me, "Oh, wasn't it your father who shot his champion cow thinking it was a lion?"

As far as I can remember, there were only two incidents in which leopards featured at M'bebi. One was when an old African hunter armed with a shotgun had successfully tracked a leopard with his dogs and shot it. The leopard was brought outside our garage. I remember going and looking at him—so beautiful, so graceful, so very dead. There were crowds of Africans milling around, thrilled at the excitement and wondering how the one-eyed old hunter had succeeded in shooting him.

Giulio, our uncle's manager of the next door farm, had been requisitioned to drive the leopard's body from the scene of his death. He became very Latin, very voluble, and very overstimulated. A photograph was taken of Giulio with his foot planted on the leopard's neck. There was no doubt in his mind, whatever the truth of the matter, who was the hero of the hour. Ultimately the leopard skin was put in the farm office.

The other incident involved Genesis. As suited his biblical name, he was the father of a huge family of twelve children. He had embraced Catholicism with fervour and was a devotee of our father and mother. One day he came into our father's office looking worried. Our father said, "What do you want Genesis?" Genesis said simply, "A leopard has broken my dogs—you must mend them."

Our father went out with Genesis, who showed him the two dogs. They were tall, whippet-like indigenous dogs, both appallingly clawed about their bodies. Their very entrails were hanging out. Our father's reaction was that the case was hopeless. Genesis was used to our mother giving medicine to his family, and to our father being the farm veterinarian. As far as he was concerned, if they could cure terrible diseases, then surely our father could do a simple thing like mend injured dogs.

The doctor was consulted by telephone. His advice was to take a needle, use good strong thread—and hope. Our father took the medical advice. Our mother held down the dogs. Their innards were pushed back into their poor broken bodies. Our father, who adored animals, did his best to sew up their skin gently. The dogs squirmed and bit during their unanaesthetized operation.

Our father said, "I am afraid that is all I can do, Genesis," and returned sorrowfully to his office, never expecting to see the dogs again.

A couple of weeks later Genesis reappeared at the office door. Frisking about with their tongues lolling and tails wagging were the two dogs, as good as new.

Genesis said: "They were broken and you have mended them."

Death and Hope

There were inevitable human tragedies on our quiet Rhodesian farm.

One day in 1949 my father, wearing his eternal sombrero and scratching the back of one of his favourite large black pigs, was approached at the pigsties by the Number One Foreman D'soka. It had been reported to him that a disaster had been located down by the river. My father must go down tonight to investigate further.

My father lost no time. At that stage he was fulfilling his dream of becoming a Canadian Mountie, which had led him to emigrate to Rhodesia in the first place, by riding around on horseback. He got mounted and rode over to the river, which lay beyond the marshy *vlei* at the foot of the Mazoe Mountains.

He later described to us how he rode along the riverbank until he came to a spot which was sheltered from view. He was horrified by what he saw.

On the bank of the river lay the body of a long-dead woman. The water lapped at her legs, and there was a knife sticking out from below her left breast. A dead baby lay on her bosom. Nearby, a man's body dangled from a rope tied to the branch of a tree. His eyes and tongue stuck out.

My father did not quite know what to do. Clearly he must call the police. The man must have murdered the woman and then in his despair hung himself. The child had presumably died of exposure subsequent to this human drama.

Knowing that he must not touch anything before the police arrived, my father went to look at the woman to make a guess at how long she had been dead. He was startled to see a very slight movement in the baby's left arm. He rushed over to the child and picked it up. There was a very faint heartbeat. The child's eyes and ears were crawling with maggots, but it was alive.

My father stripped off his khaki tunic, wrapped the girl child in it, and galloped from the river, past the *vlei,* across the old Mazoe road, and up the back drive to our house. He called for my mother, explained the situation to her, handed her the baby, and went to telephone the police.

All medical matters on the farm were in my mother's hands. She had no medical training, but she had common sense, a syringe and some basic medicines for normal ailments. Clearly this was beyond her; equally clearly, time was crucial. She carried the baby to the constantly ringing telephone in the middle of the house. For once there was nobody on the party line.

My mother rang the doctor at the Mazoe Citrus Estate. She told him that she thought of giving the baby coffee and brandy and a little soup, and she asked his advice. Dr. Simms Davies was against the brandy. He thought it might lead to permanent blindness. He was deeply disturbed about the maggots on the baby's eyes and ears.

My mother baptised the baby, and fed her coffee and soup. Slowly the baby regained consciousness and began to improve, and my mother drove her to the hospital. After a week she was well enough to be handed over to her mother's family.

In those days we had no resident chaplain. A Catholic priest called Father Longrigg used to attend to the spiritual needs of the little community. Father Longrigg had once been bitten by a crocodile on the bank of a river. (We children maintained that the crocodile had died as a result of the encounter.) He liked things to be "nice," "tidy," and "just so."

About ten years later, Father Longrigg visited the farm school which M'bebi now boasted. He went into the class of older children and explained that he was going to prepare them for baptism. He asked whether any of the children had been baptised. To his astonishment, one little hand was raised at the back of the class.

Father Longrigg said, "But that is impossible, child. What priest baptised you?"

The little girl replied, "Lady Acton was the priest, Father."

A gleam of comprehension came into Father Longrigg's eye. "And what is your name, child?"

"My name is Hope."

"WILL A LION COME?"
MEMORIES OF EVELYN WAUGH

My parents, John and Daphne Acton, were friends of Evelyn Waugh from 1936 until the writer's death thirty years later. I knew nothing of him in the earlier years, as I was born in 1941. After the Second World War, our vast family emigrated from England to Southern Rhodesia, today's Zimbabwe, and in 1958 and 1959 Waugh paid us two memorable visits there. The following year I stayed with Waugh at his house in Somerset.

Waugh in middle age has been portrayed as jaded. The Waugh we saw in Rhodesia was usually amused and always stimulating. At times, certainly, he was bored, but for the most part he was in good spirits. Not only did he make us laugh, but he laughed himself a great deal.

In 1936 Waugh was thirty-two and an acclaimed novelist. He had marooned himself in the English county of Shropshire to work on a travel book, *Waugh in Abyssinia* (1936). My parents then lived in Shropshire at our ancestral home, Aldenham Park. My father's sister, Mia Woodruff, brought the writer to Aldenham that April, and Waugh wrote to my mother: "I absolutely loved my visit."

Soon after that Waugh came for another weekend. On the Sunday afternoon, my father proposed that they go for a walk. My father was immensely proud of a waterbird called the great crested grebe which nested on our lake—the Shore Pool—and he wanted to show the grebe to Waugh. The latter was violently opposed to the plan. Alcohol had flowed that day, and Waugh objected that "the poisons ought to be allowed to settle."

My father won, and my parents set off, dragging their reluctant guest with them. Eventually the party got to the Shore Pool and sighted the great crested grebe. Waugh was furious at its inadequacies and gave vent to his feelings: "It's a pathetic bird, a miserable bird, a wretched bird," he said.

A few months later Waugh began to write *Scoop* (1938), his classic satire on journalism, and the grebe became immortal. William Boot, the hero, first appears while he is writing a weekly nature column called "Lush Places." William is in despair over an article on badgers. His sister, out of mischief, had substituted "the great crested grebe" for "bad-

---

ger" throughout his piece, and William had received indignant complaints from his readers. One nature lover "challenged him categorically to produce a single authenticated case of a great crested grebe attacking young rabbits"—and so William's adventures begin.

Sent to Africa to report on the war in Ishmaelia, William is a hopeless war correspondent. As the book reaches its climax, the grebe has become a god. William, in a slough of despond, bows his head: " 'Oh, great crested grebe,' he prayed, 'maligned fowl, have I not expiated the wrong my sister did you ... ?' " The grebe answers William's prayer, and as a result, William gets the "scoop" of the title.

But even this mockery of the grebe did not appease Waugh's fury over the infamous walk with my parents. Twenty years later he wrote *The Life of Ronald Knox* (1959). Contempt for the great crested grebe smolders in Waugh's description of the Shore Pool, "a lake which has afforded pleasure to ornithologists."

On one of Waugh's visits to Aldenham, my mother's younger brother, Hedley Strutt, was a fellow guest. After dinner, Uncle Hedley beamed and said: "I am going upstairs to see Nanny." Waugh was riveted. "Why is he going to do that?" he asked. My mother explained that Nanny Galer, who looked after my sister Pelline, had been Uncle Hedley's nanny. Nanny had brought him up, and although now in his early twenties, Uncle Hedley still doted on her. Waugh showed such interest that my mother believes the episode contributed to the bond between Sebastian Flyte and his nanny in *Brideshead Revisited* (1945), Waugh's novel about an aristocratic Catholic family.

The friendship between the novelist and my parents continued to grow. My father, whom Waugh later described in one of his books as "a light-hearted, sweet-tempered, old-fashioned, horsy young man," adored roulette. Waugh accompanied him and my mother to Ostend in Belgium so that my father could indulge himself at the casino. When Waugh was to remarry, he brought his fiancée, Laura Herbert, to meet my parents at Aldenham.

The Second World War ended such weekends, and after the war my parents sold Aldenham and emigrated to the colony of Southern Rhodesia. They bought a farm called M'bebi, twenty-five miles from the capital Salisbury (today's Harare). There they settled with their family of six children, which by 1954 had grown to ten.

Evelyn Waugh re-entered my parents' lives when Ronald Knox—Ronnie to our family—died in 1957. Ronnie was an eminent priest and scholar, and had entrusted Waugh, a Catholic convert, to write his biography. During his eight years at Aldenham as chaplain to my mother, Ronnie had translated almost the entire Bible, starting with Genesis on the day my sister Catherine was born in 1939. As my mother had known Ronnie so well, Waugh flew out to Rhodesia in early 1958 and spent a month cross-examining her at M'bebi.

My first glimpse of Waugh was striking. My father's idea of dressing for dinner after his business day in Salisbury was to remove his jacket and come into the drawing room in open-necked shirt and trousers. We boys wore khaki shirts and shorts and had bare feet, often streaked with mud from the farm. On the evening the novelist reached M'bebi, I came straight from the dairy and wandered into the drawing room barefooted and dressed as usual. A vision greeted me of a short, stout, red-faced man wearing an immaculate white dinner jacket, a garment I had only seen in films. When my mother introduced us, he glared at me. Shamed, I rushed off, put on socks and shoes, combed my hair, and reappeared. Evelyn Waugh had arrived.

We children studied our guest intently. Our ashtrays were in much use, as many of us chain-smoked cigarettes, and Waugh added to the overflow by constantly smoking huge cigars. I was now, at sixteen, officially allowed to drink alcohol. But Waugh astonished me by drinking beer at breakfast. We concluded that this was because he found our family so stunningly boring.

Although only fifty-four, Waugh made a pantomime of being an old man. His chief prop was an enormous ear trumpet, which he laid in front of him at meals. At lunch one day, the conversation turned to vocabulary. For reasons which are beyond me, I announced that I had a large vocabulary. This was too much for Waugh. His eyes blazing, he picked up the ear trumpet and put it to his right ear. Omitting to make me repeat myself, he said: "My dear boy, you only know about 200 words." I still cringe when I hear the word "vocabulary."

Waugh was diverted by all of my sisters, who used various methods to make an impression on him. Catherine, two years my senior, determined to get on Christian name terms with him. For somebody with her charm, this would not have been a very difficult task. But she made certain of it by bellowing "Mr. Waugh" towards the ear trumpet at the end of every sentence she uttered. Eventually he gave in. "Won't you call me Evelyn?" he suggested graciously.

My little sisters Mary-Ann and Jane decided that what our guest needed was entertainment. Waugh would sit trying to read his book, but found it impossible as the little girls danced before him in varying degrees of dress and undress. Waugh produced coins to persuade them to go away. But he never forgot their dancing, and he ever after referred to them by the collective nickname "the nautch girls"—Indian dancers.

Waugh was especially entranced by my sister Jill, known as Tickey. He conceived a plan that she should marry his eldest son Auberon. His letters to my mother for years are full of Jill. "My love to all your hordes, especially Tickey." After she had had an operation on her toes, he demanded furiously, "Why have you cut off Tickey's feet?" Then he complained of a photograph "showing dear Jill in a very bad light. Young Auberon is not so keen & wants a nautch girl instead." Waugh was only to abandon his dream in 1961, when Auberon got engaged.

Twenty years earlier in England, Waugh had lost the battle of the visit to the great crested grebe. Now in Rhodesia he won the battle to visit my married sister Pelline, whom he had known as a little girl at Aldenham. My mother had pointed out that Pelline could not travel, as she was heavily pregnant and had three tiny sons, so Waugh insisted on going to see her. My mother urged that this was an impractical scheme, as Pelline had only three modest bedrooms. But the author was adamant.

So my mother packed Waugh, Father Maxwell (whom Waugh had written of as the "ever present tremendously boring ex-naval chaplain"), and her five youngest children into our Volkswagen bus and drove the hundred miles to Pelline's house. Pelline's entire family huddled into one bedroom; Waugh had another, Father Maxwell the third. My mother slept on the sofa and her little children in the bus.

After dinner Waugh grew bored and went to bed early. He took a formidable sleeping draught of paraldehyde, and soon terrible snores penetrated the thin ceilings and bounced off the tin roof. His roars woke my three-year-old nephew Denes. "Will a lion come?" he asked his parents.

Early in his visit to M'bebi, I showed Waugh the schoolroom which housed most of our books. Examining the shelves, he kept laughing. He was amused by the haphazard way some great classic stood next to a book which he dismissed as rubbish. I had always thought our books perfectly well arranged, but his laugh was so infectious that I found myself laughing with him.

Drinking tea on the stoep (as we called the veranda at M'bebi), my mother and I talked to Waugh about books. I was reading *Mansfield Park* at school and asked him what he thought of Jane Austin. "Very complete," Waugh nodded. My brother Charlie and I adored P.G. Wodehouse, and Waugh thought well of our taste. He quoted a sentence from Wodehouse: "I could see that, if not actually disgruntled, he was far from being gruntled." No other author could possibly have written those words, Waugh emphasized with a chuckle.

My innocence at sixteen emboldened me to ask Waugh some direct questions about his own books. When I had read *Brideshead Revisited,* it had struck me that Sebastian's mother, Lady Marchmain, was—like my mother—a beautiful Catholic peeress. So I blurted out: "Is Lady Marchmain based on Mummy?" Waugh, who had the highest opinion of my mother, but not of Lady Marchmain, burst out laughing. "No, no," he said.

My next question was more successful. "What was the most difficult thing you ever did as a novelist?" I asked. Without hesitation, Waugh said: "Turn a woman into a man." I persisted: "Who was the man?" "Beaver in *A Handful of Dust,*" Waugh replied.

My sister Catherine and I had always laughed together at Beaver, the villain of the book. He had no personality and no job, but sat by the telephone hoping for invitations to meals. He was called "London's only spare man." Catherine had a fantasy that when I left school, I would become Salisbury's only spare man. Now we knew that the model for Beaver was a woman.

The sequel to this story came thirty years later. I had read an article about *A Handful of Dust* (1934) by Evelyn Waugh's son, Auberon, himself a distinguished writer. Auberon explained that Beaver, who had wrecked the hero's marriage, was based on a man called John Heygate, who had wrecked his father's first marriage. I wrote to Auberon and told him of the conversation I had had with his father.

Auberon replied: "What you say rings a tiny bell. I believe that I may have heard my father say that ... Baby Jungman ... was at one time London's spare girl, waiting on the end of a telephone. It is possible that he shifted this one characteristic on to Heygate. If so, it might have been a double revenge, as he had been in love with Baby Jungman at one time. A curious idea."

Waugh went back to England in March of 1958, and at Christmas that year, my mother proudly sent a family photograph to all her friends and relations. Waugh's response was biting: "I say, what a photograph!

I have been telling my family how pretty you all are & now you send them this very disillusioning group. Not like human beings at all."

Waugh's nostalgia for M'bebi was evident when he wrote: "It was touching to see the stain of the red earth of M'bebi on your letter," and he duly returned to M'bebi in March 1959. This time he made a sponsored trip to east and central Africa as an excuse to spend a fortnight with us. The fruit of this second expedition was *A Tourist in Africa* (1960). In this book, he described his first day back at M'bebi: "The teeming life of the house, as in a back-street of Naples, rages round me from dawn to dusk, but I remain in my chair, subject to interrogation, and the performances of conjuring, dancing, and exhibitions of strength, but for one day at least immovable."

Much of Waugh's second visit was taken up with sightseeing. He, my mother, Father Maxwell, and a young tycoon friend set off by car to see something of Rhodesia. The conspicuously red faces of Waugh and Father Maxwell inspired my father to christen the group, "the Lobster Quadrille," after the dance in *Alice in Wonderland*. All went well until they got to the magnificent Zimbabwe ruins. At their hotel, the manageress insisted she had only one room with a bath. Waugh insisted that *four* rooms with baths had been booked. Their voices grew more and more heated.

The manageress sought to clinch the argument. In a tone suggesting that they take their business elsewhere, she said: "We like our guests to be happy ... " Waugh trumped her: "I shouldn't think that happens very often." My mother as usual resolved the matter—Evelyn Waugh got the room with the bath.

During the Lobster Quadrille tour, Waugh found a way to tease our luckless chaplain, Father Maxwell, who summed up his intellectual life in the words, "I read people, not books." The priest, as his figure attested, enjoyed a glass of beer, and he was particularly fond of a cold Castle—Rhodesia's leading brew. At their first stop, Waugh asked Father Maxwell what he would like to drink. "A co' Cuss'ell," Father Maxwell replied with his heavy Manchester accent. From then on, every time they ordered drinks Waugh would triumphantly add: "And a co' Cuss'ell." His imitation made the poor chaplain squirm.

But if Waugh mocked the man, he treated the priest with respect. After his son Auberon had been shockingly injured in an accident, a grateful Waugh wrote to my mother: "Please thank Father Maxwell awfully for saying Mass for Bron."

Waugh had the virtue of generosity, which at times rewarded him materially. At the end of his second visit to Rhodesia, he gave a fine dinner party at a Salisbury restaurant in honor of my nineteen-year-old sister Catherine. After his return to England he reported gleefully: "My income tax man passed the bill for Catherine's Portuguese wine as a necessary literary expense."

In his letters, Waugh joined in our family jokes. Our local doctor greeted every malady from an ingrowing toenail to a burst appendix with the same hallowed words: "There is a lot of it about." Waugh seized on this catch phrase. He wrote that a friend "is down with melancholia. There is a lot of it about."

A special joke was born over *The Life of Ronald Knox,* which came out in 1959. Waugh dedicated the book to Katharine Asquith and my mother. Mrs. Asquith, whose guest Ronnie had become when we emigrated to Rhodesia, read the book in proof. She wrote to my mother that it was a masterpiece. My mother in turn wrote to Waugh, "Katharine says the book is a masterpiece." From then on, Waugh always referred to the book in his letters to my mother as "Masterpiece."

Waugh turned the joke into a bibliophile's treat. On publication of the biography, he sent my mother two copies. In the ordinary edition he wrote: "This for bottom shelf." He inscribed the special edition: "For Daphne with my love & gratitude from Evelyn. This one is for the top shelf." The title page read: "The Life of the Right Reverend Ronald Knox ... A MASTERPIECE by Evelyn Waugh." The author had had this unique volume specially printed for my mother. My brother Edward is now its proud owner; my mother, seeing my envy, presented me with the "bottom shelf" copy.

My mother's brothers, and indeed my father, had gone to Cambridge University; my mother's friends had gone to Oxford. She was more impressed by the education of her friends than her relations. So in 1959, she persuaded me to try for Trinity College, Oxford. Waugh joined in the plan, and on a visit to Oxford, sought to insinuate me into Trinity. He reported to my mother: "I told the President how lucky he was to be getting a promising scholar like Richard. He said: 'Yes, I hope very much he gets in.' Not an absolutely satisfactory answer."

I will never know if Evelyn Waugh influenced the result, but I managed to pass the Trinity entrance exam. I wanted to tour Italy and France before going to England, so my mother asked Waugh if he could suggest any friends to entertain me on the continent. Complaining as usual about my Rhodesian accent, Waugh pointed out some of my other inadequacies: "Poor chap he has lived among bungalows and skyscrapers and won't know the difference between Classic, Gothic, Baroque." As to hostesses in Europe: "I don't see Richard being at all easy in cosmopolitan society—e.g., Nancy Mitford or Diana Cooper or Pam Churchill. He must get some English polish before we put him into circulation." Waugh sensibly concluded: "Richard shall take Europe very slowly and humbly."

After some months on the continent in the first half of 1960, I arrived in England. Masses of English people had stayed at M'bebi and, as a naive eighteen-year-old, I expected reciprocal invitations to flow. They did not. However, Evelyn Waugh came up trumps, and promptly asked me to stay at his house, Combe Florey, in Somerset.

I had a happy weekend there. Auberon Waugh told me about Oxford, and I told his mother about the Jersey cows at M'bebi. Evelyn Waugh talked of people and books, expressing particular admiration for the work of Muriel Spark. I played chess with Auberon, and there was a dinner party for relations on Saturday night. On Sunday, I went to Mass with the Waughs.

We had a conversation at lunch on Sunday about thank-you letters. I loathed writing letters and asked in a voice of despair if I had to write and thank for the weekend. Laura Waugh kindly said no; Evelyn Waugh firmly said yes. He went on to suggest possible topics for my letter, and made me rock with laughter. After much discussion, he concluded that it would be best for me to make some uncontroversial remarks about the weather and the Sunday sermon.

I did write a thank-you letter, and Waugh wrote his own letter about the weekend to my mother: "I asked [Richard] with the promise that there would be a house-party but one by one the other guests chucked & took ill and in the end he was alone. He was a pineapple of politeness. The last year has transformed him from a Rhodesian schoolboy into a pre-1914 undergraduate. His accent has almost gone, his spots entirely. ... How cleverly he disguised his boredom which must have been acute."

I was not in the least bored at Combe Florey, but I was, as always, daunted by my host. Having lost my watch, I was terrified of being late when the family set out for Mass on Sunday. Waugh discovered me pacing the hall ages before the appointed hour. He wrote to my mother: "[Richard] has no watch and is disconcerted by English habits of punctuality."

My mother appears to have had little faith in my capacity to apply myself at Oxford, and Waugh agreed with her. During my first month at Trinity College, in the autumn of 1960, he replied to her worries: "Richard will not be sent down [expelled] for a year. There is a new, uncivilised system by which undergraduates are expected to pass a preliminary exam at the end of their first year."

I confounded these prophets of doom by surviving at Oxford for the full three years. But in my last term, I faced my final exams ("Schools") with panic. My mother relayed these tidings to Waugh. He consoled her: "Don't take seriously Richard's fuss about Schools. No one ever fails unless ... he deliberately insults the examiners." This prediction proved accurate. I scrupulously avoided insulting the examiners and just scraped through my exams.

Waugh's one communication to my father which survives shows to perfection his mastery of succinct prose. Waugh knew that in Rhodesia my father sorely missed the roulette wheel. From Monte Carlo, the author sent him a picture postcard of the casino. The message consisted of one word: "Homesick?"

From the time he was engaged on *The Life of Ronald Knox* (1959), Waugh made pithy comments to my mother about his work. "When I am writing a novel I know all about my characters and what they are doing when they are not on the stage. I just record what seem the most interesting incidents. I am rather doing that with Ronnie." When the book came out, he wrote: "The reviews have been jolly decent to me. A few beasts, notably Graham Greene, have been beastly about Ronnie. It is selling like warm cakes ... "

Waugh had nothing good to say about *A Tourist in Africa* (1960), the book which described his second visit to M'bebi. "I am trying to write about my African jaunt. It is hard going because I can only be funny when I am complaining about something and everyone was so decent to me." And when the book was published, he wrote: "I've sent you a copy of Pot Boiler, because it would have been impolite not to, not in the hope of causing any pleasure or interest."

Waugh's next book was *Unconditional Surrender* (1961) (published in America as *The End of the Battle*), the final volume of his Second World War trilogy. He complained to my mother: "Midwinter past and here I am stuck in my novel longing for Monte Carlo and Umtali and Kashmir but I can't move until the book is finished. I interrupted it to translate a little life of La Veuve Cliquot (paid in champagne) and can't get started again." But ultimately, he took pride in the book. "I can't remember, did I send you a copy ... If I didn't, I am very sorry & will send you one at once. It has some funny bits."

Then Waugh started the first (and only) volume of his autobiography, *A Little Learning* (1964). "I am toiling & tinkering away at an autobiography. The trouble is that I am (genuinely) not interested in myself & that while my friends are alive I can't write candidly about them." Later, he was less negative. "I have finished the first volume of an autobiography. No 'Masterpiece' but it has some comic bits ending with an unsuccessful attempt at suicide at the age of twenty-one."

The last letter from Waugh to my mother was in January of 1964. The Queen had just made my father a Companion of St. Michael and St. George (a C.M.G.). Waugh wrote: "I was much amused to see that the Queen had decorated John for services to Rhodesian agriculture. As I remember it he served a [foreign] company manufacturing bags out of imported materials. Surely someone has been pulling the royal leg? I am jealous."

Waugh ended his letter: "All love to you & Jill & the C.M.G. and the nautch girls."

Evelyn Waugh died on Easter Sunday, 1966, at the age of sixty-two. To the world at large, he was a ferocious literary lion. We were lucky; to our family, he was much more than that. He was warm and generous and stimulating and funny. When I think of Evelyn Waugh, I remember how I held him in awe. But above all, I remember his infectious laugh.

A RIP VAN WINKLE AT OXFORD

Trinity College is one of the oldest and one of the smallest of the thirty-six colleges in the university city of Oxford. A rich civil servant named Sir Thomas Pope founded the college in 1555 during the reign of Mary Tudor. An earlier college on the same site had been suppressed during Henry VIII's dissolution of the monasteries.

Today, Trinity College, with fewer than 300 undergraduates, stands

---

"A Rip Van Winkle at Trinity College, Oxford," to be published in *British Heritage*, 1998.

between its ancient rival, Balliol, and Blackwell's, one of the finest book-shops in Britain. The college faces onto Broad Street—always referred to as "the Broad" in my day. For I spent three blissful years at Trinity from 1960-1963.

Recently I decided to revisit my old college haunts. I knew that vast changes had taken place since my undergraduate days—the greatest being the admission of women to the men's colleges. When I was at Trinity there were no female students, and indeed, visitors from the women's colleges had to leave by 7:00 P.M.

During the 1970s and 1980s, the men's colleges started to admit women, and today about half of the students at Trinity are female. Feeling that I would be a Rip Van Winkle in this changed world, I arranged for my niece Natalie—who is reading Politics, Philosophy and Economics at New College, Oxford—to accompany me. (New College is so called because it was "new" in 1379.)

We met at Trinity's beautiful iron gates that date from 1737. At the porter's lodge, I looked for my old friend Clifford, a porter from the 1960s. Time plays tricks, as Clifford would be nearly a hundred by now. I told today's friendly porter that I was a graduate of the college. He waved us in, ignoring the one pound fee. "Be my guests," he said.

Oxford colleges are divided into quadrangles—open spaces around which the buildings are clustered on four sides. We made for the building in the Front Quadrangle that houses the Junior Common Room (the JCR). In my day, undergraduates relaxed in the JCR, reading newspapers and magazines and debating every possible topic. During my first term, I wrote a letter suggesting that a television would cheer the place up. A senior student objected to my request, on the grounds that our JCR shouldn't exist courtesy of the BBC. He ended his letter: "Acton must go."

When my niece and I tried to get in, we found the JCR was locked, but a friendly woman student produced a key. A vast television set now dominates the room. It's nice to be vindicated.

Our next port of call was the Chapel, built in the 1690s. The architect is unknown, but the building looks like one of Sir Christopher Wren's churches. The interior has stunning wooden carving and paneling, possibly wrought by the great Grinling Gibbons. On the right of the altar is an alcove designed for the college's then only woman—the wife of the president—to pray by herself.

We went on to Durham Quadrangle and entered the Dining Hall. On the panel outside is a wonderful portrait of Michael Maclagan, fellow in modern history from 1939 to 1981. He had tutored me in early English history, and I felt as if I was stumbling on an old friend. He had adored heraldry, and here he was, dressed in a splendid red and gold costume covered in heraldic lions.

The Dining Hall (built in 1620), with its long tables and wooden benches, seemed to have shrunk since my time. We inspected a portrait of the ill-fated Lord North, the prime minister who lost the American colonies, which was balanced by a portrait of another Trinity man, William Pitt the Elder, one of Britain's greatest prime ministers.

When I was up at Trinity, servants known as "scouts" served us lunch. A lobster cost three shillings and sixpence (about thirty cents). My niece, an animal rights activist, was horrified when I told her this important piece of information. Today's students line up to collect their own lunch, and Natalie was relieved to find something called "vegetable bake" on the menu.

We passed through into the Garden Quadrangle, which has buildings on three sides and opens out onto a vast and magnificent lawn. My old rooms on the ground floor face the lawn, but alas, the door was locked. We peered through the window, and I remembered my old-fashioned record player. Today's inhabitant had a massive TV, a video machine, a refrigerator, and any number of other luxurious appliances.

As we wandered towards the garden, I was startled to see chalked above a doorway, "LADIES 1ST VIII," apparently referring to a Trinity women's rowing team. My niece smiled at my surprise. "My friend is in the Ladies 1st VIII at New College," she said.

We crossed the lawn with all its memories of summer parties. Then we meandered back to the lodge, thanked the porter, and left through the door next to the main gate. When I was at Trinity, this door was firmly locked at 11:00 P.M. If you wanted to get in after that time, you had a problem. I took Natalie round past the White Horse, Trinity's pub, and Blackwell's bookshop, to show her how we used to solve that particular problem.

The Trinity gardens face onto Parks Road; next to the gardens is the New Bodleian Library, belonging to the university. A huge iron gate with vicious spikes on top stands adjacent to that library. My niece looked in amazement as I explained that, if we wanted to get into the college after the front door was locked, we had to climb that gate. Carefully avoiding the spikes, we would hop over onto the nearby roof and thence clamber down into Trinity gardens.

As I reminisced, Natalie kept looking at the height of the gate, at the spikes, and at my middle-aged girth. It was clear what she was thinking: "You would have done far better to have come to Oxford in the 1990s. The students all have keys to the front door nowadays."

In accordance with Trinity tradition, we adjourned to the White Horse pub—even Rip Van Winkle's modern-day Oxford niece gets thirsty.

Lords, Commons,
and Crown

MY FATHER DIED *just under a year after Patricia and I married in Iowa. He was a good man, and I shall always miss him.*

My father was a hereditary peer—the third Lord Acton. As his eldest son, I inherited his title and our family's seat in the House of Lords. His grandfather, Sir John Acton, had become the first Lord Acton. He was a Catholic intellectual, a historian, a linguist, a former member of the House of Commons, and a colleague and friend of the Liberal Prime Minister William Gladstone.

In 1869, on the latter's recommendation, Queen Victoria made my great-grandfather into a peer, and he sat as a Liberal in the House of Lords. His son, who succeeded him, was a diplomat and joined the Labour Party as the second Lord Acton. His son, my father, was not a political creature—he liked farming, business, and charitable work. But on his rare visits to the House of Lords, he sat as a Conservative. When he died in 1989, I took my seat as a Cross-bencher—as independents in the Lords are called. Thus, in four generations, my family had sat in every conceivable party and grouping in the House of Lords.

In May 1997, a British general election brought the Labour Party under Prime Minister Tony Blair to power. Although it has no plans to abolish titles, Labour has promised that, "The right of hereditary peers to sit and vote in the House of Lords will be ended by statute." How long Labour will take to fulfill this pledge remains to be seen.

My years in Parliament have been immensely interesting. The high point was the greatest parliamentary occasion since World War II—the 1990 speech in the House of Commons which led to the end of Margaret Thatcher's career as prime minister. Another highlight three years later was the largest vote ever cast in the House of Lords to decide whether to have a referendum on a closer European Union. Pieces concerning these two events appear in this chapter, along with other sketches of the House of Lords, the House of Commons, and the monarchy.

At the beginning of each session of Parliament, the Queen, the Lords, and the Commons come together for the State Opening of Parliament. The occasion is brimful of history and pageantry. My wife Patricia attended one of these ceremonies, and the chapter ends with a description of that most memorable of State Openings.

FIRST DAY IN BRITAIN'S HOUSE OF LORDS

In December, with my Iowan wife and my English son watching from the gallery, I took my seat in the House of Lords—the British equivalent of the United States Senate. The method of gaining entry to those two bodies could not be more of a contrast. To enter the Senate requires years of activity in party politics, a vast sum of money, a tremendous amount of hard work, and finally, the majority of votes cast in a state.

I got into the House of Lords in a simpler if sadder way. A year ago my father, the third Lord Acton, died. As his eldest son, I automatically inherited his title and his right to sit in the House of Lords.

Most members of the House of Lords gain their seats by inheritance. Some, known as "Life Peers" and "Law Lords," are appointed by the Queen on the prime minister's recommendation for life, and their titles die with them. Some bishops of the Church of England also sit in the Lords.

A very few ancient titles pass in the female line—if a lord from one of these families dies leaving a daughter but no son, she can inherit the title. But most titles, such as that of my family, can never go to a woman. I have often wondered what my eldest sister thinks of a system whereby, although she was born nine years before me, I as a male inherit the title and the seat in the House of Lords.

In America, the Senate is the senior of the two Houses of Congress. In Britain, the elected House of Commons dominates; the House of Lords can only delay legislation for up to a year. The Lords' main role is in revising bills, often rushed through the Commons without proper consideration.

Although the power of the House of Lords is much less than that of the American Senate, it is nonetheless very important. In the United States, there is a separation of powers—the president and his cabinet are independent from the Congress. In Britain, the prime minister and most of the cabinet sit in the House of Commons (the remainder sit in the House of Lords). With a healthy majority of members in the House of Commons, whatever bill Margaret Thatcher's Conservative government submits is automatically passed. Thus the only effective brake on the British executive is the House of Lords.

Des Moines Register, February 16, 1990.

This comes about despite there being a built-in Conservative majority of hereditary peers, because many of these do not attend. The result is that a coalition of opposition party peers and independents and government rebels can and periodically do defeat the government.

Few people really think the composition of the House of Lords is satisfactory. Certainly no other country would dream of imitating it. But the various plans this century to abolish the Lords and replace it with a more democratic second chamber have always come to nothing. The real reason is the fear that the result will be a more effective upper house, and thus a greater limitation on the power of the House of Commons. The present leadership of the opposition Labour Party says that if it becomes the government, it will replace the House of Lords with an elected Senate. Time will tell.

Meanwhile, the present composition does have some advantages. Cross-benchers—of which I am one—are beholden to no political party or interest. They can speak and vote exactly as they think right, and are a distinctive feature of the British upper house.

I am a very junior member of the House of Lords—just *how* junior was highlighted by an incident when I took my seat. As a new member, I was honored by being given the front right-hand seat of the Cross-benches, opposite the throne. A voice from my right on the Senior Labour bench greeted me with the words, "You need an Order Paper," and the peer handed me his own. It was the former prime minister, now Lord Callaghan, next to whom sat his predecessor as prime minister, Lord Wilson. Both kindly signed my Order Paper to commemorate my first day in the Lords. Former prime ministers and eminent people from many spheres sit in Britain's upper house, giving a wealth of experience and knowledge to the deliberations.

When I left the chamber my cousin, Davina Darcy de Knayth, was waiting in her wheelchair to take my wife, my son, and me to tea. She is a baroness in her own right, having succeeded to an ancient title dating from 1332. Appallingly injured in a car crash twenty-five years ago, in which her husband was killed, and without an ounce of self-pity, she devotes her public life to speaking up from her wheelchair for the disabled (and many other worthy causes) in the House of Lords.

An elected Senate would doubtless be more rational. But until such time as it comes, these examples show that the curious composition of the House of Lords can have its advantages. Certainly, having become a member by the accident of birth, I mean to do my very best to play a part in that ancient institution.

[Author's note: I sat as a Cross-bench peer for nearly eight years. In 1997, after the election of Prime Minister Tony Blair's Labour government, I moved to the Labour benches.]

SURPRISES ABOUND IN THE HOUSE OF LORDS

The House of Lords is full of surprises, great and small.

When I went to take my seat last year, the liveried attendant announced that I should hang my overcoat on my father's peg in the entrance hall. My father had not sat in the Lords since he emigrated to Africa in 1947, but sure enough, there was the peg marked with his name solemnly awaiting his return.

The ceremony to introduce a hereditary peer such as myself is simple. Wearing a suit, you take the oath of loyalty to the Queen, sign the roll, and shake the Lord Chancellor's hand. So long as you don't sign the Lord Chancellor's hand and shake the roll, you can't really go wrong.

In contrast, a newly ennobled peer performs an elaborate pageant. Recently I witnessed Black Rod and Garter King of Arms enter the chamber, followed by a new peer and his sponsors wearing scarlet and ermine robes and carrying black cocked hats. The new lord and his sponsors bowed to the Cloth of Estate, which marks the place on the throne where the Queen sits to open Parliament. They then paraded around the chamber. At the end of the ceremony, they sat and stood three times doffing their hats to the Cloth of Estate. As the new peer exited, a sudden roar greeted him: "Hear, hear!"

After this ceremony, the House proceeded briskly with its business. First came questions put to the various government ministers, and then the debates of the day. I was amazed that many peers seemed to be asleep, leaning sideways in their benches. But when I tried it myself, a voice echoed loudly from the back of the bench. Hidden microphones carry the speeches to the hard-of-hearing.

The language of the debates is striking. The House of Commons is never mentioned by name—it is always "Another Place." The self-disci-

Des Moines Register, October 3, 1990.

pline is also striking. There is none of the rowdiness of the Commons—peers refer to each other as "the noble Lord So-and-So" and speak with great courtesy.

An octogenarian peer, Lord Longford, recounts how far this courtesy can be taken. He once heard a lord describe another as: "redolent of oleaginous hypocrisy ... without, of course, any desire to be personally offensive to the noble Lord, for whom I have such a high respect."

Lord Longford himself, an old and true friend, represents many facets of the House of Lords. Uniquely, he was made a peer in 1945 and later inherited his elder brother's title as well. He has been leader of the Lords and has held many high offices of state. Among innumerable careers he has been an Oxford don, a writer, a publisher, a banker, and a crusader. The newspapers christened him "Lord Porn" because of his war on pornography.

Lord Longford took me under his wing from the outset, introducing me to attendants, policemen, and waitresses. He escorted me to my first tea in the peers' dining room. There you sit at a long table eating wafer-thin cucumber sandwiches. I asked the peer next to me the question of the hour—how long would the prime minister survive? "That's politics," he snorted. "I am here for the National Health Bill." Discerning a medical man, I hastily changed the subject to the difficulties of giving up smoking, which drew a happier response.

After tea, Lord Longford set off at a great pace to show me the library. As I puffed along beside him, he suddenly stopped and said with a disarming grin: "I think that I should give you the advice that a ninety-year-old peer gave me when I first came here. 'In the House of Lords, *always* walk VERY, VERY SLOWLY. You will live longer.'" Then he galloped away. I dawdled behind, reflecting on the wisdom of that ancient peer, who must have been born when Victoria was a young Queen.

On another day Lord Longford and I were in the guest dining room. Suddenly there was a terrific din. "There's the division bell. Come on, we must vote," said Lord Longford, and off we dashed.

Voting in the Lords is done on foot. "Contents" and "Not Contents" follow intricate routes through the chamber and along different passages, where tellers record the votes. Geography not being my strong point, I was terrified I would vote the wrong way by mistake. Fortunately, my cousin Lady Darcy de Knayth and I were supporting the same side. I pushed her wheelchair while she called directions.

We lost the vote, and repaired to the peers' dining room to console ourselves. I'm not sure what American Senators do after losing a vote, but in the House of Lords, there's nothing to revive the spirits like crumpets and a good cup of tea.

THE SPEECH THAT BROUGHT DOWN A PRIME MINISTER

On Tuesday of this week, the 372 Conservative members of the British House of Commons voted in the first round of their leadership contest. Although Prime Minister Margaret Thatcher received 204 votes, she was not fifteen percent clear of her challenger, former Secretary for Defense Michael Heseltine, as required by party rules. The latter received 152 votes, while sixteen members of Parliament abstained.

The prime minister now has resigned, and the Conservative Party is openly split. A second vote for the leadership is due to be held on Tuesday, November 27th. In this round, the winner requires a simple majority of 187 votes.

Margaret Thatcher's problems have multiplied over the last two years. She has had deep-seated differences with colleagues in the Conservative Party. She has alienated European leaders with her constant objections to greater economic unity. The electorate was up in arms over her poll tax and economic policies, which had produced soaring inflation, interest rates, and unemployment. But Mrs. Thatcher's gravest political problem has been her high-handed approach towards her fellow cabinet ministers—not one survived from the original 1979 team.

Matters reached a climax when the deputy prime minister, Sir Geoffrey Howe, resigned at the beginning of the month. I learned in the morning newspapers on November 13th that Sir Geoffrey was to make a special resignation statement in the House of Commons that afternoon. I decided to avail myself of the privilege of sitting in the peers' gallery in the Commons to hear his statement.

Des Moines Register, November 24, 1990.

I arrived early and witnessed the prime minister's entrance to the jeers of the Labour Party. She sat in her customary place, apparently composed. However, she betrayed her nervousness by constantly kicking her crossed leg—clearly visible from the gallery, but not to her fellow members in the House.

Sir Geoffrey Howe came in, and for the first time in twenty-five years, sat on the back benches instead of the front benches reserved for ministers. His hands were pressed on his knees, knuckles white with strain.

Then Michael Heseltine took his seat. Everyone present knew that he was considering challenging Mrs. Thatcher for the party leadership. The tension in his whole body reminded me of a racehorse or greyhound awaiting the start.

Sir Geoffrey rose to speak. The House—normally uproarious—was hushed.

Sir Geoffrey began by recalling his long relationship with the prime minister and their joint early successes. Then he turned on her, blasting Mrs. Thatcher's "nightmare image" of Europe as "a continent that is positively teeming with ill-intentioned people, scheming ... to 'extinguish democracy.' "

Mr. Heseltine nodded vigorously.

Sir Geoffrey attacked the prime minister's opposition to a European common currency. He used a cricketing metaphor to describe the appalling effect of her utterances on the diplomatic efforts of the Chancellor of the Exchequer and the Governor of the Bank of England: "It is rather like sending your opening batsmen to the crease only for them to find, the moment the first balls are bowled, that their bats have been broken before the game by the team captain."

Mrs. Thatcher smiled.

But the prime minister looked increasingly grim as Sir Geoffrey described the impossibility of serving in her cabinet: "I realise now that the task has become futile, ... trying to pretend that there was a common policy when every step forward risked being subverted by some casual comment or impulsive answer."

Then Sir Geoffrey explained his resignation: "I have done what I believe to be right for my party and my country. The time has come for others to consider their own response to the tragic conflict of loyalties with which I have myself wrestled for perhaps too long."

He ended. The Conservative members sat in shocked silence. Mrs.

Thatcher walked quickly out of the chamber. The elderly peer on my left turned to me and said: "You are fortunate to have been here. That is the most important speech in the House of Commons for fifty years."

I understood what he meant. In 1940, a member of Parliament had destroyed the Conservative Prime Minister Neville Chamberlain and brought Winston Churchill to power with the words: "Depart, I say ... in the name of God, *go.*"

I looked along the bench at Viscount Whitelaw, the Conservative Party's great and popular elder statesman. When he had sat down before the speech, he looked cheerful. Now he was sheet white.

As I left the gallery, I was certain that Michael Heseltine would challenge Mrs. Thatcher for the party leadership.

Perhaps Conservative members of Parliament, and whomever they choose as their new leader, will think hard about the unquestioning support they have given the prime minister for eleven and a half years. In so doing, they may find the words of my great-grandfather, the first Lord Acton, singularly apt:

"There is no worse heresy than that the office sanctifies the holder of it."

[Author's note: Subsequently the Conservative members of Parliament chose John Major to succeed Margaret Thatcher. Thatcher was made a peer, and now sits in the House of Lords as Baroness Thatcher.]

THE PRIME MINISTER'S QUESTION TIME: "A VERY ODD AFFAIR"

Members of Congress have no opportunity publicly to cross-examine the president of the United States. By contrast, the British prime minister submits himself twice a week to questions from the House of Commons.

Des Moines Register, August 19, 1994.

Conservative Prime Minister John Major recently said that the British public regards Prime Minister's Question Time as "a very odd affair." Many Americans, watching it on the C-Span television channel, must find the institution thoroughly bizarre.

Every Tuesday and Thursday afternoon from 3:15 to 3:30, Members of Parliament (M.P.s) crowd the green leather benches of the Commons for the high point of the parliamentary week. Ten questions for the prime minister are listed on the Order Paper. Almost invariably, they are "open" questions, all asking the same thing: "If he [the prime minister] will list his engagements for [the day's date]."

The Speaker, Betty Boothroyd, calls the name of the first questioner, who shouts out the number of his or her question. In response, the prime minister recites his schedule for the day. Then the Speaker calls the questioner's name again, and the M.P. asks a supplementary question. This is the real point of the exercise—the question can be about anything from Bosnia to unemployment.

John Major replies, and the Speaker calls one or two other supplementary questioners. Then she moves on to the next question on the Order Paper. Major refers to his previous answer about his day's schedule, and the cycle is repeated.

The centerpiece is when the leader of the opposition asks questions. After the untimely death of Labour Party leader John Smith in May, then-deputy leader Margaret Beckett handled this task with great aplomb. Whenever Margaret Beckett asked or John Major answered a supplementary question, the green leather benches erupted in cheers or jeers. The spectacle is positively gladiatorial.

The first recorded question of the prime minister was in 1721. The system has been constantly developing ever since.

For example, the peculiar "list his engagements" form of question has evolved over time as the most "transfer-proof." If the M.P. listed a specific question, say about education, the prime minister could transfer it to the Secretary of State for Education for a reply, and thus the M.P. would lose the opportunity to question the prime minister. A list of the prime minister's engagements can't be transferred—hence its popularity.

After an illness in 1953, Winston Churchill reduced the number of question times from four to two. Tuesdays and Thursdays have been the designated days ever since.

Few prime ministers can match Churchill's wit on these occasions. Once asked to divide the Ministry of Agriculture and Fisheries,

Churchill refused, adding: "After all, there are many ancient links between fish and chips."

Former Prime Minister Harold Wilson wrote that every prime minister awaits questions with apprehension. A predecessor, Harold Macmillan, used to be physically sick or nearly so before Question Time. Even the "Iron Lady," Margaret Thatcher, is reputed to have dreaded questions.

Prime ministers prepare themselves thoroughly for the ordeal. Often Conservative questioners reveal their supplementary questions in advance to the party whips, or accept planted questions. Then John Major can open his briefing book and read out remarkably detailed answers.

As for opposition questions, the prime minister's advisors have to guess. They prepare a profile of listed questioners, detailing their interests. They then draft answers on fifteen to thirty current political topics.

From his briefing book, and from his general command of government policy, John Major answers questions. He usually is able to respond effectively even to the supplementary questions of opposition M.P.s, whom the Speaker selects at random.

Major has recently called for the abolition of the "open question" asking for his engagements. He proposes instead that substantive questions be submitted in advance. This proposal is likely to meet with resistance.

Apart from the matter of transferability, M.P.s like to hide behind open questions. They like to ask follow-up questions along the whole range of policy. With a specific question submitted in advance, they would be limited to asking supplementary questions on the main topic. Also, M.P.s fear that the spontaneity of the prime minister's answers would be replaced by the damage-limiting replies drafted by the civil service for other government ministers to give in Parliament.

An old story illustrates the civil service attitude to parliamentary questions. Two senior civil servants, touring in the English west country, were discussing the ideal parliamentary answer. They arrived at an unmarked crossroads. The driver called to a very rustic-looking farmhand: "Can you tell us where we are?" The farmhand replied: "You be lost."

The driver was about to upbraid the man, when his colleague gripped his arm in excitement. "Don't you see?" he said. "That was the *perfect* parliamentary answer. It was brief; it was accurate; and it added not one iota to existing knowledge."

However eccentric and noisy Prime Minister's Question Time may be, it makes the prime minister directly accountable to even the newest and humblest member of Parliament. And that, at least, is something to commend it.

[Author's note: In May 1997, the new Labour Prime Minister, Tony Blair, changed Prime Minister's Question Time. It now takes place once a week, on Wednesdays, for thirty minutes.]

THE SUFFRAGETTE IN THE BROOM CLOSET

Women peers play a leading part in the House of Lords. For example, in debates on foreign affairs, Baroness Chalker, the minister of Overseas Development, speaks for the Conservative government.

Opposite her is the Labour Party's principal speaker on foreign matters, Baroness Blackstone, a distinguished academic. On the same side of the chamber is Baroness Seear, the deputy leader of the Liberal Democrats, who enlivens debates with her eloquence.

Looking across the red leather benches, you sometimes see Baroness Thatcher—former Prime Minister Margaret Thatcher—seated on the Conservative front bench reserved for party dignitaries, listening intently to the speeches.

Baroness Thatcher is the only woman prime minister Britain has had. But if you go over to the House of Commons, you find increasing numbers of women in other prominent positions—both in Prime Minister John Major's cabinet and in the Labour Party's shadow cabinet.

Seeing all these eminent women in Parliament takes my mind back to Virginia-born Nancy, Lady Astor. In 1919, she became the first woman to take a seat in the House of Commons. When I was eighteen and Lady Astor was a fiery old lady, I met her at a luncheon party. Although at the time she petrified me, now I look back on the occasion as an exhilarating encounter with history.

Most people have heard of Nancy Astor and Margaret Thatcher, but

what about those women whose efforts made it possible for such remarkable pioneers even to be in Parliament? For instance, how many
people know of the woman who spent the night in a broom closet at the
House of Commons for the sake of women's suffrage? Recently I learned
about an obscure memorial to this intriguing feat and decided to search
it out.

I set off from the House of Lords and walked to the central lobby,
thronged with people waiting to go into the chamber of the House of
Commons for Prime Minister's Question Time. From there I passed
through the columns of marble statues, which line the narrow St.
Stephen's Hall, and turned right into the vastness of Westminster
Hall.

This great hall was completed in 1099. Here the law courts were
born, and state trials—including that of Charles I—were held. Here the
bodies of monarchs and prime ministers have lain in state. My heels clat-
tered on the cold stone floor and echoed from the vaulted roof.

By a small door was a sign that read: "St. Stephen's Crypt—peers
and M.P.s please ring the bell." I did so, and eventually an old man appeared. He inspected my identity badge, opened the door, and let me
through.

Several flights of steps led down to the medieval chapel of St. Mary
Undercroft, ornamented lavishly during the Victorian era. At the back of
the chapel was a darkened antechamber. I groped for the handle of another door, and switched on the light.

I found myself in a tiny closet. A broom and a bucket draped with
rags leant against the wall. An old rolled-up carpet occupied one corner,
and a battered music stand another.

On the back of the closet door was a small metal plaque. Above it
was a photograph of a woman against the purple, white, and green
colours of the suffragette movement. I read the inscription on the
plaque:

IN LOVING MEMORY, EMILY WILDING DAVISON

In this broom cupboard Emily Wilding Davison hid herself illegally
during the night of the 1911 census. She was a brave suffragette campaigning for votes for women at a time when Parliament denied them
that right. In this way she was able to record her address on the night
of that census as being "The House of Commons," thus making her
claim to the same political rights as men.

Emily Wilding Davison died in June 1913 from injuries sustained when she threw herself under the King's horse at the Derby to draw public attention to the injustice suffered by women. By such means was democracy won for the people of Britain.

I left in silence, thinking of Westminster Abbey and Nelson's Column in Trafalgar Square. And I realized that this broom closet—in its simple and lowly way—was also a national monument.

THE LORDS' HISTORIC VOTE

History is about to be made in the House of Lords, Britain's upper house of Parliament. The Lords shortly will vote on whether to put the Maastricht Treaty on European Union to the British people in a referendum.

Ten of the twelve European Community countries have ratified the Maastricht Treaty (three of these—France, Ireland, and Denmark—after holding referendums). German ratification awaits the result of court challenges to the treaty. That leaves Britain.

The House of Commons after months of wrangling has essentially agreed to the treaty, and the House of Lords in principle concurs. But the Lords now face the great constitutional question of whether to hold a referendum—which opinion polls show a huge majority of people want.

The former prime minister—now Baroness Thatcher—leads those in the Lords who urge a referendum. All Britain's political parties supported Maastricht in last year's general election. Hence Lady Thatcher argues: "No elector in this country has been able to vote against Maastricht—*none.*"

Peers who agree with Lady Thatcher point to the example of the 1975 referendum, when the British people voted in favor of staying in the European Economic Community. Peers who support Prime Minister

Radio Commentary, Weekend Edition, Monitor Radio, the broadcast edition of *The Christian Science Monitor,* July 9, 1993.

John Major say ratification is a matter for Parliament alone.

Already more lords have spoken on Maastricht than during any debate in the 600-year history of their House. The forthcoming vote is likely to be the largest ever.

Twelve hundred peers have seats in the House of Lords. A majority of the 350 who regularly attend seem to oppose a referendum. However, nobody knows how many of the remaining "backwoods" lords will appear on this historic day ... or how they will vote.

Many "backwoods" peers live in the countryside, and don't attend the House of Lords from one year to the next. Their views on the referendum might be colored by unusual political considerations. For example, a keen fox-hunting lord—despite supporting a referendum—might fear that a "no" majority in a referendum would bring the Labour Party to power. Labour might abolish fox-hunting—hence that peer might prefer not to vote on the referendum question at all.

I spend part of each year surrounded by wild turkeys and deer in the backwoods of Iowa. I *will* fly back to London especially for the referendum vote, because I consider it so overwhelmingly important.

Many peers who desire a referendum—like Lady Thatcher—oppose Maastricht. I broadly support the treaty, because I want Britain to influence Europe's future. But I think the electorate should take such a major constitutional decision, so I will vote with Lady Thatcher.

The chances are that the referendum vote will fail. Still, great excitement lies ahead.

[Author's note: The vote was overwhelmingly against a referendum, by a majority of 445 to 176—by far the largest number of votes ever cast in the House of Lords.]

A NEW RECRUIT TO THE ORDER
OF THE GARTER

An item of news with overtones of medieval England does not seem to have made its way onto America's modern information highway. Recently, Baroness Thatcher—the former British prime minister, Margaret Thatcher—has become a Lady Companion of the Most Noble Order of the Garter.

The Garter is Britain's oldest order of chivalry, having been founded by King Edward III in 1348. Its nearest rivals in age rejoice in the names of the Order of the Thistle and the Order of the Bath. But they pale by comparison to the grandeur and antiquity of the Garter.

Edward III during his reign was embroiled in wars with France. A lover of the tournaments and jousting of knights, he conceived the idea of founding an order of knighthood modeled on King Arthur's fabled Knights of the Round Table.

But whence came the improbable name of "The Garter"?

During the 1340s, so the story goes, King Edward held a grand tournament at Windsor Castle. During a ball that evening the King danced with the Countess of Salisbury.

As the couple danced, one of the Countess's garters fell off. Edward chivalrously swooped down to rescue the garter from the floor. Seeing the knowing looks and nudges of the other dancers, Edward said in his best medieval French: "*Honi soit qui mal y pense.*" (For those whose medieval French is rusty, this translates as: "Shame on him who thinks evil of it." Or, "Evil be to him who evil thinks.")

The king then put the garter on his *own* leg, saying that soon the garter would be held in such high esteem that they who were permitted to wear it would account themselves fortunate.

Edward proceeded to found his order of knighthood, with the garter as its emblem and *Honi soit qui mal y pense* as its motto. The order was limited to 24 knights, so as to comprise two teams of 12 knights for jousting—mock battles on horseback using lances. Each knight was given his own stall in the chapel at Windsor Castle.

Over the centuries, the number of Knights Companions of the Garter has remained fixed at twenty-four; only upon a vacancy occasioned by death will the sovereign appoint a new knight. In addition, the

---

Des Moines Register, July 6, 1995.

monarch has periodically made special appointments from the British and foreign royal families which, during the twentieth century, came to include royal ladies of the Order such as the Queen Mother and Princess Anne.

In 1990, Queen Elizabeth II appointed Lavinia, Duchess of Norfolk, a major figure in the world of charities, as a Lady Companion of the Garter. She thus became the first woman in the order's 650-year history to be one of the twenty-four core, non-royal members.

The current knights include former prime ministers and other elder statesmen, former governors of the Bank of England (equivalent to chairmen of the Federal Reserve), an admiral, a general, and other grandees.

The longest serving Knight of the Garter today is the Earl of Longford, a former Labour cabinet minister, a prolific writer, and an ardent crusader against pornography and other social evils. (Incidentally, he's also very kind to peers who sometimes live in Iowa.) Lord Longford shows a spirit Edward III would commend, as, in his ninetieth year, he runs a sedate four miles every morning.

On June 19th, Baroness Thatcher and Sir Edmund Hillary—the conqueror of Mount Everest in 1953—were invested as Companions of the Garter during a private ceremony at Windsor Castle. Before the recent fire, this would have taken place in St. George's Hall, but now—shades of the medieval Countess of Salisbury—the ceremony is held in the ballroom.

There Queen Elizabeth placed the insignia of the Order on the new Companions. The knights and ladies were resplendent in blue velvet mantles, crimson velvet hoods, and black velvet hats with a plume of ostrich feathers surrounding a tuft of black heron's feathers.

The garter itself is about one inch wide and made of dark blue velvet edged with gold, bearing the motto, *Honi soit qui mal y pense* in gold letters. The knights wear the garter below the left knee, while the ladies wear it above the left elbow.

After the investiture, the knights and ladies marched to St. George's Chapel. In a public ceremony there, Queen Elizabeth commanded Baroness Thatcher and Sir Edmund Hillary to take their own stalls in the chapel, thus formally "installing" them. So Margaret Thatcher became the second ever Lady Companion of the Order of the Garter and may place the initials "LG" after her name—representing Britain's highest honour.

Many centuries have intervened between Edward III and Baroness Thatcher, LG, but it seems singularly apt that Lady Thatcher should have joined the king's Order. Having spent so many years jousting with the opposition parties during Prime Minister's Question Time in the House of Commons, she will now spend the rest of her life in an English order dedicated to the art of jousting itself.

THE TOWER OF LONDON AND THE MONARCHY STILL STAND

[Author's note: The following article was written as an impression of the British monarchy's position at the end of 1992. Many events since—above all, the tragic death of Diana, Princess of Wales in 1997—have rendered some of the facts in the article out-of-date. But the piece is included as a snapshot of an important historical period.]

The Tower of London is the oldest royal palace in Europe. William the Conqueror, who founded the modern English monarchy, built the original Tower of London—the White Tower—in 1078. From the beginning, large black ravens have hopped about the Tower grounds. The legend is that without the ravens the Tower will fall—and so will the kingdom.

Does the separation of the Prince and Princess of Wales mean that the ravens are poised to leave the Tower? Certainly the international press gives the impression that the royal separation has provoked a great constitutional crisis.

The key point to remember is that Her Majesty Queen Elizabeth II is only sixty-six years old; her mother is ninety-two. The Queen, a lover of country pursuits, is in good health, and is likely to live another twenty years. Nobody appears to believe that Queen Elizabeth is suddenly going to lose her throne. Thus, there is no constitutional crisis, but there is widespread disillusion with the royal family.

Des Moines Register, January 1, 1993.

For all of her forty-year reign, her majesty has been a model of public duty and a popular sovereign. However, during 1992 she and her family have faced a barrage of difficulties.

On the Queen's accession to the throne—as in case of her father, King George VI—the government agreed that she should pay no tax. Britain's current economic depression and massive unemployment made her exemption from tax completely out-of-step with the times. Following a newspaper campaign that stressed the anomaly of this arrangement, the Queen decided to pay taxes. In future, she also will relieve the government from the cost of supporting minor members of the royal family.

Another bone of contention concerns Windsor Castle, recently ravaged by fire. The castle belongs to the state, rather than Queen Elizabeth personally, so the government announced it would foot the bill for restoration. Many taxpayers feel strongly that the Queen should pay. Doubtless as a compromise, her majesty eventually will make a major contribution.

But the royal marriages have been the matter on which the media have concentrated. Princess Anne has divorced and—unusually for a member of the royal family—remarried. The Duke and Duchess of York have separated, and day after day the press has reported the antics of the Duchess.

The real drama concerns the Prince and Princess of Wales. In announcing their official separation to Parliament, the Prime Minister, John Major, stressed that the constitutional position was unaffected, and that the Princess could still become Queen. However, questions about their future have been raised.

Although she may become Queen in name, Princess Diana seems most unlikely ever to be *crowned* Queen. The decision as to whether his wife is crowned belongs to the King. The last four of King Henry VIII's six wives were not crowned, and in 1821 King George IV went so far as to bar his separated wife, Queen Caroline, from his coronation in Westminster Abbey.

Another question is whether Prince Charles will, indeed, succeed his mother. Having just separated from his popular and glamorous wife, his fortunes are at a low ebb. Some recent polls indicate many people would prefer that the Prince of Wales step aside in favor of his ten-year-old son, Prince William.

However, this reaction is in the emotional aftermath of the royal separation. A more balanced judgment on the standing of Prince Charles—an intelligent and serious man—will be possible in a few years time. Meanwhile, the constitutional position is plain—Prince Charles remains heir to the throne.

If the Prince and Princess of Wales were to divorce and the Prince sought to re-marry, then under the Royal Marriages Act of 1772, he would have to obtain the Queen's permission. No doubt the Archbishop of Canterbury and the prime minister would advise on the religious and popular consequences.

The archbishop might indicate that he could never crown a divorced and re-married head of the Church of England. If so, Prince Charles might then consider giving way to Prince William. Some commentators suggest that to avoid this contingency, the monarch should cease to head the Church of England.

The monarchy has survived the Wars of the Roses, the beheading of King Charles I, and the interregnum of Oliver Cromwell. It has survived the ousting of King James II in 1688, and the abdication of King Edward VIII in 1936. It has survived the great unpopularity last century of King George IV and, in her middle years, Queen Victoria.

Doubtless the English monarchy will have to adapt to changing circumstances, as it has done for the last nine hundred years. Perhaps in time it will slim down to something more like the Scandinavian or Dutch royal houses.

But despite the recent headlines, it is going too far to assume that the royal mishaps of 1992 foreshadow the fall of the House of Windsor. Unless an unexpected tidal wave of republicanism arises, either King Charles III or King William V will succeed Queen Elizabeth II.

The ravens show no sign of abandoning the Tower of London yet.

THE UNHAPPIEST OF ROYAL WEDDINGS

[Author's note: In recent years, the failure of royal marriages has been the subject of much speculation and comment. My review of Flora Fraser's book, The Unruly Queen: The Life of Queen Caroline *(London: Macmillan, 1996) outlines the story of the miserable marriage two centuries ago between King George IV and Queen Caroline.]*

As a young woman in 1794–95, Caroline made two terrible mistakes from which great misery was to flow. First, she consented to marry the Prince of Wales, the future George IV. Second, on the day the couple actually met for the first time, she failed to wash.

For an unmarried 26-year-old German princess, the prospect of becoming the future Queen of England must have been irresistible. She greeted the formal request for her hand from the emissary, Lord Malmesbury, happily enough. Malmesbury, who conducted the bride to England, asked her lady-in-waiting to explain to Caroline that "the Prince is very delicate, and that he expects a long and very careful *toilette de propreté,* of which she has no idea. On the contrary, she neglects it sadly, and is offensive from this neglect."

But when the engaged couple met in St. James's Palace, and the Prince embraced his future wife, Malmesbury recorded that the Prince "said barely one word, turned round, retired to a distant part of the apartment, and calling me to him, said, 'Harris, I am not well; pray get me a glass of brandy.' " The reason for this grotesque greeting was simple—Caroline had not washed, and the Prince later complained of her "personal nastiness."

The wedding that followed was ghastly. The Prince was like a man going to execution and completely drunk. Caroline said several times to her new husband: "What is the matter my Prince? You have such a sad face on." The drunken Prince passed most of the marriage night with his head under the grate. After two or three weeks, the pair ceased to live as man and wife. Nonetheless, Caroline had managed to conceive Princess Charlotte.

The royal couple described their mutual detestation rather well. The Prince, longing for a separation, declared "he had rather see toads and

---

"'To the Princess of Wales's Damnation,'" *[London] Literary Review* (March 1996).

vipers crawling over his victuals than sit at the same table with her." On her side, Caroline (whose father was known for valour) when warned that there would be a pistol shot in an opera she attended, rejoined: "When the daughter of a hero marries a zero, she does not fear gunfire."

The author of *The Unruly Queen*, Flora Fraser, relates in fascinating detail the whole appalling epic of the marriage. The couple separated, and Caroline—who went to live at Blackheath—was prevented from bringing up her daughter. She sought solace from the Prince's ceaseless vile behavior in a series of lovers.

During 1814, the Prince became Regent. Caroline, having suffered endless humiliation, decided to go abroad. The charming Regent toasted this news with the words, "To the Princess of Wales's damnation and may she never return to England."

After a period in Brunswick, Caroline went to Italy, and for the first time she found a measure of happiness. Deciding she needed a courier and interpreter, Caroline found one in Bartolomeo Pergami, a dream of good looks. In Naples, he became her lover, and after she had bought him a Sicilian Barony, her Chamberlain. Caroline settled first at Lake Como, and subsequently at Pesaro on the Adriatic. Her behavior in Italy was not that of a princess. On a visit to the Empress Marie Louise in Parma, Caroline gave a yawn so vast that she fell off the chair and burst out laughing. Marie Louise was unamused.

When George III died in 1820, the new Queen was appalled when she was refused a guard of honor and a papal audience in Rome. Moreover, the new King had her name omitted from prayers for the Royal Family. After six years abroad, a livid Caroline returned to England. In contrast to her loathed husband, she was a popular heroine.

George IV had a bill introduced in the House of Lords to dissolve the marriage. The issue before the House was that the Queen had carried on "a licentious, disgraceful and adulterous intercourse" with Pergami.

The climax of the book is the Queen's "trial" for adultery, dramatically described by the author. At the end of it, peer after peer in speech after speech said that while convinced of the Queen's guilt, they would not vote for the bill while it contained a divorce clause. At second reading, the government's majority for the bill was only 28, and on third reading, a bare nine. The government then dropped the bill; thus the Queen was "acquitted."

Colossal crowds supported Caroline and lit up the cities in rejoicing.

But when Parliament voted her a 50,000 pound annuity, and she accepted, her popular support vanished.

Thus it was that George IV, without provoking a huge outcry among his subjects, was able to bar the Queen from his coronation in the famous scene used by the author as the Prologue to her book. Within three weeks of the coronation, Caroline was dead from an intestinal blockage.

Flora Fraser's splendid biography, *The Unruly Queen: The Life of Queen Caroline,* does justice to a fascinating woman—tragic, brave, likeable, humorous, and indeed, unruly.

A CURTSY FOR THE QUEEN

One of the great occasions of the British calendar is the State Opening of Parliament. Wearing the crown jewels, the Queen announces her government's legislative plans for the forthcoming session in a speech from the throne in the House of Lords. The peers, dressed in scarlet and ermine robes, sit with other dignitaries on the red leather benches surrounding the throne; the members of the House of Commons stand in the back of the chamber.

Since I became the fourth Baron Acton after my father's death in 1989, I have been privileged to attend three State Openings. The ceremony of May 6, 1992 was especially memorable, because my American wife was there.

A ballot is held among peers' spouses who wish to sit in the chamber, and my wife proved lucky. She consulted the secretaries to the Gentleman Usher of the Black Rod—the official who organizes the event—about the protocol required. They explained that she needed an evening gown and a tiara.

Endless shopping expeditions in London produced a magnificent black and gold evening dress, ideal for Patricia's dark Mediterranean looks. She was in near despair over the tiara. Then, at an antique fair in her hometown of Cedar Rapids, Iowa, she found a simple gold and pearl

"A Curtsy for the Queen," *British Heritage* (October/November 1994).

tiara which perfectly matched her dress. She was ready for the occasion.

We arrived at the House of Lords soon after 9:00 A.M. on the day of the State Opening. There we met a young peeress even newer and more nervous than my wife. Boosting each other's confidence, the two new-comers went off to watch the preparations, while I put on my robe in the library. Then I stood in the Prince's Chamber behind the throne and looked down the Royal Gallery towards the Queen's Robing Room.

Under television lights, elegantly dressed peers' guests were being seated in the Royal Gallery. Yeomen of the Guard, in red uniforms, stood at regular intervals in front of the seats. After a procession of Her-alds came past, I went into the chamber of the House of Lords and took my place.

The diplomatic corps was arrayed near the throne in formal dress—some ambassadors wore the traditional flowing robes of their Arab and African nations. The judges in their full-bottomed wigs sat immediately below the steps of the throne. The chamber began to fill with scarlet-clad peers.

Patricia was in the row ahead of me, her dark hair set off by the blonde baronesses next to her. Soon Princess Margaret and the Royal Dukes and Duchesses of Kent and Gloucester took their seats opposite the diplomatic corps.

At 11:27 A.M., with a flourish of trumpets, the Queen started her progress through the Royal Gallery. A few minutes later, the Heralds and various dignitaries entered the chamber. The Earl Marshall and the Lord Great Chamberlain walked in backwards, preceding two peers bearing the Sword of State and the Cap of Maintenance.

The Queen made her entry, wearing the purple imperial crown and the royal robes. She was escorted by the Duke of Edinburgh in naval uniform, and followed by her pages and ladies-in-waiting.

I had a moment of panic. Did my wife, or indeed any American woman, know how to curtsy? I had reckoned without Miss Dieman's and Miss Bennett's admirable ballet school in Cedar Rapids, Iowa. In perfect unison with the other peeresses, Patricia executed the elegant curtsy her childhood dancing instructors had taught her. The Queen took her place on the throne and said: "My Lords, pray be seated."

At a signal, Black Rod went to summon the Commons. They clat-tered in at the back of the chamber. The Prime Minister, John Major, fresh from his general election triumph, stood next to Neil Kinnock, the Leader of the Opposition. All eyes turned to the first woman Speaker of the House of Commons, Betty Boothroyd. She gave a huge and charming smile.

The Queen put on her spectacles and read a short speech. She described her plans for state visits and outlined the business for the parliamentary session. After about fifteen minutes, Her Majesty finished speaking, and the royal procession departed from the chamber.

The peers milled about, and my wife and I greeted various friends. Then we went to thank Black Rod's secretaries for all their help. The young women admired Patricia's costume, and as we said good-bye, one of them called out to her: "Iowa would be proud of you."

After a vast buffet lunch by the River Thames, we listened to a brief ritual debate, and took our leave. Only then did the exhilaration begin to fade, and real life intrude. The policeman near the door looked at us with an amused smile. "I am afraid you will find it impossible to get a taxi," he said.

America, America

IN JANUARY 1966, at the age of twenty-five, I paid my first visit to the United States. I was working then in colonial Rhodesia for a packaging company which was bought out by a major American corporation. The order came from New York: "You had better come over and see how we do things here." I came over.

On my first day in New York, I took the subway. Confused by the geography, I turned to the man next to me and said: "Excuse me, please, but can you tell me how many stops to East 42nd Street?" He looked at me and snarled: "Why the hell should I tell you?"

Were all Americans going to be like that?

Then I went to Pittsburgh. My hotel was some way from the box plant, and the question of transport arose. A father and son, both workers in the plant, volunteered to drive me. They did this every day for two months, even though it meant they had to get up half an hour earlier in the morning as my hotel was off their direct route. All Americans were not like the man in the New York subway.

Years went by, and then in 1984 I made another lengthy trip to the United States. By now I was a lawyer for the government of independent Zimbabwe (as Rhodesia had become). The United States Information Service invited me to come to America on their Overseas Visitors Program. For a month I crisscrossed the country, seeing law schools and legislatures, judges and politicians. In Raleigh, North Carolina, I attended a Jefferson-Jackson Day Dinner. In Lincoln, Nebraska, the legislature made me an honorary citizen. But New Orleans is the city that stands out in my memory.

I arrived late one evening and had dinner in the French Quarter. At about midnight, I decided to walk back to my hotel, and after getting directions, set off. Soon I was lost, and found myself in a street where all the buildings were high-rise and all the people looked very tough.

Suddenly, the toughest man in the street loomed in front of me. He had scars on one cheek, he wore a wide-striped jacket, and he bounced on the balls of his feet.

"You're wearing a three-piece suit," he said accusingly. I nodded. "And I can see the outline of your wallet in your pocket." I began to pray.

"You must be crazy," he said. "Don't you realize it's dangerous here? Where are you staying?"

I told him the name of my hotel. "Follow me," he said, and through the streets of New Orleans we walked.

When we arrived at the hotel, I got out my wallet and said, "Can I give you something for your trouble?"

"I don't want your money," he said. "Just don't be so dumb," and he vanished into the night. Americans quite definitely are not all like the man on the New York subway.

Over the last decade—my Iowa phase—I have enjoyed several trips up and down the Mississippi River. As a result, this chapter records visits to Hannibal, Missouri, and Minneapolis, Minnesota. Occasionally we've gone farther afield—to New York City to see my brother-in-law's musicals, or to Boston to visit the Freedom Trail, and some pieces describe those visits as well.

But most of the essays that follow are about a variety of ordinary features of American life which for one reason or another have intrigued me. They range from cable television, non-dairy creamer and the film Jurassic Park, to Americans' attitudes towards their holidays and a Halloween hayride. They all find their natural home in a chapter called ... "America, America."

SURVIVING AMERICAN HOLIDAYS

The enthusiasm of Americans for their holidays seems to know no bounds. For a start, a special day appears to exist for every conceivable occasion—Secretary's Day and Boss's Day first entered my life when I came to Iowa. But American exuberance on the three giant holidays of Independence Day, Thanksgiving, and Christmas strikes an Englishman as truly remarkable.

The Fourth of July is a day of great confusion for me. I am married to an American, I am a visitor in America, and I like Americans. However, on that holiday flags fly, people parade, bands play, rockets and fireworks whoosh—all to celebrate liberation *from Britain.*

As a remnant of the British Empire, I inevitably feel foreign and out of it on the Fourth of July. The barrister in me is tempted to debate Anglo-American history with everybody I meet. Yet frankly, it is difficult to make a terribly strong case for the colonial taxation policies of King George III.

Sometimes silence is the only appropriate response. I long to be a tiny island of frigid Britishness in the midst of a sea of happy Americans.

But people are so hospitable that I never quite achieve my dream. "*Do* come to our party," "*Do* come and watch the marathon," "*Do* come and see the fireworks," they say. Despite my doubts—and humming "Rule Britannia" to the last—I invariably fall in with their plans.

We Britons have our own fireworks day. Guy Fawkes Day on November 5th commemorates a 1605 plot by Fawkes and other Catholics to blow up the Protestant King James I in the House of Lords. I have a mixed reaction to this fireworks day, too. As a Catholic, I lean towards Guy Fawkes. As a staunch monarchist, I am appalled.

The English regrettably have no holiday comparable to Thanksgiving. I love Thanksgiving. I love the warmth of people and the sense of family. I even feel a rare urge to accompany my wife to her church.

The spirit of Thanksgiving helps me to overcome the two great drawbacks to Iowa—static electricity and ice. After church, ignoring my dread of electric shocks, I stand on a nylon carpet and shake hands with friends, while blue sparks crackle at our touch. I disregard my terror of

Des Moines Register, December 18, 1991.

slipping on the ice as, like a fly, I edge my way gingerly around the car. I just feel so good.

A splendid Czech friend always starts Thanksgiving Day on the right note. She gives us kolaches she has baked that morning, a greedy beginning to a greedy day.

Normally Americans spend their lives pursuing an illusion of immortality. People revere diet and fitness. They talk of cholesterol and calories and saturated fat. They encourage one to jog and do aerobics. Then suddenly at Thanksgiving, everybody suspends their preoccupation with the perfect physique. Exercise is forgotten. For one glorious day in the year, everybody hurls themselves into eating as much as possible.

My mother-in-law is a superb cook who remembers the happy, far-off days when the route to a man's heart was through his stomach. Pumpkin pie had always sounded dubious to my English ears; at her table, I learned to appreciate the nobility of this historic dish.

The proximity of Thanksgiving to Christmas seems to heighten, rather than diminish, American zeal for the latter holiday. Intense merrymaking is concentrated on December 25th. Britons, on the other hand, spread out their celebration over Christmas Day, Boxing Day (December 26th), and on to New Year's Day. Precious little work gets done between Christmas Eve and January 2nd.

Christmas shopping is an even more sacred pastime for Americans than for the British. Certainly it inspires my American wife all the year round. As early as January, she will buy some unbelievably boring item in London, like a packet of English tea. By December, when she finally wraps the tea in America, it has become an exotic gift.

My wife's family makes a ritual out of opening presents around the tree. Only one person opens a package at a time, slowly removing the ribbon and wrapping. Then they all exchange ecstatic "oohs" and "ahs," transforming the shirt or the book into something truly extraordinary.

To tease them, I describe my childhood Christmas. My mother used to spread a huge sheet on the floor and pin the names of each of her ten children to it. Presents were piled near each name tag. When my mother signalled, we children dived for our piles, and ripped open the packages as fast as we could. With ten of us, the gift-by-gift method would have taken the rest of our lives.

Sometimes I pretend to dislike the fervor Americans display during this season. In truth, I find it infectious. I will never be a child with my brothers and sisters again. But my American family's enthusiasm makes me feel like a child at Christmas, and that is as it should be.

SPEAKING THE QUEEN'S ENGLISH IN AMERICA

Every airport in the United States ought to display a sign:

English Speakers Beware!
American is a Foreign Language.

After I began to spend a lot of time on my wife's side of the Atlantic, I wished I had had such a warning. I soon discovered that words can have different meanings in England and America—with potentially disastrous results.

One day I needed to correct an article written in pencil. In English terms, I wanted to "rub out" the mistakes. Off I went to a nearby shop that seemed to supply everything. In a ringing English voice, I asked: "Do you sell rubbers?"

A deathly hush fell upon the customers and all eyes turned towards me. The shop assistant slid a box across the counter.

I recoiled. "No, no, no—not that!" I said, and drew pictures in the air. "Oh," said the man. "You mean an *eraser*," and produced one.

I am still mortified.

My mother-in-law, who is a wise and good woman, came to the rescue. She presented me with a British/American language dictionary.

With my new book, I was able to perform simultaneous translations. Curtains were drapes, cupboards were closets, gardens were yards. The rubbish became the garbage, and dust bins became trash cans.

Des Moines Register, September 26, 1991.

Motoring life was especially fraught. I, who had always bought petrol from a garage now got gas from a filling station. In England, the car had a bonnet and a boot. In America I learned that a hood was not only a crook, nor a trunk an enormous suitcase.

More confusing lessons took place in supermarkets. What I called "jam" was in a jar marked "jelly." What I called "jelly" was in a box marked "Jell-O." I searched in vain for British treats like bath buns and digestive biscuits.

My dictionary defined wonderful words not used in my native tongue—like antsy, bodacious, and crackerjack. For the first time I understood palooka, picayune, and popsicle.

The book was also an awful warning. So many wholesome English words became filthy or insulting when they crossed the ocean. To spell out those words in a family newspaper would be to court the disaster the dictionary teaches you to avoid. But armed with this book, Britons in America can escape what might delicately be termed the "eraser" trap.

Linguistic problems lie as much in pronunciation as in meaning. In my youth, the film *The Ten Commandments* shocked me into realizing the chasm between English and American inflection. When Moses went up Mt. Sinai to receive the Ten Commandments—*God spoke with an American accent!* I was appalled. Surely everybody knew that God spoke with an English accent.

That arrogance had to go when I found myself in the land of Charlton Heston. American accents were the norm; British accents were comparatively rare. This has its advantages for someone like me who loves to talk. People everywhere say: "I just *adore* your accent. *Please* go on talking." I invariably oblige.

However, there are also disadvantages. Some people find me incomprehensible. Certain phrases lead to constant trouble. "Diet Coke"—the nectar of the middle-aged—is one of them. Apparently I swallow the "t" in "Diet," which baffles my hearers.

The most striking Diet Coke problem occurred in a Greek-American restaurant. At the bar I said: "Can I have a Diet Coke, please?" The young man looked like a startled rabbit.

"I'm terribly sorry, Sir, but I've only been here for two weeks," he apologized. "I just don't know all these Greek drinks yet."

Despite such failures to communicate, I try to keep calm about my bilingual shortcomings. After all, language is only one aspect of the complexity of life. The poet Christopher Morley had the right idea when he wrote:

"Life is a foreign language; all men mispronounce it."

IT'S NO LONGER GROWN-UP TO SMOKE

Tobacco was king in Rhodesia (today's Zimbabwe) where I was brought up. Rich white tobacco farmers employed large black labour forces. They drove enormous imported American cars to the tobacco sales and took expensive holidays abroad. The merits of smoking were promulgated from every side—newspapers, magazines, radio, and cinema. One simple message got through to this Rhodesian child: It was "grown-up" to smoke.

My parents, noting my unruliness, sent me at a tender age to a Jesuit boarding school. The Jesuits—doubtless to distract from temptations of the flesh—made smoking *the* crime. Somewhat illogically, many of the Fathers chain-smoked themselves, and the eighteen-year-old school prefects were actually allowed to smoke. But for the rest of us, the cigarette was forbidden fruit.

By the time I was ten I found that my thirteen-year-old contemporaries talked mostly of girls and admired two things in their fellows—sporting prowess and disobedience. Girl talk was a puzzle to me, and I was puny and a poor games player. Disliking Jesuit discipline, I found one simple means of not only being disobedient, but popular and grown-up as well. I took up smoking.

"Tom Tom" and "Star" cigarettes made from the sweepings off the tobacco floors (and intended by white-owned companies for black consumption) sold for a penny for eight. I smoked them enthusiastically. Sometimes one found pieces of wood in them, and on one occasion I found a small nail, but I smoked them with increasing pleasure.

Des Moines Register, March 8, 1990.

And so I smoked my way through school. By the time I was myself a prefect—and allowed to smoke—I had graduated to boxes of fifty sophisticated "Matinee" cigarettes. Thus prepared, I embarked on all the vicissitudes of life. Thirty years passed. Despite the ups and downs, there was one constant—tobacco.

And then everything changed. I married an Iowan.

Suddenly I found myself limited to ten cigarettes a day and confined to smoking in one room of the house. Local officialdom stopped me smoking in public buildings, in shops, in cinemas. Social pressure was amazingly anti-smoking. The polite question, "Do you mind if I smoke?" was answered rudely with, "Yes!" Two young women students of my wife's told me they could *never* marry a man who smoked. I was appalled.

The climax came at a dinner party. The host forbade me to smoke even in his garage, thus driving me into the snow. The ten-year-old Rhodesian schoolboy—now in his deep forties—rebelled. I swore undying loyalty to the cigarette.

Very slowly things changed. Patricia had originally and with varying degrees of subtlety tried to persuade me to give up smoking. Then she left it alone. A mystery writer—a natural smoker if ever there was one—told me that he had given up smoking for health reasons. A doctor friend pointed to a full ash tray and gently asked, "What are you doing to your lungs?" Some mornings I woke up wondering if perhaps the Surgeon General had a point—and then hastily smoked two cigarettes to banish the worry.

Finally I went to a friend and poured out my thoughts. She summarized them: "You love your wife, you are very happy, and you want to live. Do you really want to kill yourself with cigarettes simply to be *naughty?*"

My eyes were opened. My doctor friend recommended nicotine chewing gum. After lunch with him on January 2nd, I threw my cigarettes away.

The most positive thing about giving up smoking is that your wife glows with happiness. Friends encourage you, and even strangers congratulate you. You feel some sense of overcoming yourself. On the other hand, you have a constant craving. You eat too much. Your concentration wanes. Your temper deteriorates.

The real test will come if I am run over by a truck tomorrow. I undoubtedly will hear the voice of a small Rhodesian boy saying: "You poor fool. You could have smoked 590 more cigarettes!" But I hope also to hear an American voice:

"At least you tried to grow up."

THE DECLINE AND FALL OF AN ANTI-TV BRIT

Television did not exist in colonial Rhodesia when I was growing up in the 1950s. Our farmhouse had plenty of books, and after a time we got a radiogram. The radio crackled and the gramophone gave electric shocks, but we ten children thought it the height of sophistication.

One magic day, our father brought home a 16-millimeter film projector. The trial movie was Alfred Hitchcock's *The Lady Vanishes,* and we watched it no less than ten times that first week.

From then on we saw innumerable films. We cheered our cowboy heroes and developed crushes on our favorite film stars. But if you had cross-examined us about contemporary American television shows like *I Love Lucy* or *Ozzie and Harriet,* we would have greeted your questions with puzzled stares.

With such a background, how should a newcomer approach modern American TV? I decided my attitude would be one of lofty disdain. I would get my news from the BBC on the radio. I would get my entertainment at the cinema and the theatre. The television could mind its own business.

Things modified slightly because of the wonders of American video stores. I found films I'd always wanted to see and classics I didn't even realize existed. After all, viewing them on a television screen was just a matter of convenience—it was certainly not watching TV.

The jump from videos to television films was a very small one. This was just the cinema at home—much the same thing as our trusty 16-millimeter projector.

Des Moines Register, October 16, 1993.

Of course, I had to deal with the problem of leading a double life in Iowa and in England. The relationship between the pound sterling and the dollar was a source of constant fascination. One of the cable stations broadcast London business news early each morning, and I classified my bleary-eyed attendance as "financial necessity."

Equally, as a loyal Englishman, I was eager to keep up with British politics. C-SPAN regularly showed Prime Minister's Question Time in the House of Commons. Watching this performance was nothing to do with television—it was fulfilling a political obligation.

As a guest in the United States, I thought it churlish not to know something of American politics, too. The McLaughlin Group was the obvious source of information, as they were the only TV commentators who yelled as loudly as the members of the House of Commons. But my motive in observing their antics was just good manners towards my American hosts.

Then the question of local patriotism arose. Roseanne Arnold, like me, was a sort-of Iowan. Was it not my duty periodically to monitor *Roseanne*? Of course, hers was a situation comedy, but I followed it out of loyalty, not as television.

The "Nick at Nite" station was devoted to the TV programs of the past. At last I saw the *I Love Lucy* of my deprived youth—and also managed to squeeze in a few episodes of *Mary Tyler Moore*. I tucked both shows away under the heading, "classical film history." I still listened to my BBC news on the radio, but had discovered a miracle. "Headline News" and CNN were 24-hour news stations. You could look up from your book every few minutes and learn whether the world had changed. This, I told myself, was just a diverting new method of reading.

After a long day in the State Historical Society library, I found the intellectual stimulus of *Wheel of Fortune* vital therapy. Occasionally I even managed to beat my mother-in-law to a word.

I had so many duties to perform. I had a duty as an Englishman to watch tennis from Wimbledon. If I wanted to dwell peacefully in eastern Iowa, I had a duty to keep a watchful eye on the fate of the Hawkeyes.

Devotion to research on modern American life led me to the violence of *Murder She Wrote,* where more or less everybody is a killer, a suspect, or a dead body. Anyway, the stories reminded me of the Agatha Christie books I read during my carefree, television-free childhood in Africa.

With so many essential obligations, I discovered the heaven of the remote control—what I call the flicker box.

FLICK, FLICK.
"Sshhhh, Patricia, I'm trying to concentrate."
FLICK, FLICK.
"Let's eat on trays in here tonight."
FLICK, FLICK.

Of course, I still don't actually *watch* television. And how I dread the coming of 500-channel TV sets. Just *think* of all the work!

FLICK, FLICK, FLICK.

WHAT MAKES THE HANNIBAL IN HANNIBAL?

I used to think that the name *Hannibal* had to do with elephants crossing the Alps. But a recent trip to Mark Twain's hometown on the Mississippi River opened up a whole new Hannibal to me.

Everything in Hannibal, Missouri, has to do with Mark Twain—the pen name of Samuel Clemens, whose boyhood there inspired his classic book, *Tom Sawyer.* Driving into the town, we passed the Tom and Huck Motel, the Huck Finn Shopping Center, and the Mark Twain Hotel.

Our bed and breakfast, The Fifth Street Mansion, sounded Twain-free. But no—inevitably, Samuel Clemens had dined there on his final visit to his hometown. At that same long-ago party was Laura Hawkins, known to Hannibal and literature as Tom Sawyer's Becky Thatcher.

Inspired by Clemens's ghost, I rushed up to the bedroom to read *Tom Sawyer.* I was determined not to leave Hannibal the only tourist who had never read a Mark Twain book.

Next morning we began our pilgrimage at the vast Mark Twain cave. Here Tom and Becky were lost for three days. What prompted

Radio Commentary, Weekend Edition, Monitor Radio, the broadcast edition of *The Christian Science Monitor,* September 9, 1994.

Miss Mamie Fraaman of Moline, Illinois, in 1922 to scrawl her name on the cave wall? I was tempted to scribble myself, until our young guide announced that today a signature can earn a year in prison.

Lunch presented a terrible dilemma—should we try the Becky Thatcher Restaurant or the Mark Twain Dinette? The latter's advertisement on a huge revolving root beer mug seduced us. I gobbled up the specialty—Mark Twain Fried Chicken.

During the afternoon we walked round the tiny rooms of the Mark Twain Boyhood Home. There we learned the vital information that Samuel Clemens wrote in bed. Also that he was the first famous author to use a typewriter. But did he actually type in bed? Alas, no one in the Mark Twain Boyhood Home seemed to know.

My favorite spot was the legendary white fence, which Tom Sawyer tricked the other boys into whitewashing. A row of us tourists gazed at it in awe. Like Tom Sawyer, I would have made friends with Huckleberry Finn and fallen in love with Becky Thatcher. But I would never have had the gumption to get my contemporaries to do my painting for me.

We crossed the street to the home of Clemens's childhood sweetheart—now immortalized as the Becky Thatcher Book Shop. I paid my respects by purchasing a copy of *The Wit and Wisdom of Mark Twain*. It was time to say good-bye.

Mark Twain once said of Hannibal: "All that goes to make the me in me is in a small Missouri village."

As we left behind the Hotel Clemens, Huck's Pipes and Coins, and the Mark Twain Antiques & Collectibles Gift Shop, I could only reflect that nowadays, all that makes the Hannibal in Hannibal is in Mark Twain.

LOST IN THE MALL OF AMERICA

Shopping for me always brings to mind a narrow street of small shops in Britain shortly after World War II. My mother would lead my sister and me by the hand, past the rabbits hanging in the butcher's window, to collect our meat ration. A few doors down was the dressmaker who altered our clothes. Whenever we visited her, she gave each of us children a chocolate biscuit—a rare treat in those austere days. I would stare longingly at the painted lead soldiers in the window of the little toy shop, and then we would go home for tea.

The sheer size of modern shopping malls and supermarkets never ceases to astonish me. Soon after I came to Iowa, I went to buy a loaf of bread in a Hy-Vee, took a wrong turning, and in a panic thought I would never find the check-out counter again.

Recently my Iowan wife announced my education must go a stage further. We would visit Minneapolis and do some Christmas shopping at the Mall of America—the largest indoor shopping arena in the history of the universe. I was appalled.

I sought comfort in the words of the industrialist Charles Franklin Kettering: "We should all be concerned about the future because we will have to spend the rest of our lives there." Yes, but did that mean I was sentenced to an eternity in the Mall of America?

We drove through ice and snow to our hotel on the outskirts of the Mall. Punctually at 9:15 A.M. we took a shuttle bus to the Mall terminal. When we arrived, we headed for Camp Snoopy, a colossal indoor theme park, and then started our trek around the shops.

The Mall of America is a small country of its own; it is the size of Monaco and has the fervor of the Vatican City. It has its own army of security guards and cleaners, all smiling and friendly. It has its own language. "Happy Shopping!" people say to each other, and, "Meet you at Camp Snoopy."

Mall Americans have a uniform. Whatever else they may wear, they invariably put on tennis shoes. They are, like all good Americans, determined to go everywhere and do everything—and they know their feet will get tired.

Des Moines Register, December 19, 1992.

Mall Americans are a dedicated nation. As I sat on one of the mercifully plentiful benches reading my Minneapolis *Star Tribune,* the woman next to me looked at the headline. "Oh, good," she said. "The President is sending the troops into Somalia." Then she added, "I haven't seen a newspaper for two days." I asked idly, "Where have you been?" She gave an ecstatic smile. "Lost in the Mall of America!"

A few hundred shops later, I sat down on another bench. An elderly man told me that every day he drove from St. Paul to the Mall to watch the people. "Did you know," he said in a voice ringing with pride, "that since the Mall opened less than three months ago, over 11 million people have been here?" I felt a stab of guilt. I *should* have known; I should have asked. Why was there no electronic scoreboard?

We wandered on, and I looked for reminders of my childhood. I saw no butcher's shop, no rabbits, and no meat ration. But endless fast food places served meat cooked in every way that fast food chefs could devise.

I saw no miniature lead soldiers, but in the Lego exhibition, which rose through four floors, full-sized spacemen with ray guns floated overhead while vast Lego dinosaurs towered over us.

No dressmaker was in evidence, but the Mall had at least two hundred clothes shops. I know, because my wife went into them all.

Then I found something familiar. The Great American Cookie Company had a splendid selection of treats, and among them was an approximation of the chocolate biscuits the dressmaker used to give us. I bought one and munched away appreciatively.

Walking and walking through that sea of people, I realized that no one at all had jostled us. Somehow all of the shoppers were on their best behavior, determined to be polite and ensure that everybody enjoyed their day of frenzied leisure.

I wondered what working in the Mall was like, so I asked a young woman assistant. "Great," she said. "Half the people are from other states or foreign countries. Everyday I stand here selling postcards and feel as if I'm traveling all around the world."

My feet are not my greatest asset, and after seven hours, they proclaimed they wanted to rest. We carried our booty back to the shuttle bus. The people on the bus were like conquerors who had survived some epic journey. They seemed to say: "We know what it is to have climbed Mount Everest."

When we arrived at our hotel, a fresh young couple was waiting to catch the shuttle for the Mall. "What's it like?" they asked eagerly.

My answer astonished me.

"Better than I expected," I said. "Happy shopping."

A TWENTIETH-CENTURY DINOSAUR
AT JURASSIC PARK

Ten million Americans must have seen *Jurassic Park* during its first few days on the screen. Most of those ten million seemed to be at the shopping mall in Iowa City on the Saturday evening we succumbed to the madness.

An endless line snaked and coiled round the mall. My wife and I kept trying to join it in the wrong place, but helpful patrons pointed out the error of our ways. At last we found the tail. The excitement reminded me of a seething throng before the Derby or some other great sporting event.

Why had we come? Patricia likes dinosaurs, loves Steven Spielberg, and has happy memories of the *Godzilla* films of her childhood. She promised I would relish this latest monster classic.

I am from a more decorous movie tradition. As a boy, I always enjoyed wholesome films with stars like Doris Day or Debbie Reynolds. But I wanted to feel a quintessential American experience—the megamovie, the prodigious crowd, all America at play.

Kind friends who had arrived early had promised to buy our tickets. When we got to the front of the snake, my wife went to find them. In my capacity as chronicler of American customs, I went to observe the refreshment counter.

One boy of about eleven bought the ultimate container of pop. I forget if it was called "super" or "jumbo." He could not get his hands around it, so he clutched the container with both arms. Without the lid, he could have swum in it.

Next, two schoolgirls bought popcorn. The server slid two giant vats that would have fed a family of six across the counter. The girls seemed to stagger slightly under the sheer weight of their purchases.

I considered my choice. If you are over fifty and metabolically correct, you avoid chocolate. I love chocolate, and in my slender youth I always ate a bar at the cinema. But these 1990s American chocolate slabs were designed for greedy mammoths. Fearing to be so identified, I settled on a medium Diet Coke. With the grievance of a captive in the market place, I gritted my teeth and handed over two dollars.

Somehow I fought my way into the packed theatre and clambered over several pairs of knees. Nearby a voice said: "I wonder if this movie will be as good as *Jaws*?"

My heart sank. I had forgotten that Spielberg directed *Jaws*. The book was so bad that I had avoided the film altogether. I hoped this wouldn't be an ill-favored omen for the evening.

Then there was a hush ... and *Jurassic Park*. From the outset, the audience was mesmerized. Two young girls near me slumped ever lower in their seats. As they neither groaned nor fled, presumably they were enjoying the film. Others in our row gasped and shivered with satisfied terror.

My own reaction was rather more muted. The billionaire played by Richard Attenborough was mad and power-hungry. Even though Queen Elizabeth had recently made Attenborough into a lord, I just couldn't summon up any sympathy for my fellow peer.

The billionaire's two grandchildren and a couple of grown-up scientists were the other main characters. The plot of the film appeared to be: Dinosaurs nearly eat children and scientists; audience shrieks; cycle is repeated ... and repeated ... and repeated.

Fortunately for the dinosaurs, there was a lawyer in the film. Lawyers are one of the few groups in America who can safely be pilloried. Spielberg's lawyer was humiliated, degraded, and ultimately eaten by prehistoric monsters—to the huge satisfaction of the audience.

I am a lawyer, and three of my companions were lawyers. I was shocked to find that they were as entertained by the fate of their colleague as everybody else.

This seemed a propitious moment for me to buy another Diet Coke. A group of white-faced children stood outside the exit. I suspected that the untimely death of a cow in Jurassic Park, rather than the demise of the lawyer, had frightened them out of the cinema.

Fortified, I returned. I wondered if the monsters would devour Lord Attenborough? Lords are a politically safe class to insult—think of "drug lords," and "war lords," and "ten lords-a-leaping."

By now my sympathies were entirely pro-dinosaur. But as the film went on and on, the monsters had only limited success in their voracious plans. At last it was over.

Outside, I stared at the people leaving. Rapture, ecstasy and bliss, with tinges of fear, were spread across their faces. Young and old, female and male, I saw not one discontented customer. They were Americans and had partaken in an American rite. They would surely tell their grandchildren about it.

I tried to pin my lack of enthusiasm on being hopelessly British. But in my heart, I knew that wasn't the reason.

The awful truth was that *I* was the dinosaur at Jurassic Park.

AN ANGEL ON BROADWAY

I've always secretly dreamed of seeing my name up in lights on Broadway. The only drawback is that I can't act, I can't dance, and I can't sing. That left only one route to stardom. I would have to become an angel—that is, the optimistic kind of angel prepared to take a risk on theatre productions.

The chance came by way of my wife's brother, who is a composer. He spent most of the last year writing the music and lyrics for a small country musical called *Honky Tonk Highway*. When I learned the show needed investors, I couldn't resist.

Long ago my father taught me never to gamble more than I could afford. So on this occasion I compromised and became a "mini-angel." Obviously I had to fly to New York to see the show. Normally I detest the city—but this time it seemed to be bathed in a heavenly golden glow.

Brimming with enthusiasm, I volunteered to go to the half-price ticket booth in Times Square and hand out playbills for our show. Other productions had young people to distribute their flyers. Dressed in T-shirts and jeans, they kept up an endless patter with the tourists.

Radio Commentary, Weekend Edition, Monitor Radio, the broadcast edition of *The Christian Science Monitor*, July 22, 1994.

To compensate for my inexperience I had only a three-piece suit and a very English accent. I held a bemused family from Georgia spellbound as I stumbled through my pitch: "You really must ... um ... come to my ... um ... brother-in-law's musical. He is ... uh ... very talented and it's the only ... um ... country musical in New York."

At the preview that Saturday night, I eagerly studied the program. In tiny letters at the end, I found my name. It wasn't exactly the lights of Broadway, but my heart leapt. The small cabaret theatre suddenly seemed like Radio City Music Hall.

During the show, nobody could have clapped louder, nobody could have laughed louder than I. At intermission, I beamed at the other theatregoers. I couldn't find my family from Georgia, but never mind, at the end of the performance the audience applauded ardently.

In a taxi afterwards, I warbled the show's tunes in my old crow's voice. The taxi driver fumed, but I felt glorious—Broadway and all of New York belonged to me.

Back at my hotel, I spotted a rack with theatre brochures. I hastily filled it with flyers for *MY* show.

An angel's duties are never done.

THE BRITISH ARE COMING!
THE BRITISH ARE COMING!

[Author's note: The producer of Monitor Radio's Weekend Edition asked me to come to Boston and walk the famous Freedom Trail, giving my reaction as a loyal British subject to the sites made famous by the American Revolution. We started at the Freedom Trail visitors' center, where I spoke with a guide.]

I'm a visiting Briton.

GUIDE: *Well, welcome to Boston. Welcome to New England.*

Thank you very much. I'm making my first trip to Boston, and I'm making my first trip on the Freedom Trail. How would you advise

Radio Commentary, Weekend Edition, Monitor Radio, the broadcast edition of *The Christian Science Monitor*, December 9, 1994.

a very loyal Briton to approach the Freedom Trail? What spirit would you think suitable?

GUIDE: *An open mind, of course.*

RADIO ANNOUNCER: *Our commentator, Richard, Lord Acton, often talks about his observations of America on our show from his part-time home in Iowa. When he came to visit us in Boston recently, we took him out to the Freedom Trail, Boston's major historic sites from Revolutionary days. Frankly, we were watching for Lord Acton's reaction to the way America writes the history of early British/American relations.*

The site of the Boston Massacre, extraordinarily enough, is in a triangle in the middle of the road, and two *extraordinarily* noisy trucks are making the most horrendous modern noises to both take us back to the eighteenth century and bring us up to date. "Massacre" is a rather strong word, as only five people were killed. The British troops, I gather, were very very sorely provoked. Still, five people did lose their lives ...

RADIO ANNOUNCER: *We moved on to a place most tourists in Boston like to visit—the historic Faneuil Hall—the pronunciation of which is a lively subject for debate.*

Well, here I am approaching the cradle of liberty. There's tremendous argument about the pronunciation of it. My guides, and most of the people I've talked to, all say it is pronounced "Fan ... u ... ell." However, true Bostonians pronounce it "Fan ... ell," and in fact it's a Huguenot name, and my Huguenot accent isn't very good, but it should be pronounced "Fan ... a ... oo eel." So I think I'll stick with "Fan ... ell" and try to be a true Bostonian, just for this episode.

RADIO ANNOUNCER: *Inside the building, we were surrounded by relics of American history.*

Faneuil Hall really is very impressive—its tradition of public speaking and of course the history and all the portraits, and the beauty. Here, in 1764, the Americans protested the Sugar Act, and they said, "If taxes are laid upon us in any shape without our having a legal representation where they are laid, are we not reduced from the character of free subjects to the miserable state of tributary slaves?" Now this was translated into, "No Taxation Without Representation," and so that's really where this famous slogan was born.

There are portraits all over this hall, and I'm actually standing below one of George Washington looking, I may say, incredibly English, which cheers me up. The centerpiece is a huge meeting being addressed by the great orator Daniel Webster. He also looks very English, so I'm feeling really quite at home.

RADIO ANNOUNCER: *Our next stop was Charlestown, a neighborhood of Boston. Our taxi left us at the bottom of a hill, whose name gave Lord Acton a moment's pause.*

Well, we clamber up the stone steps to the monument to Bunker Hill. Forty years ago in a classroom in what was British colonial Southern Rhodesia, today's Zimbabwe, a luckless schoolmaster tried to teach me the facts of the American Revolution and the American War of Independence, and I distinctly remember him talking about the Battle of Bunker Hill. But I discovered on coming to Boston that it wasn't truly the Battle of Bunker Hill at all, but it was the Battle of *Breed's* Hill. Even in this land of euphemism, it must be the mother and father of all euphemisms to call the most famous battle by the name of the wrong hill!

RADIO ANNOUNCER: *And now from Bunker—or rather Breed's—Hill, on to Boston Harbor. On December 16, 1773, colonists disguised as Indians rode out to three ships and dumped tea into Boston Harbor, a revolutionary act known as the Boston Tea Party. At the time, it shook the British Parliament and goaded them into closing down Boston Harbor. At the site of the Tea Party, Lord Acton pondered its relevance to contemporary issues.*

We are here now preparing for the reenactment of the Boston Tea Party. The ship is a recreation of the Beaver; it's called Beaver the Second, and it was built in Denmark in 1973, and it's not that far from old Griffin's Wharf, where the actual episode took place.

I've brought along my own tea bags, which I'm going to hold onto very tight to demonstrate my loyalty to the home country and to show that I'm not an American and I'll have no part of their wicked revolution!

COSTUMED LEADER ON SHIP: *Now, why are we meeting here today; what brings us all together? Taxes. And how do we all feel about taxes? (Boos) We don't like them.*

What interests me about this whole episode, is that the Americans won, but they still have their taxes; they don't like them much. And they have their representatives, but they don't like them at all. I find that quite ironical.

FROM SHIP: *One, two, three. Dump the tea into the sea!!!*

[Fade-out to cheers]

A LAND FLOWING WITH
NON-DAIRY CREAMER

I got off on the wrong foot when I asked for "white coffee, please."
The waitress in that supermarket cafe was not going to stand for any British phrases. "What?" she said.

"Coffee with milk," I hastily corrected myself.

"I'll get it," said the waitress, and returned a minute later with a cup of coffee and two small packets. The words "Non-Dairy Creamer" were printed on their sides.

I opened a packet and spilled the contents on the table. Like Sherlock Holmes, I subjected it to minute examination. In color the powder was slightly off-white. I tasted it—it had no taste. I smelled it—it had no smell.

I looked at that powder, and I thought back to my childhood on our colonial Rhodesian dairy farm. I thought of our lovely Jersey cows. I thought of Butterdrop and of Regal Lady and of L'Etacq Rita, the grand champion cow of the entire country. I remembered the great churns brimming with their fresh, warm milk. And I rebelled.

"What is that?" I asked, pointing at the powder.

"Cream," said the waitress succinctly.

I turned over the packet. On the back was a list of chemicals that would have daunted a nuclear physicist: "Sodium Caseinate, Sodium Silico Aluminate, Dipotassium Phosphate, Monoglycerides, Sodium Tri-Polyphosphate, Diacetyl Tartaric Acid, Ester of Mono, Diglycerides, Beta Carotene and Riboflavin."

"That is *not* cream," I said. "It has never had anything to do with a cow." I knew about cream, delicious Jersey cream.

"Well, it *says* creamer," said the waitress, in the patient voice of one who has long dealt with difficult children.

"Oh, yes," I said, "but it also says sodium tri-polyphosphate and all sorts of other mouth-watering treats." I warmed to my theme. "Why don't you serve real cream or real milk?"

She shrugged. "Non-dairy creamer is good for you," she said.

"Are you saying that things like sodium silico aluminate and dipotassium phosphate and, for heavens sake, diacetyl tartaric acid are good for you?" I asked incredulously.

Des Moines Register, November 21, 1992.

"If most Americans take creamer in their coffee, it *must* be good for you," she said with impeccable logic.

I tried a different tack. "Do you remember cows—old-fashioned things with four legs that went 'moo'? I want something from a cow. I want milk!"

She was a nice woman, that waitress, and she decided to humor me. "OK," she said. "Wait a minute." She came back with a small glass jug. The jug was filled with a thin, watery liquid.

My mind went back forty years. On our farm, we used to separate the thick, yellow cream from the skimmed milk. The cream we sold; the skimmed milk we fed to the pigs.

"That's skimmed milk," I said. "I want milk, *real* milk, milk fit for human consumption."

"You don't want skim milk?" said the waitress.

"No, I don't want skimmed milk."

"OK," she said. "I'll get you two percent."

I thought longingly of our rich Jersey milk. We would have instantly banished from our herd any cow who dared produce less than five percent butterfat. But I knew when to surrender. "That would be wonderful," I said.

Soon she was back with the two percent milk and a fresh cup of coffee. I heaved a satisfied sigh and poured a little milk into my coffee cup. The waitress looked at me with an amused smile:

"Do you want Sweet 'n Low with that?"

FINDING AMERICA ON A
HALLOWEEN HAYRIDE

Reviews of the recent film, *Quiz Show,* stressed that in the 1950s America lost its innocence. I have just taken a pre-Halloween trip to a pumpkin patch and strongly recommend that the writers of those reviews do likewise. They might learn something.

Des Moines Register, October 29, 1994.

Halloween was no part of my childhood in wartime Britain or later on our farm in colonial Rhodesia. The whole idea simply passed our family by.

Since my American existence began, I've happened upon a few little goblins demanding "trick or treat." I've noticed the odd pumpkin on the doorstep, and the occasional skeleton dangling in the supermarket. However, even in America, I've never got properly involved with Halloween.

This year has proved different, thanks to my brother-in-law. He is a composer and spends most of the year in New York City, but he constantly pines for the tranquility of Iowa. This autumn—overcome by his longing to see the leaves change color—he appeared in Cedar Rapids.

My brother-in-law decided that now was the time for me to experience Halloween from the bottom up. So an expedition was arranged. "Oohing" and "aahing" at the trees on the way, we drove to a pumpkin patch on the edge of Linn County.

We started off in a sort of produce barn. A splendid assortment was on view—squashes and Indian corn and maple syrup and taffy apples. There was a smell of fresh straw. Children darted in and out.

We wandered outside and were greeted by a labyrinth made from giant corn stalks. I took my turn—most of my fellow adventurers didn't come above my knee. They got through the maze without difficulty, whereas I managed to lose myself in several dead ends before thankfully emerging into the daylight.

Next to the maze, a couple of goats looked speculatively at the audience, and a pot-bellied pig of great charm rooted about. I sat on a bench to recover from my exertions in the maze. The pig and I exchanged meaningful glances.

Beyond the animals, a crowd of people was queuing for a hayrack ride on a wooden trailer hitched to a tractor. I joined the throng and was the last to heave myself aboard. I found myself sharing a large straw bale with a self-possessed six-year-old named Carrie.

Forty of us bumped our way around the edge of a cornfield. First we passed under a sinister black spider dangling from a tree. Nearby, a sign said: "Where's Waldo?" I boomed out in my unmistakably English voice: "Who on *earth* is Waldo?" There was a stunned silence. "He's a character in a book," a kindly man explained.

My ignorance revealed, Carrie decided to take me under her wing. A gruesome creature appeared out of the cornfield. "A werewolf," announced Carrie. Then, "Look! Bats!" I looked, and instinctively ducked. Carrie, with the courage of a six-year-old, reached up. "I touched them, I touched them!"

My young guide kept up a running commentary. "Monster." "Blue fairy." "More bats." "Witch." "Skeleton." "Dracula." We passed innumerable cardboard ghouls and other unspeakable horrors. A white-clad vampire emerged from the cornfield, waving us on. Dutifully, we waved back.

Suddenly an innocent-looking youth loomed up. "There's Waldo!" everybody yelled. I heaved a sigh of relief; I need ponder the mystery of Waldo no longer. We jolted our way back to the point of departure. I thanked Carrie for her guidance.

The people on our hayride ranged in calendar age from three to seventy-three. But as they dismounted, flushed and excited, I could have sworn there was nobody aboard who felt more than ten years old.

The object of our expedition to the pumpkin patch was, after all, to get a pumpkin for Halloween. I marched off and, from among the millions of pumpkins, selected a suitable candidate. My pumpkin was not an object of beauty, and yet it had a certain misshapen character. Then, armed with our pumpkins and primed for Halloween, we drove home.

Much innocence may have been lost in America in the 1950s. But for the jaded, I can only suggest that they follow in my footsteps. For innocence is alive and well and living in the pumpkin patches of Iowa.

Bits and Pieces

NOT LONG AGO *Patricia and I paid a visit to the grave of the person responsible for our meeting. She is buried in London's Highgate Cemetery, and the words on her gravestone give a hint of the mystery surrounding her life:*

*Françoise Marie
De Bourbon-Orleans
(Opal Whiteley)
Died 17th February 1992
Aged 95 Years
"I spake as a child"*

The first essay in this chapter, entitled "To Live Again in Music: The Riddle of Opal Whiteley," tells the remarkable story of the woman who was either the child of an Oregon lumbercamp family or possibly, as she believed, a French princess. The essay was written in 1992 during the Iowa Summer Writing Festival, a splendid opportunity for aspiring writers organized each year by the University of Iowa. A classmate of mine, on reading the essay, said: "It is an Anastasia story," and certainly it has the tantalizing qualities of mystery and royalty that made the woman who believed herself to be the daughter of the czar of Russia fascinating to so many people.

This chapter comprises an assortment of subjects, and hence its title, "Bits and Pieces." One of these tells of the singer with one of the best-known voices in the history of the cinema, and yet whose own name is scarcely a household one. Others tell of such contrasting characters as F. W. de Klerk, the former president of South Africa, and a remarkable settler on the Channel Island of Sark. There are articles about united Germany and about the Moscow of Gorbachev.

Two of the pieces are part of my own family history. A radio script describes the journey of an ancestral portrait from Naples in Italy to Cedar Rapids in Iowa. And the last of the "Bits and Pieces" is the story of how my great-grandfather came to write that so often misquoted phrase, "Power tends to corrupt, and absolute power corrupts absolutely."

TO LIVE AGAIN IN MUSIC:
THE RIDDLE OF OPAL WHITELEY

The nurses were the chief mourners at her Requiem Mass. They were the last of a long line who, from 1948 until her death in February of 1992, had cared for Opal Whiteley, or Princess Françoise d'Orleans, at Napsbury Hospital outside London. They had petted her and called her the Princess, and looked after her to the end. Three of them, two English and one Spanish, wearing dark dresses, had come down to St. Etheldreda's, the oldest Catholic church in London. They walked through the imposing Gothic nave, beneath the statues of the martyrs, and then paused.

Opal's large black coffin lay at the front of the flagstoned aisle between two rows of wooden pews. A railing separated the coffin from the high altar, and behind the altar, a huge stained glass window depicting Christ the King and the four evangelists dominated the church. The nurses shyly hung back, well behind the coffin, keeping in what they thought was their place. But nobody who could have been a relation was there: no Whiteleys of the Oregon lumbercamp family, who had raised Opal, nor any of the family of Bourbon-Orleans, the royal house of France, to which Opal passionately believed she belonged. The nurses were the people who had given her love in the last of her ninety-five years. So in that tiny congregation, I took it on myself to persuade them to occupy the places of honor in the front pew.

Three men from the Official Solicitor's Office, dressed in somber suits, chose seats in the second row of mourners. Since 1948, when Opal could no longer take care of herself, their office had conducted her affairs. At the time Opal was put in the hospital, her room was stacked from floor to ceiling with books and magazines. She had spent all her money on genealogical books, determined to prove she was not Opal Whiteley, daughter of Oregon lumbercamp people, but Princess Françoise d'Orleans, daughter of Prince Henri d'Orleans and descendant of Louis Philippe, the last King of France. The storage of the books had proved too expensive, and in 1977 the Official Solicitor had decreed Opal's books be sold. However, the Solicitor still had charge of something far more precious—the copyright of the diary of Opal Whiteley

"To Live Again in Music," Iowa Summer Writing Festival, 1992.

which, seventy years before her death, had been a literary sensation on both sides of the Atlantic.

The story of how the diary came to the world began late one afternoon in 1919, in the office of Ellery Sedgwick, editor of *The Atlantic Monthly*. Opal, then a dark, slender beauty in her early twenties, had come to the *Atlantic*'s office in Boston with a nature book she had written. Sedgwick recalled that her book had no appeal for a publisher: "But about Opal Whiteley herself there was something to attract the attention even of a man of business—something very young and eager and fluttering, like a bird in a thicket." Opal told Sedgwick that she had lived in nineteen lumbercamps in Oregon. Her memories of her childhood deeply impressed the editor, and he recorded the revelation that followed:

> "If you remember like that, you must have kept a diary."
> "Her eyes opened wide. 'Yes, always. I do still.'"
> "Then it is not this book I want, but the diary."
> "She caught her breath. 'It's destroyed. It's all torn up.' Tears were in her eyes."
> "You loved it?"
> "Yes, I told it everything."
> "Then you kept the pieces?"
> "Yes, I have kept everything. The pieces are all stored in Los Angeles."

Sedgwick sent for the fragments of the diary, which Opal said a foster sister had torn up in a fit of rage ten years earlier. The pieces arrived, thousands of them, stuffed in a hatbox. Opal had written her diary in crayon on butcher paper, the backs of envelopes, any sort of paper. The pieces varied in size, from half sheets of paper to tiny scraps, and the writing was in characters that gradually changed from a childish scrawl to a more mature hand. In the early years of the diary, the printed letters ran into each other, leaving no space between words.

Ellery Sedgwick placed Opal under the protection of his mother-in-law, Mrs. Walter C. Cabot, who lived alone in a grand Brookline house. Opal's bedroom opened onto a large sitting room, from which all the furniture was removed. On the floor, inch by inch, Opal pieced together her diary, working eight hours, day in and day out, for nine months. Solving this vast jigsaw puzzle was made possible because Opal had written with a variety of colored crayons, using each until it ran out, and had adorned the borders of each page in childish patterns.

In 1920, *The Atlantic Monthly* serialized extracts from the first two years of the restored diary, written when Opal was six and seven. A few months later, the Atlantic Monthly Press published the first two years of the diary in full as a book, *The Story of Opal*. In a rapturous review, the *New York Times* said: "Opal saw life imaginatively, beautifully, lovingly. All who wish to understand childhood and all who wish to find joy in it will do well to read this ... wonderful book."

Opal's diary tells of the child and her pets and her friends. It tells of nature, of her joy and sorrows. The language of the diary is unique:

> *I did have meditations about what things the eyes of potatoes do see there in the ground. I have thinks they do have seeing of black velvet moles and large earthworms that do get short in a quick way. And potato flowers above the ground do see the doings of the field—and maybe they do look away and see the willows that grow by the singing creek. I do wonder if potato plants do have longings to dabble their toes. I have supposes they do just like I do. Being a potato must be interest—specially the having so many eyes.*

The names Opal gave her pets in Oregon are extraordinary: Peter Paul Rubens the pig, Felix Mendelssohn the mouse, William Shakespeare the old horse, Elizabeth Barrett Browning the Jersey cow, Brave Horatius the sheepdog, and Lars Porsena of Clusium her pet crow. Even more astonishing is her name for herself. Mrs. Whiteley—always referred to in the diary as "the mama"—calls her "Opal." But the little girl calls herself "Françoise."

> *The wind was calling ... "Come petite Françoise, go explores."*

> *And the boards of the bridge ... said in their squeaks, "Petite Françoise, we have been waiting a long time for you to go across the rivière."*

Opal writes repeatedly in the diary of her beloved "Angel Father" and "Angel Mother," whom she regards as her true parents. In her introduction to the published diary, Opal explains that before their death her angel parents had given her two copybooks, from which she took the names of her pets and other historical figures mentioned in her diary. Her real father, she writes, was a naturalist and explorer; her mother died in a shipwreck. "Then it was they put me with Mrs. Whiteley." Opal believed that she was a substitute for a child of the Whiteleys, also named Opal, who had died.

The diary is full of French words and expressions. Strange lists of French flowers appear:

> I did sing to [the baby] le chant de fleurs that Angel Father did teach
> me to sing, of *h*yacinthe, *é*claire, *n*énufar, *r*ose, *i*ris, et *d*auphinelle, et
> *o*léandre, et *r*omarin, *l*is, *é*glantier, *a*némone, *n*arcisse, et *s*ouci.

The first letters of this apparently random jumble of flowers spell the name, "HENRI D'ORLEANS," a French prince who was an explorer and naturalist. He died a bachelor in Saigon in 1901 (when Opal would have been four or five years old), just before he was due to travel on to America. Opal, for all her adult life, believed that Henri d'Orleans was Angel Father, her true father. The diary contains several similar lists of French words whose first letters spell the name of Prince Henri's father, Robert d'Orleans, Duke of Chartres, and other members of the d'Orleans family.

The appearance of the diary in *The Atlantic Monthly* caused a considerable stir. When Opal's diary appeared as a book, many critics hailed it as a literary wonder. Then doubts began. No child, some people said, could have written such a book. It was too sophisticated; an adult must have written it. The Whiteleys swore that Opal was their daughter, Opal Whiteley, and was not adopted. Skeptics trying to explain the diary said that all the French content and the references to Angel Father and Angel Mother were a hoax and a forgery.

Opal's greatest supporter remained Ellery Sedgwick, the editor of *The Atlantic Monthly*, who throughout his life insisted that the diary was genuine. He summarized his views in his autobiography, written in 1946: "Of the rightness and the honesty of the manuscript as the *Atlantic* printed it, I am utterly convinced; more certain am I than of the authorship of many another famous diary, for I have watched the original copy reborn and subjected it to the closest scrutiny."

Another mainstay was the former British Foreign Secretary, Lord Grey of Fallodon, an immensely distinguished international statesman and nature lover. Lord Grey had been introduced to Opal by Ellery Sedgwick, and they met at the house of a friend in Boston. Sedgwick wrote of this unusual encounter: "[D]uring the thirty years I guided the *Atlantic,* I have never watched two more delighted and understanding friends than the statesman and the child of the woods talking back and forth of wrens and pewits, of orioles and cuckoos."

When *The Diary of Opal Whiteley* was published in Britain in September 1920, Lord Grey wrote in a glowing introduction, "I have read the book with sheer delight." In Britain, as in America, many critics acclaimed the book. The *Times Literary Supplement* called it "the most complete picture of a child's inner life that can be imagined." But after a few months, like a shooting star, Opal's diary vanished from public view on both sides of the Atlantic. Forty years were to pass before the diary was reprinted in England as part of a book, *Opal Whiteley: The Unsolved Mystery,* by the British author Elizabeth Bradburne.

When she learned of Opal's death, Elizabeth Bradburne made the journey from her home in Dorset to attend the Requiem Mass. She had such deference for Opal, and such humility herself, that she certainly was not going to sit in a front pew at St. Etheldreda's. Small and spirited, she took her seat farther back. Elizabeth Bradburne had read the diary and was fascinated by Opal's story. She described her first meeting with Opal at Napsbury Hospital in 1958: "I saw a small rather rotund little person, aged about sixty, with greying hair and very large, soft brown eyes. Though shabbily dressed in a badly fitting brown woollen jumper and skirt, she had undoubted graciousness and charm. She held out her small hand to me, a gesture which almost made me feel I should bow over it."

In her book, Elizabeth Bradburne explains how Opal came to England in the 1920s, after the publication of her diary there. Soon afterwards she is believed to have visited Prince Henri d'Orleans' mother, the Duchess of Chartres. Although details of the meeting are unknown, Bradburne records it as "fairly well authenticated" that in 1925 the Duchess paid for Opal to make a trip to India, where Prince Henri had journeyed. In India, Opal was befriended by an Indian prince, the Maharana of Udaipur. An American woman who knew Opal was astonished to see her in Allahabad in an open carriage drawn by white horses and accompanied by royal outriders.

The Duchess died before Opal returned to England, and no other member of the d'Orleans family gave her any measure of recognition. However, Opal continued to see friends in English high society who believed her story—people she had met through Lord Grey of Fallodon and the chairman of her London publishers, Constant Huntingdon. In her quest over the next twenty years for what she believed was her d'Orleans ancestry, and in the face of continued public rejection, Opal became unbalanced. Eventually she half-starved herself, spending all her money on genealogical books, and in 1948 she was put in Napsbury Hospital.

As to the diary, Elizabeth Bradburne presents a forceful case for its authenticity. The wording is that of a child, the paper is pre-1914, and the crayons are of a type in use then. The diary's outlook and expressions are that of a child. Moreover, by the time she met the editor of *The Atlantic Monthly*, Opal had lost the ability to write as she had in the diary. Her nature book, which Ellery Sedgwick rejected, had none of the diary's special sparkle. Bradburne challenges the case of those who maintain that Opal forged her diary when in her early twenties. Such a plot would have meant that Opal, having conceived the extraordinary idea of a hoax diary, wrote many thousands of words in a child's capital letters, carefully misspelling the bulk of them, and changing her writing as the diary progressed. Then Opal would have to have torn the whole thing up, presumably realizing that it would take months to put it back together again.

Despite Elizabeth Bradburne's powerful argument that the diary is genuine, she recognizes that the question of the French language in the diary (the grown-up Opal was totally ignorant of French) and the whole d'Orleans connection remain mysterious. She writes: "The story of Opal—difficult to believe and yet impossible to dismiss—is unfinished. The mystery baffles still."

Another mourner at the Requiem Mass was my Aunt Mia, the Honourable Mrs. Woodruff. An indomitable eighty-six-year-old, she had commandeered a car and chauffeur to drive her from her house near Oxford. She had known Opal since the 1930s, and to my Aunt Mia, her friend has always been and will always be "Françoise." At one time Aunt Mia had sheltered Françoise in her house. My aunt is absolutely certain that whatever the truth of the child's origin, she was not the daughter of Oregon lumbercamp people. Aunt Mia believes Françoise was French, and that the strange language in the diary was the result of the child translating from French into English in her head. The chauffeur and another man carried Aunt Mia's wheelchair up the worn steps of St. Etheldreda's, and then pushed it next to the front pew, to the left of the coffin. Aunt Mia, dressed entirely in black, sat composed. At eighty-six she was used to death.

A cousin who accompanied my Aunt Mia sat behind her. Nearby sat two devotees of Opal. One was an Englishwoman who had come from Cambridge. Long captivated by Opal and her diary, she prized among her possessions some of Opal's correspondence, which the Official Solicitor had given her. The other was an American translator of literature. She, of all the thousands of people over the years who have read Opal's diary, was the only member of Opal's general public who had managed to attend the Requiem Mass. This woman had been enchanted by the diary, which she only had discovered the previous year. When she read Opal's obituary in *The Independent,* she counted herself fortunate to be working in London and thus able to go to St. Etheldreda's.

The priest gestured my wife and me to sit next to the nurses in the front pew. We had met because of Opal. My wife's brother, Robert Lindsey Nassif, an American composer, had loved the diary and over the last decade had made several trips from New York to visit Opal in Napsbury Hospital. Determined to write a musical based on the diary and to discover all he could about Opal, Robert had sought out my Aunt Mia, with whom I was then staying. He had brought his sister with him for the visit, and subsequently she and I had fallen in love and married.

Robert's musical, *Opal,* had gone into rehearsal off-Broadway the week before Opal died. Had she but lived a few more weeks, Opal would have had the satisfaction of knowing that *The New York Times* was as enthusiastic about the musical of her childhood as it had been seventy years earlier about her diary: "Mr. Lindsey's lovely music and several memorable songs, combined with the odd, French-infused language of the famous diary of Opal Whiteley, draw one into a place of magical transformations. ... This splendid little musical ... is a rare achievement."

The news of Opal's death had saddened Robert, who had become devoted to her. Unable to come to London himself, he had asked me to represent him at the Requiem Mass. My wife was at St. Etheldreda's in her own right. She originally had met Opal through Robert and, a few months before Opal's death, had gone alone to visit her at Napsbury Hospital. Together, we brought a spray of white lilies, which we laid on the coffin.

A Requiem Mass in the old Latin was the right way to say farewell to Opal. In her English life from the 1920s onwards she had been

Catholic, but clearly, she had been a Catholic long before. The Whiteleys were a Protestant family. The flavor of Opal's Catholicism from her
earliest days is shown in endless places in her diary:

> Today I did go in quick steps to the tree I have planted for Louis
> Philippe, roi de France, for this is the day of his borning in 1773. I
> did have prayers. Then I did light my little candle. Seventy-six big
> candles Angel Father did so light for him, but so I cannot do, for
> only one little candle I have. It did burn in a bright way. Then I did
> sing, "Deo Gratias." ... Then I did sing "Sanctus, sanctus, sanctus,
> Dominus Deus."

The all-male choir of St. Etheldreda's Church sang their part of the
traditional Latin Mass for the Dead, chanting—like Opal in the Oregon
forest—"sanctus, sanctus, sanctus." The priest, wearing black vest-
ments, said the Mass in the ancient rite.

A television producer had been making a film about Opal's life
when she died. His camera crew set up their equipment to the right of
Opal's coffin, near a niche bearing a statue of a Catholic martyr. The
producer directed his cameraman to swing his camera around the
church during the celebration of Mass. The priest murmured his Latin
words at the altar; the television producer murmured his directions to
the cameraman.

As part of the ritual, the priest asked me to read from the Book of
Wisdom in the Old Testament. When I finished reading, I looked up
from the text—the vaulted roof and stone walls of St. Etheldreda's
dwarfed the handful of mourners. Then Elizabeth Bradburne went to the
lectern and read a passage from Opal's diary in which the little girl, longing for her dead Angel Mother and Angel Father, reflects on heaven:

> I wonder if honeysuckles grow about the gates of heaven. I've heard
> they are made of precious jewels. I have thinks there will be flowers
> growing all about. Probably God brought the seed from heaven when
> he did plant the flowers here on earth. Too, I do think when angels
> bring babies from heaven to folks that live here below, they do also
> bring seeds of flowers and do scatter them about. I have thinks that
> they do this so the babies may hear the voices of the loving flowers
> and grow in the ways of God.

Thereafter the priest gave a brief tribute to Opal. He summed up the whole mystery of her life in a masterly understatement: "I gather there was some doubt as to who this lady really was." Soon the Mass was over. The coffin was taken to London's Highgate Cemetery, where the graves of George Eliot and Karl Marx are situated. There Opal was buried.

Four days later, my wife and I arrived in New York to see a preview of the musical *Opal*. That afternoon we took a taxi to the Lamb's Theater near Broadway and walked through its white portico to find Robert. We peered into the theater, where two little girls were sitting, dangling their legs over the edge of the stage. The six-year-old actress cast as Opal and her eight-year-old understudy were going through their lines with the director. Robert tip-toed over to join us. Outside the theater we took photographs of the signs that bore the simple name, "Opal."

That night my wife and I returned to the Lamb's Theater for the preview performance. The musical is set in a lumbercamp in the Oregon forest, and tells the story of the little girl Opal and her friends, the animals and people of the camp. The story is of the harshness of Opal's life and her remarkable resilience and joy.

As the child actress sang a ballad, "Angel Mother, Angel Father," I thought of Opal. I thought of her diary as a seven-year-old and this musical which caught its sense of wonder. I thought how a television film of Opal's life was being made in England, and how an abridged version of the diary was now in print in America.

I had not cried at the Requiem Mass. A very old lady had died, which did not seem to be a matter of great sadness. But the spark of her life as an extraordinary child goes on. And that is why, as I listened to the little girl sing "Angel Mother, Angel Father," I found tears starting in my eyes.

A CYNIC AT THE CINEMA

I believe in Santa Claus. I have an open mind on the whereabouts of Elvis. If the tooth fairy existed in British culture, no doubt I would believe in the tooth fairy, too. I like my illusions.

The German poet, Christoph Martin Wieland, summed up my attitude: "An illusion which makes me happy is worth a verity which drags me to the ground."

One of my happiest illusions concerned musical films. Whenever I saw a movie star singing on the screen, I always believed that it was *that* man or woman doing the singing. Various people at various times tried to convince me that my notion was not always right, that sometimes a professional singer dubbed the voice of the star. I dismissed such people as dreary spoilsports.

Then I got married, and everything changed. My wife's brother, Robert, writes music and spends his entire working life in the world of musicals. One fateful day in Iowa City, he told me that it was indeed true—dubbing was a widespread practice. Then he asked me if I had ever heard of Marni Nixon.

I looked blank. Robert said: "Well, you are very familiar with her voice. Did you see the movie of *My Fair Lady*?"

I said, "Of course."

He said, "It was not Audrey Hepburn who sang the part of Eliza Doolittle; it was Marni Nixon."

I was shocked. I had always been impressed with how well Audrey Hepburn had varied her voice from Cockney flower girl to Mayfair lady.

Robert went on. "Did you see *West Side Story*? Natalie Wood did not sing Maria's songs; it was Marni Nixon." He was remorseless. "You think Deborah Kerr sang the part of Anna the governess in *The King and I*, don't you? Well, you're wrong; it was Marni Nixon."

He concluded: "I hate to disillusion you, but I know Marni, and what I say is true. *Time* magazine called her 'the Ghostess with the Mostest.' "

Unfortunately, Robert is not a liar, and he really does know an enormous amount about musicals. With great reluctance, I felt obliged to believe him.

Sometime later, I borrowed the autobiography of the great lyricist

"Shattered Illusions," *Iowa City Magazine* (April 1993).

Alan Jay Lerner from the public library. In the book he told the story of the making of the Lerner and Loewe film, *Gigi,* which won nine Academy Awards. Lerner described how the French film star Leslie Caron played the title role. She had a singing voice which was "not a pretty noise," so they sent for Marni Nixon to dub her.

Leslie Caron, who thought well of her own singing, was furious. She went to André Previn, the musical director, and insisted that she supervise the recording. Lerner wrote: "By mid-afternoon, Marni Nixon was on the verge of hysteria and André halted the session out of concern for her health. By the following day the worst was over, and at sundown Marni under Leslie's direction completed the dubbing."

Thus I learned that Marni Nixon was the ghost for even more heroines than Robert thought. Moreover, she was versatile enough to sing with a French accent and give a very convincing imitation of Leslie Caron.

Earlier this year, I watched Marni Nixon perform in one of my brother-in-law's musicals off-Broadway. She confirmed her range by singing with an authentic Scottish accent. After the show, Robert introduced me to her. I said, "How thrilling to meet Eliza and Maria and Anna and Gigi."

Marni smiled and shook her head. "Not Gigi," she said.

"But you *were* Gigi. I know you were. Alan Jay Lerner says you were in his book."

"I wasn't," said Marni. Then she explained: "Another young woman sang the part of Gigi. She had a difference with the studio and brought a lawsuit. When Lerner wrote his book, he was nervous of using her name. So instead he used mine." She shrugged. "I didn't mind."

My head spun. This was a case of a dubber dubbing for the dubber. I insisted on written evidence, so she signed my program: "Marni Nixon—not Gigi."

I still believe in Santa Claus. But I have lost my faith in the magic of musical films. I now suspect that all of the heroines' voices have been dubbed. If I read that a dubber has dubbed for the star, I have to assume that the writer has deliberately misled me, and that a different dubber did the dubbing.

When it comes to movie musicals, I am now a sad and embittered cynic.

SOME THOUGHTS ON A UNITED GERMANY

One looks at history through one's own spectacles. My family is partly German. My father's grandmother was Austro-Bavarian, and from another ancestor I inherited the German surname Dalberg. Nonetheless my family's loyalties were clear when war came. For the first four years of my life, my father was away fighting Nazi Germany.

I was born in England in 1941, and we lived in Shropshire far from the bombs of London. But one of my earliest memories is of donning a gas mask and going into the cellar as a precautionary drill against the danger that Germany would use poison gas. To a little child, Germany was to be feared.

On the other hand, there was Alfred. As part of the war effort my mother worked furiously farming our ancestral acres. Alfred was a German prisoner of war allocated to assist her in 1945. Alfred was immensely hardworking and kind. I used to "help" him feed the pigs. Alfred taught me how to count in German; he taught me how to swear in German; he even tried to teach me how to sing in German. I adored him.

From my earliest age there were two Germanys. The Germany my father was fighting, and the Germany of Alfred.

Which Germany can the British expect in the future? The Germany that sought to dominate Europe militarily in two world wars? Or the democratic and economically astonishing West Germany of the last forty-five years?

These questions have been in the forefront of British politics recently. Mr. Nicholas Ridley, a senior Cabinet Minister and close ally of Prime Minister Margaret Thatcher, caused a furor with an interview he gave to a weekly magazine in July. The article was headed, "Saying the Unsayable About the Germans," and bore a cartoon of Margaret Thatcher reacting with horror to a poster of West German Chancellor Helmut Kohl bearing an unmistakable Hitler moustache and forelock.

In the article, Ridley said of moves towards European monetary union: "This is all a German racket designed to take over the whole of Europe." Later in the interview, he was asked: "But surely Herr Kohl is preferable to Herr Hitler. He's not going to bomb us, after all?" Ridley replied: "I'm not sure I wouldn't rather have ... the shelters and the

Des Moines Register, August 29, 1990.

chance to fight back, than simply being taken over by ... *economics.* ...
I mean [Kohl will] soon be trying to take over *everything.*"

There was uproar in Britain and Germany. A few days later Prime
Minister Thatcher, with apparent reluctance, accepted Ridley's resignation. Then a memorandum written by Thatcher's private secretary
appeared in the press. It was the secretary's record of a meeting the
Prime Minister had held in the spring with a group of experts about Germany.

The general tone of the memorandum was optimistic about the effects of a united Germany. But much public attention focused on a list
of attributes described as "an abiding part of the German character."
These were cited as: "their insensitivity to the feelings of others ... their
obsession with themselves, a strong inclination to self-pity, and a longing to be liked." Then came an alphabetical list: "angst, aggressiveness,
assertiveness, bullying, egotism, inferiority complex, sentimentality." Inevitably, this part of the memorandum was highlighted in Britain and
around the world.

British opinion polls taken after Ridley's resignation showed ambivalence about his startling public comments. The polls indicated that
most Britons favored a united Germany, while at the same time most
would be "worried" if a unified Germany became the dominant power
in Europe. Apparently public opinion still supports Britain's move towards closer European economic integration, despite fears of German
preeminence.

Some of the British ambivalence is a matter of generations. For example, my father's eldest sister is a splendid 85-year-old. She has vivid
memories of the carnage of the First World War and the horrors perpe-
trated by the Nazis in the second. She—like many other Britons of the
older generation—reacted simply to Mr. Ridley's concern about German
economic dominance: "He is quite right!"

In contrast, nothing in the lifetime of my son—born in 1966—has
given him reason to fear a united Germany. To him, West Germany is a
European neighbor with an enviably successful economic record. His
chief rivalry with his young German friends takes place on the international soccer field. He and many others of his generation label any
British nervousness about German reunification a "Fourth Reich men-
tality."

As a member of the middle generation, I have watched West Germany since the Second World War with admiration. It has built a colos-

sal economy out of rubble. It has stuck meticulously to its constitution. Nothing in its behavior since 1945 worries me more than any other western European country. Yet my childhood experience leaves me with a nagging doubt.

If I were to give advice to my nieces and nephews about the prospect of a united and sovereign Germany, I think I would say: Learn from all of our family. Learn from my aunt to be wary of Germany's past. Learn from me to respect Germany's progress. Learn from my son to hope for Germany's future.

MOSCOW SERVICE: WAIT, WAIT, AND WAIT

The democratic world applauded the tens of thousands who took to the streets of Moscow in August and defied the coup. When they had won, and President Mikhail Gorbachev was back in office, an unhappy thought came to mind. What about the millions of Muscovites who had shown no resistance?

Moscow has known centuries of rule by the tsars followed by decades of communism. Thus one can understand why the vast bulk of the citizens of Moscow greeted the coup with apathy or fear. But their inaction does not augur well for the political future.

Apathy also has pervaded the Soviet economic system. Lack of management, lack of incentive, lack of efficiency have led to forecasts that the Soviet republics may fail to distribute enough food in the coming winters to sustain their people.

My experience in a Moscow hotel during the late 1980s highlighted the reality of the Soviet economic system. The hotel is a symbol of the lethargy that will make the move to a free market so difficult.

My brother-in-law was the Moscow correspondent for the London *Daily Telegraph*. He, my sister, and their three children filled their apartment. I wanted to visit them, so I took a package tour with a seven-night stay in a major Moscow hotel.

As our party stood in a slow line at the reception desk (all of life in

Moscow is a slow line), a Romanian next to me announced that the hotel had 4,000 beds and had been built for the Olympic games. The hotel was for foreigners only—the guests were mainly East European, with a sprinkling of Westerners. The staff were Russians, as were the police, who kept all other Russians out.

I spent most of my waking hours with my family or sightseeing. But in the short time I was actually in the hotel, several incidents drove home the chronic inefficiency of Moscow.

One afternoon I longed for a drink. On the ground floor was a huge bar. A sign on the counter read: "Foreign Currency Only." Behind the counter, a row of barmen stood chatting.

Eventually I got one man's attention. He gestured that the bar was closed. Surprised, I asked where to get a drink, and he pointed upwards. I clambered up the stairs and found another bar. Here a notice said roubles would be accepted.

The four men behind this counter were doing nothing at all. I ordered a drink, and the barman replied with the dread word, "nyet"— Moscow's favorite expression. He insisted that the bar was shut. I asked where I could quench my thirst. The man pointed downstairs towards the first bar. I gave up in despair.

The next night, I decided to have dinner in the hotel's grand restaurant. I stood in line for two hours, growing more and more hungry. Finally I was shown to a table, which I shared with some Bulgarians. The menu was elaborate, with scores of exotic dishes, and I studied it greedily.

Time passed with no sign of service. Then suddenly one of the Bulgarians toasted me: "Peace and friendship," he said. I raised my glass of water and responded: "Peace and friendship." ("And food," I silently implored.)

After nearly an hour, a waitress appeared and spoke in Russian to the Bulgarians. I prepared to order a splendid meal. Then my tablemate announced gloomily: "She says there is only soup, two sorts of fish, and beef stew." My hopes crumbled. After another hour, some tasteless stew arrived.

The final episode came at breakfast the day before I left Moscow. Huge vats of hard-boiled eggs were brought around. Hungry after a night out with my relatives, I took three.

I cracked open the first egg. The contents slithered onto the plate. The egg was completely raw. Amazed, I cracked open another egg; it, too, was raw.

I picked up the third egg. Then I looked around the vast dining room. All the guests were furiously showing the hotel staff that their eggs had not been cooked. Somehow, hundreds and hundreds of eggs had managed to get to the breakfast table without going near a stove.

None of the staff seemed shame-faced; none of them seemed surprised; nobody apologized. With shrugs, the waiters removed the raw eggs and, after a long delay, returned with bread and cheese.

These incidents were not catastrophic, as we tourists were hardly going to starve. However, the hotel earned much foreign currency and should have been a showpiece for visitors. Instead, it was ghastly. Even in that era when *glasnost* and *perestroika* were meant to improve all aspects of Soviet life, basic reliable service just did not exist.

Now an era of democracy appears to be dawning in the Russian federation. Hopes are high that political change will usher in a western-style market system. But how will a new economic attitude be born? How will the people develop initiative and efficiency?

And how long will it be before the eggs in that Moscow hotel come to the breakfast table cooked?

THE CHANNEL ISLAND THAT HONORS AN ENEMY

The hell of ethnic strife in Bosnia makes one wonder how people with a history of enmity can ever live together in peace. On a recent trip to the island of Sark, I learned of an instance where a former enemy was made welcome, thrived, and today is honored.

Sark—the smallest inhabited Channel Island—lies between Britain and France. A feudal Seigneur, whose privileges go back to 1565, and a parliament called the Chief Pleas, rule the 560 inhabitants.

The island is three miles long and at most a mile wide. It supports a unique community. Cars are banned; people travel by bicycle or horse and cart. Tractors do the heavy work.

Des Moines Register, June 11, 1993.

The Sarkese pay no income, property, or inheritance tax. Most revenue comes from a tax on tourists. The Seigneur, who is descended from a pirate, collects some feudal dues and pays Queen Elizabeth £1.70 a year for his ancient privileges. He alone can breed dogs or keep pigeons.

The island employs a doctor, but no dentist. Toothache means taking a boat to the neighboring island of Guernsey.

A few weeks ago, my wife and I visited Sark. We approached the sheer cliffs by boat. A tractor dragged us up Harbour Hill in a wagon with wooden seats called the "Toast Rack."

We bicycled along Sark's one and only avenue of shops, passing the schoolhouse where the Chief Pleas meets, and the jail—supposedly the smallest in the world.

The beauty of the countryside is breathtaking. Sark has the greenest of green fields. Yellow and white Guernsey cows watched us pedal by. The only sounds were the clip-clop of horses and the cries of seagulls.

Sark is tranquility itself. Yet it was not always so.

In 1940, the German army invaded the island and occupied it for the rest of the Second World War. The people lived under curfew and were forced to report daily to German military headquarters. The Germans laid barbed wire and thousands of mines on the cliffs and beaches.

Allied commando raids led to German reprisals. Fifty of the tiny population were deported to prisoner-of-war camps. The Sarkese suffered hunger and want. Men wore shirts made of curtains; young women wore blanket coats. Five long years went by.

All this seemed ancient history as we sat in the sunshine at the far end of the island, feasting on Sark crab salads. On our return journey, we noticed the Sark ambulance parked outside a house. A kindly woman beckoned us to come and look at this remarkable contraption. It is the body of an ambulance with the engine and front section replaced by a trailer hitch. A tractor tows it around the island's winding roads.

Our new friend explained that her husband performs the island's ambulance duty. She added, "He replaced Werner."

"Who is Werner?" I asked.

"He is our German," she said with a fond smile. Then she told us his story—a story I later amplified from articles in the *Guernsey Evening Press*.

During the Second World War, Werner Rang was a young soldier in the German army. He was early decorated with the Iron Cross for a daring rescue from a mine field in France.

In 1943, Rang came to Sark as a member of the enemy occupying forces. He served as a corporal in the medical corps, assisting the doctor with both German and Sarkese patients. On their rounds, Rang met a young island woman with tonsillitis, called Phyllis Baker. She spoke German and was the island's interpreter.

After six months, Rang was posted to Guernsey, where he remained until the German surrender. Then he was made a prisoner of war in Britain and subsequently worked on a farm there. In 1948, Phyllis joined Rang in England, where they married. The following year they went back to Sark.

The island people had known Werner Rang as an enemy medical orderly in wartime. Now they welcomed the young couple. Rang worked for his father-in-law, and then for the formidable Dame of Sark (grandmother of the current Seigneur). Later he opened a jewelry shop, which he still runs today.

In 1977, the Chief Pleas appointed the former German corporal to a year's term as Connétable—police chief of the island. Since then, he has been repeatedly elected as a deputy in the Chief Pleas.

Rang took over the Sark ambulance in 1961. He was on 24-hour duty and was paid 50 pence per call. During the next twenty-nine years, he made over 1,200 calls.

The pinnacle of Werner Rang's public life came after he retired from ambulance duty at the age of seventy. In 1991, Queen Elizabeth rewarded his devoted service with the British Empire Medal—a singular honor for a holder of the German Iron Cross.

As we bicycled back to the "Toast Rack," I longed to meet the island's legendary German. His story gave me a glint of hope that erstwhile enemies can live side by side in harmony.

AN UNEXPECTED MEETING WITH DE KLERK

Improbably, I have just met President de Klerk of South Africa in London. Twenty-five years ago, I worked in South Africa for six months. I had an opportunity to see apartheid close up, and intensely disliked what I saw. Little did I realize that at the same time I was looking at apartheid, the South African authorities were looking at me. They apparently disliked me with equal fervor, for soon after leaving the country I was declared a prohibited immigrant.

Over the succeeding years I became a firm supporter of the international campaign of sanctions against South Africa. This seemed to be the only alternative to terrible bloodshed between the races.

For a long time I despaired of the future of South Africa, as racist president succeeded racist president. When de Klerk came to power in 1989, he spoke much of "reform." I had grave doubts about him—I thought his talk of reform was a cynical device to try to achieve the lifting of sanctions.

But since then, my opinion gradually has changed. De Klerk released Nelson Mandela and his senior colleagues. He legalized the ANC (African National Congress) and a host of opposition organizations. A start was made on the dismantling of apartheid with the desegregation of libraries, swimming pools, and other municipal facilities.

In early February of this year, de Klerk announced his intention to repeal all of the remaining apartheid legislation in South Africa. This statement prompted me to make a speech about South Africa in the House of Lords.

I advocated a step-by-step approach to lifting sanctions. As President de Klerk removed major apartheid legislation, some sanctions should be removed. De Klerk and the ANC had recently agreed on a program for the release of political prisoners and the return of exiled opponents of the South African government. When these agreements were fulfilled, more sanctions should be removed. Finally, when a new constitution was agreed to and implemented, the last sanctions should be abolished.

As a prohibited immigrant, I was surprised to receive an invitation to hear President de Klerk speak at South Africa House in London on April 22nd. After some hesitation, I decided to go.

Outside South Africa House there was a knot of demonstrators

Des Moines Register, May 8, 1991. ·

holding signs saying "One person one vote NOW" and "Abolish Apartheid IMMEDIATELY."

I thought of the number of times I had signed the petitions of such anti-apartheid demonstrators or contributed money. Now I felt lonely.

I proceeded to the small lecture auditorium. The audience was composed mainly of right-wing Conservative members of Parliament. I had been fighting them for years over southern African issues.

But I felt less lonely when a friend—one of Britain's two Asian women members of the House of Lords—came and sat next to me. Born in India, she is a powerful fighter against racism, and her presence was a real boost.

President de Klerk talked for half an hour. He spoke of violence, of negotiations, of a new constitution. He spoke of sanctions, of land, and of his far right-wing Conservative Party opposition. After a period of questions and answers, the meeting broke up.

I went over to President de Klerk and introduced myself. After congratulating him for his courage in setting South Africa on a new course, I decided to probe. "You are the first politician in history who is prepared to write himself out of power," I said.

President de Klerk blinked, smiled, and inspected my name tag. "I would not be too sure about that, Lord Acton," he said. "I am going to win the black vote."

As I left the building, it struck me what an amazing statement that was. Only two years ago, there seemed little hope of black South Africans even getting the vote. Now a white president was actually expecting to receive black votes.

South Africa is changing.

THE MAN WHO GAVE IT ALL AWAY

[Author's note: De Klerk introduced a constitution based on universal suffrage, and in 1994, Nelson Mandela and the ANC won the subsequent elections and came to power. The following review of Patti Waldmeir's Anatomy of a Miracle: The End of Apartheid and the Birth of the New South Africa *(London: Viking, 1997) tells something of the extraordinary circumstances which led to the new South Africa.]*

In May 1995, the all-white South African rugby team, the Springboks, took the field in their homeland for the final of the World Cup. Behind them came an astonishing figure—President Nelson Mandela, wearing the green and gold jersey belonging to their captain. The crowd of mainly white South Africans chanted: "Nel—son! Nel—son!" Then the crowd sang the African nationalist song—now the national anthem of South Africa—*Nkosi Sikelel'i Afrika*. To complete a dream, the Springboks went on to win the World Cup.

How did this incredible scene come about? In *Anatomy of a Miracle,* Patti Waldmeir seeks to explain the unparalleled transfer of political power in South Africa, whereby Mandela succeeded F.W. de Klerk as president. She calls this transfer "the negotiated revolution." The author, who had known some African National Congress leaders in exile in Zambia in the 1980s and was head of the *Financial Times* bureau in Johannesburg from 1989-1995, was in a position to observe the extraordinary events during those years. One of the most striking features of the saga is that the government and ANC participants in the negotiations seemed so often to have had a remarkable understanding—even sympathy—for each other. Although this was not true of Mandela and de Klerk, it was true of ANC leaders like Thabo Mbeki and Cyril Ramaphosa and the white South African negotiators with whom they held endless meetings.

The author has the highest regard for Nelson Mandela. She quotes and echoes the views of an Afrikaner who was a warden at Robben Island, where Mandela and other ANC leaders were imprisoned: "Mr. Mandela was a prisoner but also a leader, anybody could see that ... the

"The Man Who Gave It All Away," *[London] Literary Review* (April 1997).

moment he walked into a room, his manner, his way of speaking, his dress, you knew he was a leader."

But in many ways, the exploration of F.W. de Klerk and his motives is the most interesting part of the book. In a chapter entitled, "Why the Boers Gave It All Away," the author examines what made this conservative leader of the party of apartheid decide to free Mandela, raise the ban on the ANC, and enter into negotiations with that party. De Klerk is explained as a man of logic, and—although the author did not warm to him personally—a good man. He set out to preserve as much power for his Afrikaner people as possible, and in the end he gave power away.

A long-time friend of de Klerk asked him why he took that initial great leap. De Klerk replied: "[T]here are certain crevasses in my mind which even my friends do not have the right to probe." The author thinks that de Klerk's actions came from a combination of a sense of injustice and pragmatism. Apartheid had failed; hence, it was immoral and must be replaced. Therefore, he must negotiate with the ANC, and he must free Mandela. Mandela must lead a legal organisation, so the ban on the ANC must end.

To right-wing Afrikaners, de Klerk was guilty of treason. Remarkably, it seems not a single attempt was made on his life. In fact, the worst that happened was when de Klerk had finally agreed a new constitution with the ANC in November 1993. One of his cabinet ministers seized him by the shirt and yelled: "What have you done! You've given South Africa away." De Klerk calmed him down, and even got him to remain in his National Party.

One particular mystery is why de Klerk managed to win more than two-thirds of the vote in a referendum among the white electorate for "change" in March 1992. The author doesn't devote a great deal of space to this referendum, and yet de Klerk rightly called it a fundamental turning point. Analysis of the referendum result will doubtless be the subject of future books.

Anatomy of a Miracle is essential reading for anyone interested in South Africa. It confirms that the transfer of power without the long-predicted massive race war truly was a miracle. If de Klerk had not been de Klerk, if Mandela had not been Mandela, if either man had been assassinated—the list of things that could have gone wrong was endless—then this book would have had a very different title.

SIR JOHN IN IOWA

The portrait of my great-great-great grandfather, Sir John Acton, appears to have made the long journey from the Kingdom of Naples to the State of Iowa without too much of a cultural shock.

Sir John's arrival in Iowa, it seems to me, is just one more phase in an extraordinary life.

Born in France in 1736 of a French mother and an English father, the young John Acton served in Italy in the navy of the Grand Duke of Tuscany. He proved so adept at chasing pirates that the Grand Duke recommended him to his sister, the Queen of Naples, to strengthen the Neapolitan navy. He was a huge success and soon rose to be Prime Minister of Naples.

Naples then was the romantic capital of the world, for the wife of the British ambassador was none other than Emma, Lady Hamilton, legendary paramour of Britain's great hero, Admiral Lord Nelson.

John Acton's own romantic life was, to say the least, unique. When his family in England died out, he became a baronet with extensive English lands. The 64-year-old Sir John hit on a novel method to keep the property entirely in the family—he'd get a papal dispensation and marry his 14-year-old niece.

The couple married in 1800 on Nelson's flagship, with Sir William and Lady Hamilton as witnesses. Sir John and his niece-wife had three children, who remarkably could say that their mother was also their first cousin, and their father was also their great uncle.

What relation the children were to each other I've never been able to work out, but happily the inbreeding doesn't seem to have done any lasting harm.

When Sir John died in 1811, his niece-wife took her children from Italy to live in England. And with her she brought a portrait of her husband.

Last month, Sir John's portrait made another change of country, and he now surveys a midwestern cornfield. Gazing at the picture makes me realize how short the centuries really are.

Radio Commentary, Weekend Edition, Monitor Radio, the broadcast edition of *The Christian Science Monitor,* June 23, 1995.

As a little boy, I can remember my Great-Aunt Mamie, then a very old lady. And as a little girl, *she* had known another very old lady—her great-grandmother, Sir John's niece-wife.

Maybe the eighteenth-century kingdom of Naples and the twentieth-century state of Iowa aren't so very far apart after all.

DOES ABSOLUTE POWER REALLY CORRUPT ABSOLUTELY?

Some years ago, soon after I had inherited our family title, I visited the Library of Congress in Washington, D.C. I filled in a request form, and under "Name," wrote: "Lord Acton."

The man behind the counter looked at the form, looked at me, and—evidently well-versed in history—said: "No, you are not."

"Not what?" I asked.

"Not Lord Acton."

I knew what he meant. My great-grandfather, the first Lord Acton (1834-1902), was an eminent historian with a high-domed forehead and a huge, bushy beard. My new acquaintance was obviously thinking of him.

So I said: "I am *a* Lord Acton. But I am not *the* Lord Acton."

The Lord Acton was a Victorian Catholic of immense erudition. It has been calculated that he read one thick volume for every single day of his life. He planned to write a definitive History of Liberty, but as he insisted on knowing everything about the subject, he never wrote the book. What has come down to us is a body of essays, lectures, reviews, notes, and correspondence.

Many sayings of my great-grandfather are to be found scattered in books of quotations, but one in particular has immortalized him: "Power tends to corrupt, and absolute power corrupts absolutely."

Although this quotation has passed into common usage, few people know its origin. In February 1887, a fellow historian named Mandell

Creighton had published volumes 3 and 4 of *A History of the Papacy During the Period of the Reformation: The Italian Princes, 1464–1518.* Creighton was a scholar and a Church of England clergyman who later became a bishop. He was, in addition, the editor of an intellectual periodical named *The English Historical Review.*

Creighton asked my great-grandfather to review the new volumes in the *Historical Review.* Acton loathed the books, and warned: "[Y]ou must understand that it [the review] is the work of an enemy."

On receiving the review, Creighton wrote to a friend that it "reads to me like the utterances of a man who is in a furious passion." He added: "I think the public would be greatly amused at an editor inviting and publishing a savage onslaught on himself."

The two men continued their correspondence, and on April 5, 1887, Acton wrote a letter in which he condemned the medieval Popes for the Inquisition. He criticized Creighton for ignoring the Inquisition's torture chambers and for his undue deference to those in power. Acton wrote: "[I] cannot accept your canon that we are to judge Pope and King unlike other men, with a favourable presumption that they did no wrong. ... *Power tends to corrupt, and absolute power corrupts absolutely.*"

A century later, you often find this phrase quoted—and misquoted—by politicians and the press. Frequently the words "Power tends to corrupt" are misstated as "All power corrupts." This error makes me grind my teeth with frustration, for it warps the meaning of the original phrase. A *tendency* to corrupt is quite different from the *certainty* of it.

More to my taste is my uncle's play on the words: "Power tends to corrupt, but absolute power is much more fun."

I myself have been the victim of the quotation. Apparently it was said of me by contemporaries at Oxford University that "power tends to corrupt, but Richard Acton is absolutely corrupt."

A cartoon from the *New Yorker* adorns our refrigerator in Iowa. It shows a king, wearing his crown, and answering a telephone call with the words: "Corrupted absolutely—and you?"

I am amused by such variations, but sometimes I'm forced to defend the family maxim. Recently during Question Time in the House of Lords, a Liberal Democrat peer asked a question of the government which began: "Does the Minister agree that it is not conservatism that corrupts, but power ... ?" He had left out the vital word "tends," and lightning flashed before my eyes.

Boldly I leapt to my feet to correct him. "My Lords, is the Minister aware that power does not corrupt? Power *tends* to corrupt." The Chamber erupted with laughter at my impassioned defense of the family phrase. The Minister replied: "I have it from the horse's mouth!"

I am not always quite so sensitive about my great-grandfather's famous words. For when people say to me: "Are you related to the man who wrote about 'power and corruption'?" my answer reflects more pride than pedantry.

I tend to reply: "Absolutely."

Fragments of Iowa's Past

WHEN I WAS GROWING UP *in Africa, an old judge said to me: "When you set out on a journey, what you need is a map. History is the only map of life there is."*

I've always loved history, and at Trinity College, Oxford, modern history was my subject. Wherever I have lived, histories of the place have found their way onto my bookshelves.

In Iowa, intrigued by the origins of the state's nickname, "Hawkeye," I researched and wrote an article on the subject for the Palimpsest, *produced by the State Historical Society of Iowa. This led to many other articles on Iowa's history in the* Palimpsest, *the* Annals of Iowa, *the* Iowan, *and the* Des Moines Register. *Ultimately, in 1995, my wife and I wrote a book called* To Go Free: A Treasury of Iowa's Legal Heritage.

The essays chosen for this chapter represent a small selection from these various publications, including some of my earliest researches and favorite topics. For example, Thanksgiving in my view is the greatest of American celebrations. It was tremendous fun unearthing the story of Iowa's first Thanksgiving, as seen through the eyes of newspaper editors in Burlington and Davenport.

The pieces chosen are meant to be as much of a mixture as possible. Thus, the story of the abolition and restoration of capital punishment in the 1870s appears side by side with the history of the Cherry Sisters, notorious for their appalling vaudeville act. The attempt of Governor Harding to ban foreign languages during World War I is juxtaposed with Bonnie and Clyde's shoot-out near Dexter, Iowa.

One article gave me special pleasure to write—an account of the suffragette Sylvia Pankhurst's visit to Iowa in 1911. The piece was written to coincide with the seventy-fifth anniversary of American women getting the vote. Imagine what a joy it was that Sylvia Pankhurst was English! After many hundreds of hours researching and writing about Iowa's history, this was the very first article devoted to somebody from my native land.

This book began with a variety of observations about life in modern Iowa. It seems fitting that it should end with a look at some fragments of the state's past. They are all part of the map I'm drawing of my Iowa journey.

"HAWKEYE": WHAT'S IN A NAME?

When I came to Iowa from England to marry my Hawkeye bride, I asked her why Iowa was the Hawkeye State, why Iowans were called Hawkeyes, and why the University of Iowa sports teams were christened the same name. She had no idea. Other Iowans could not answer the question either. So I tried to find out for myself.

Various diverting theories have been advanced to explain why the name Hawkeye was given. For example, a writer in the 1870s stated:

> The hawk came in for notoriety in all localities, on account of his constant vigilance and keenness of sight. ... In these early days of Iowa, the people had to be as vigilant as hawks, in watching government officers, Indians, and intruders ... [and so] gradually grew the appellation or application of the name of Hawk-Eyes.

The evidence reveals, and historians generally agree, that it was actually the brilliant pioneer lawyer David Rorer who suggested applying the name Hawkeye to the people of the future Territory of Iowa in early 1838. Born and educated in Virginia, Rorer moved to Little Rock, Arkansas, in 1826 and established a law practice there. In 1835, he freed his slaves and, with his wife and four young children, set out for a new life on the Iowa frontier, settling the following year in the hamlet of Flint Hills—the Burlington of the future. There he practiced law and built the first brick house in what was to be Iowa.

In 1839, Rorer successfully represented a former slave in the first reported decision of the Iowa Territorial Supreme Court, *In the matter of Ralph*. He appeared in innumerable important cases and, late in life, wrote three weighty legal tomes. A *Chicago Tribune* obituary in July 1884 described him as one of the ablest lawyers and most learned law writers at the American bar.

David Rorer was active in the early push for territorial status. At the Burlington Territorial Convention of November 1837, he chaired the committee that drafted the petition to Congress to create a separate territorial government for the Iowa District (then part of the Territory of

Originally published as " 'Hawkeye': What's in a Name?" *Palimpsest* 70, no. 3 (Fall 1989), pp. 114–20. Adapted by permission of the publisher.

Wisconsin). Rorer knew that the inhabitants of other new Midwestern states had acquired rather unfortunate nicknames—"the Suckers" of Illinois and "the Pukes" of Missouri. One historian records that the people of the Iowa District lacked sufficient barbers and razors and were already being called "the Hairy Nation." Rorer wanted to adopt a dignified name for the people of the anticipated Territory of Iowa before an unflattering one was cast upon them.

The key to where David Rorer got the name Hawkeye lies in his leisure pursuits. His colleague at the bar, Edward H. Stiles, described Rorer as "an omnivorous reader" with a "well-developed taste for general literature." Rorer, like thousands of his contemporaries, had undoubtedly read the most popular author of the period—James Fenimore Cooper.

Cooper's best-known work was *The Last of the Mohicans*, which first appeared in 1826 and was a phenomenal best-seller. In the 1820s, only nine books had the distinction of having total sales exceeding one percent of the population of the United States in the decade in which they were published. Five of these were by James Fenimore Cooper, and the easy leader was *The Last of the Mohicans*.

It is inconceivable that a well-read man like David Rorer was not thoroughly familiar with James Fenimore Cooper's works. There is even evidence that in 1838—the year Rorer suggested the name Hawkeye—Cooper and *The Last of the Mohicans* were still popular in Rorer's hometown of Burlington. In June 1838, the only American novels reported missing from the Wisconsin Territorial Library, established at Burlington the previous year, were both volumes of Cooper's works. Later that year, Theodore S. Parvin, the territorial governor's private secretary in Burlington, was sent *The Last of the Mohicans* for Christmas by a friend in Ohio.

The overwhelming popularity of Cooper's books helps to explain what inspired Rorer to choose the name Hawkeye for the future Territory of Iowa. Cooper's greatest creation is the hero of the frontier known to his Indian friends as "Hawkeye." The character Hawkeye (also known as Leatherstocking and other names) appeared first in *The Pioneers* (1823) and then in *The Last of the Mohicans* (1826).

Uncas, the Indian hero of *The Last of the Mohicans,* gives a glimpse of Hawkeye's qualities in the following dialogue:

> Uncas took the scout by the hand, and led him to the feet of the patriarch.

"Father," he said, "look, at this paleface; a just man, and the friend of the Delawares."

"Is he a son of Miquon?"

"Not so; a warrior known to the Yengees, and feared by the Maquas."

"What name has he gained by his deeds?"

"We call him Hawkeye," Uncas replied, using the Delaware phrase, "for his sight never fails."

When David Rorer suggested the name Hawkeye for the people of the forthcoming Territory of Iowa, he was undoubtedly giving them the name of Cooper's frontier hero. Yet the name also had an echo of another contemporary hero—this one a real, rather than a literary, figure.

Black Hawk, the Sauk war chief, had long resisted the advance of the settlers. In 1832, he had fought and lost the Black Hawk War in Illinois and Wisconsin. The ensuing treaty compelled the Sauk and Meskwaki to cede the nucleus of Iowa, and the settlers poured in from 1833. The area became known as the Black Hawk Purchase.

Black Hawk himself was taken as a prisoner to Jefferson Barracks, Missouri, and thence to Washington, D.C., to meet President Jackson. His subsequent tour of Eastern cities and the publication of his autobiography made him a national figure. By 1838, he was living out his old age near Fort Madison.

The ring of the name Black Hawk in "Hawkeye" evidently appealed to David Rorer and his colleagues who helped launch the nickname. Rorer was responsible for suggesting the name to one of these colleagues—James Gardiner Edwards.

Edwards in 1838 was about to launch the *Fort Madison Patriot*. On March 24, 1838, he published the first edition of the paper, and on page two he wrote of the congressional bill to separate "the proposed Iowa Territory or Black Hawk Purchase" from the Territory of Wisconsin. He then wrote: "If a division of the Territory is effected, we propose that the Iowans take the cognomen of Hawkeyes. Our etymology can then be more definitely traced than can that of the Wolverines, Suckers, Gophers &c., and we shall rescue from oblivion a memento, at least, of the name of the old chief. Who seconds the motion?" On the same page, there were no less than four stories about Black Hawk, referred to in some as "the old chief."

The name did not catch on immediately. The following winter, Rorer, Edwards, and Rorer's law partner, Henry W. Starr, decided that they must find a way to popularize the nickname. Edwards (who had moved from Fort Madison) suggested a bald announcement in his new Burlington newspaper, but David Rorer, with greater subtlety, thought that the best way of promoting the name Hawkeye would be to get people to take it for granted. He decided to send a series of letters to territorial newspapers, thus planting the nickname in the readers' minds. Rorer composed four lengthy letters anonymously signed, "A Wolverine Among the Hawkeyes." Fellow lawyer Shepherd Leffler copied them so that Rorer's handwriting would not be recognized, and they were sent off to Iowa newspapers in early 1839.

The four letters, given huge prominence in the Dubuque and Davenport newspapers, were purportedly written by a traveler from Michigan visiting Iowa. The term "Hawkeye" was used frequently and favorably, as in "that charming lustre of the eye and healthful glow of cheek peculiar to the Hawkeye people" and "the enterprise and industry of the Hawkeye farmers."

The letters are written in a literary, educated style, with romantic detail of Iowa's beauty and fertility, but they are mercilessly critical of certain aspects of the territorial scene. The Wolverine was incredibly rude about Governor Lucas, Edwards's rival Burlington newspaper, and the town of Bloomington (now Muscatine), which resulted in letters to the press and editorial comment. The Wolverine letters created a stir, and historians date popular acceptance of the name Hawkeye to their publication. Indeed, shortly after the second Wolverine letter, Parvin, the governor's secretary, wrote in his diary: "Mother confined with a daughter—a young Hawkeye." In September 1839, Edwards changed the name of his newspaper to *The Hawk-Eye and Iowa Patriot.*

In May 1841, Iowa's new Whig governor, John Chambers, put his own stamp of approval on the nickname. Responding to a formal speech of welcome in Burlington, he said: "Let us ... be citizens of Iowa—'Hawkeyes,' if you please, in spirit and in truth. I will be a 'Hawkeye' and in the discharge of my official duties will endeavor to do impartial justice to all."

In 1977, State Representative James D. Wells of Cedar Rapids proposed that the nickname of Iowa be enshrined in law. In an editorial entitled "We're the Hawkeyes," the *Des Moines Register* commented that official sanction was not needed: "We like the name Hawkeyes, and we imagine that most Iowans do. For well over a hundred years—without benefit of legislative exertion—the people who came here have been heirs to a nickname that wasn't embarrassing to them."

As a twentieth-century traveller in this state, not unlike the Wolverine, I am delighted that my wife and her fellow Iowans should be known by the name of Hawkeye—a just and brave hero of fiction, with the added echo of Black Hawk, a remarkable man in Iowa's history.

IOWA TERRITORY BORN ON THE
FOURTH OF JULY

On the Fourth of July, 1838, the Territory of Iowa—carved out of the Territory of Wisconsin—celebrated its birthday. Statehood lay eight years in the future. For now, the pioneers rejoiced in the founding of the new Territory.

Rain-drenched Iowans from the summer of 1993 would have found Dubuque on that day all too familiar. The *Iowa News* recorded: "The day was stormy—indeed there was a continual falling of rain from 2 or 3 o'clock in the morning, which prevented our country friends from joining us."

At half past one that afternoon, a procession marched to the Dubuque Catholic church. The audience listened to a reading of the Declaration of Independence, followed by an oration. Then they sang patriotic songs.

One hundred and fifty people moved on to an arbor, where they partook of a "substantial repast." Afterwards they drank twenty-eight toasts, including several to the birth of the Territory. The *Iowa News* put a temperate gloss on the libations: "Nothing occurred to mar the harmony of the day, and we are pleased to say that that immoral practice of drinking spirits to excess was unknown here on that occasion."

In the new Territory's capital of Burlington, the townspeople sat down to a sumptuous banquet "provided by that excellent caterer, Mrs. Parrott of the Wisconsin Hotel." Forty-six toasts were drunk—eight of them honored Iowa, while the citizens rose five times in praise of the Territory's farmers.

Cyrus S. Jacobs, the editor of the *Iowa Territorial Gazette and*

Des Moines Register, July 4, 1993.

Burlington Advertiser and a candidate for the new territorial assembly, proudly reported: "Half savages, as we are represented to be, we as a whole conducted ourselves in a manner both as regards minds and morals, in a way that would not disgrace ... the best specimen of American society."

But the most memorable gathering was in Fort Madison, and this because Black Hawk—the legendary Sauk war chief—was in attendance. In 1813, his siege of Old Fort Madison had forced the troops to burn the fort and evacuate. He had finally been conquered in the 1832 Black Hawk War, which resulted in a vast stretch of Sauk and Meskwaki lands along the western bank of the Mississippi River being opened to settlement.

In July 1838, Black Hawk was living near Fort Madison. There he made the last public appearance of his long life at the settlers' celebration.

In his report of the occasion, the editor of the *Fort Madison Patriot*, James Gardiner Edwards, emphasized its importance: "The fact that the birth-day of the new Territory of Iowa was to be celebrated at the same time [as Independence] made the day appear doubly interesting."

First the citizens assembled in a new building for the ringing of a bell and the reading of the Declaration of Independence. Then a local lawyer gave an endless oration, after which the townspeople enjoyed a celebratory meal.

Edwards described the occasion in the *Patriot*: "At 3 o'clock, a large number of ladies sat down to Dinner in an Arbor, prepared for the occasion on the bank of the Mississippi. ... Among the invited guests at the table, the old Indian Chieftain BLACK HAWK stood prominent."

After the cloth was removed and the ladies had retired, there was a plethora of toasts. Edwards, a temperance enthusiast, wrote hopefully: "[A]lthough wine was placed on the table, not more than two bottles were drunk by a large company. The majority drank their sentiments in cold water."

Then Edwards himself proposed a toast: "*Our Illustrious Guest* Black Hawk.—May his declining years be as calm and serene as his previous life has been boisterous and full of warlike incidents."

After the toast was drunk, Black Hawk rose to respond:

> It has pleased the Great Spirit that I am here today—I have eaten with my white friends. The earth is our mother—we are now on it— with the Great Spirit above us—it is good. ...

Rock River was a beautiful country—I liked my towns, my corn-fields and the home of my people. I fought for it. It is now yours—keep it as we did—it will produce you good crops. ...

I was once a great warrior—I am now poor. ... I am now old. I have looked upon the Mississippi since I have been a child. I love the Great River. I have dwelt upon its banks from the time I was an infant. I look upon it now. I shake hands with you, and as it is my wish I hope you are my friends.

Black Hawk closed his speech. Five final toasts followed, including, "Uncle Sam's Youngest Daughter—Iowa." The festivities ended.

Thus did Iowans in the Mississippi River towns launch the new Territory on July 4, 1838.

CELEBRATING IOWA'S FIRST THANKSGIVING

In 1844, six years after its birth, the Territory of Iowa celebrated its first official Thanksgiving.

The previous century, Presidents George Washington and John Adams had declared days of thanksgiving. However, the national holiday had dwindled away, and by 1844 Thanksgiving had become a local festival in New England and other states.

On October 12th of that year, Iowa's second territorial governor, John Chambers, issued a proclamation which began: "At the request of many of my Fellow Citizens, I have deemed it proper to recommend that Thursday, the 12th day of December next, be observed throughout the Territory, as a day of general Thanksgiving to Almighty God for the many and great blessings we enjoy as a people."

It is not surprising that many of the governor's "Fellow Citizens" asked for a thanksgiving celebration. For in 1844, territorial Iowans had particular reason to feel grateful. While Illinois and Missouri experienced terrible floods that year, Iowa had the good fortune to escape the worst of them.

Des Moines Register, November 21, 1993.

In early May, James G. Edwards—the editor of the *Burlington Hawk-Eye*—wrote: "The Mississippi is higher than the writer ever saw it. The opposite bottom lands are entirely inundated, and the torrents, from the distant North, whirl and eddy round the cabins and trees in fine style."

At much the same time, Alfred Sanders, the editor of the *Davenport Gazette,* journeyed along the Mississippi River. He passed houses in Missouri and Illinois whose owners travelled from their front doors by canoe. Sometimes he saw a house on the prairie amid a great spread of water that extended for miles and made cultivation impossible.

However, Sanders reported in the *Gazette* that Davenport had been spared the full force of the flood: "[T]he high water did no injury, save partly filling the cellars on Front street. ... [I]t has shown the necessity for grading that street, and throwing up an embankment on the water's edge to guard against a similar evil."

By the end of June, the whole levee in St. Louis was inundated, while many stores and houses held four feet of water. On July 4th, the *Davenport Gazette* described the entire southern country as one vast sheet of water which had swept away years of work and deprived families of their homes.

In contrast, Davenport's 1,750 inhabitants had every reason for gratitude. Sanders wrote: "We, of a more favored clime ... surrounded with a country inhabited by an industrious population, and teeming with provisions more than adequate to our wants, should feel grateful towards our God that he has so favored us above our fellow creatures."

From mid-April to the end of June, almost incessant rain had fallen in the Davenport area. The newspapers of Davenport and Burlington alike reported poor prospects for the corn—but the wheat crop was prolific. The news from Bloomington (later renamed Muscatine) was that the wheat was a bit disappointing. However, the hitherto sickly corn had improved, and a good yield was anticipated.

Further to the west, Johnson County was blessed with bumper crops. The wheat was the most abundant ever, while the corn, oats, barley and potatoes were unusually fine. An Iowa City newspaper announced that a four-pound carrot had been left at its office. Among the splendid vegetables at C.C. Morgan's grocery store was a beet weighing 15 1/2 pounds. But the champion vegetable in the store—variously described as a South American Squash and a Pumpkin—weighed no less than 141 pounds.

The population of the whole territory had grown from 22,859 in

1838 to 75,122 in 1844. In the latter year, Iowa City—the new territorial capital—boasted 915 inhabitants. However, Burlington (the original capital) remained the largest town.

Indeed, in September 1844, the *Hawk-Eye* claimed that Burlington was the fastest-growing city on the Mississippi north of St. Louis. Its population had increased from 1,831 in the previous year to 2,300. Fifty new buildings were going up. The town bustled with 27 general merchants, 5 grocers, 4 bakers, 3 saddlers, 3 dealers in boots and shoes, 9 physicians, 1 dentist, and many tailors, carpenters and masons.

Burlington also had livery-stable keepers, barbers, a hatter, a watchmaker, stone cutters, plasterers, cabinet-makers, gunsmiths, butchers, blacksmiths, "and all the other trades and professions of which the world is composed." But the *Hawk-Eye* emphasized one notable decline: "There are but 11 lawyers located here now; a year or two ago, there were 25."

With thriving towns, with a burgeoning population, with fruitful soil, ample crops and a merciful avoidance of the worst of the floods, small wonder that Iowans in 1844 pressed Governor Chambers to declare a day of thanksgiving.

The territorial newspapers welcomed the governor's Thanksgiving proclamation. The *Davenport Gazette* was delighted: "The former residents of New England, where the time-honored custom of setting apart a day of thanks to the Giver of all good, prevails, will be rejoiced to see that our Governor has introduced the custom west of the Mississippi river."

The *Burlington Hawk-Eye*—which normally disagreed with everything the *Davenport Gazette* wrote—greeted Thanksgiving with equal enthusiasm. Similarly, the *Iowa City Standard* was "glad to welcome the good old Pilgrim custom to our midst."

Thanksgiving day was December 12th. In Davenport that morning, the *Gazette* announced: "We presume religious exercises, appropriate to the day, will be observed in most of the churches."

The *Burlington Hawk-Eye* was lyrical in anticipation: "Glorious patron saint of the Pilgrim festal rite! ... Preside on this, your privileged anniversary, over the fragrant roast and the savory stew. Scoop out generously, from the rich plum pudding. Deal out unstintingly of the inviting pastry and the delicious sweet meats, and above all, give us the lightsomeness of contented and grateful hearts."

The *Hawk-Eye* laid out a full program for the day. Public services in each of the churches would be followed by family thanksgiving dinners.

The evening would bring a musical entertainment, and then Mr. C.C. Shackford would lecture on music. Thereafter, the "beauty and chivalry" of Burlington would attend a dance at the City Hotel.

The article concluded: "These, with the accompaniments of shooting Deer on the bottoms, knocking over Prairie chickens and netting Quails, make up a very respectable sum total for our day's duty."

Thanksgiving in Burlington turned out as enjoyable as hoped. Reverend Hutchinson's sermon in the Congregational church earned a golden review from the *Hawk-Eye*. In the evening, a large audience packed the Methodist church to hear the music. Mozart's Military Waltz and a mournful song called "The Grave of Bonaparte" won special praise. Mr. Shackford's address on music was eulogised as "poetry without rhyme and metre."

Finally came the dance. "Of the doings at the City Hotel, we cannot speak, but we saw the next day several whose eyelids hung heavy—the inference is easily drawn."

Alfred Sanders, the editor of the *Davenport Gazette*, was shocked by Burlington's revels. Sanders—who thought the fitting way to observe the holiday was to give thanks in church—wrote sarcastically: "We certainly misunderstood the intention of this day." He reproved Burlington for the shooting of deer and prairie chickens, the lecture of Mr. Shackford, and the ball at the City Hotel.

The *Hawk-Eye* scoffed at the rigidity of its Davenport rival. No statute forbade shooting after church on Thanksgiving day. As to the venerable Mr. Shackford's address, "it will be long before the Davenport boys can commit the sin of listening to such." And as for dancing, even the most puritanical law "placed no penalty against cutting a 'pigeon wing' or balancing to partners in the tune of Money Musk, on Thanksgiving Eve."

But despite their different attitudes about the day, both newspapers were eager for Thanksgiving to be a permanent event in Iowa. The *Davenport Gazette* said: "May it long prevail with due observance," while the *Hawk-Eye* said, "We can wish the day, with all its pleasurable occurrences, to be duplicated with each returning December."

And no doubt both newspapers would have been delighted that—a century and a half later—Iowans even now are preparing to celebrate the Thanksgiving festival.

THE MAGIC OF UNDISCOURAGED EFFORT: THE DEATH PENALTY IN EARLY IOWA

Most Iowans know that their state abolished the death penalty in 1965. Fewer realize that this had happened once before—nearly a century earlier. Although this first abolition of capital punishment was short-lived, it was remarkable in having largely been achieved through the efforts of a single reformer in response to the imminent hanging of a condemned prisoner.

Controversy about the death penalty is as old as the Territory of Iowa. In 1838, Governor Robert Lucas in his message to the first Territorial Assembly declared himself an opponent of "sanguinary punishments." But he reluctantly suggested that capital punishment be enforced until a penitentiary was built. The Assembly thereupon passed a law punishing murder with death.

Seven years later, in 1845, the first legal executions took place. The Hodges brothers from Nauvoo, Illinois, were convicted of murder in Burlington, and a crowd of ten thousand people watched them hang. One brother took ten minutes to die. A few months later, a large meeting launched the Iowa Anti-Capital Punishment Society. The Society denounced the death penalty as barbaric, vengeful, brutalizing of spectators, and contrary to Christianity.

The climax of the early reformers' efforts came in 1851, when Iowa very nearly became the first state to abolish capital punishment for all crimes. The legislature was considering the first Code of Iowa, and there were powerful reformers on the Code Commission and in both legislative houses. Upon its second reading, The House of Representatives and the Senate approved a provision abolishing the death penalty. Headlines of "Capital Punishment Abolished in Iowa" greeted the news. However, a forceful sermon by an Iowa City Presbyterian minister supporting the death penalty changed the minds of many members of the House of Representatives. Within days the House reversed itself and voted to retain capital punishment.

The 1851 Code did introduce a notable reform. Henceforth, second degree murder would be punished only by imprisonment. Premeditated murder in the first degree would continue to be punished by death.

Despite the failure of the legislature to abolish capital punishment in

Originally published as "The Magic of Undiscouraged Effort: The Death Penalty in Early Iowa, 1838-1878," *Annals of Iowa* 50, no. 7 (Winter 1991), pp. 721–50. Adapted by permission of the publisher.

1851, the goal remained on the state agenda. In six votes in the House or Senate between 1856 and 1870, those who sought to abolish the death penalty consistently obtained about forty percent of the vote.

Then in 1872 everything changed. A man named George Stanley was convicted of first degree murder. The Iowa Supreme Court refused Stanley's appeal, and Governor Cyrus Carpenter set April 12 as the date for his execution.

Stanley had become a Catholic while he was in prison, and his parish priests begged the governor for mercy. Two Quaker petitions "numerously signed" supported these pleas. Governor Carpenter replied that although he was personally against the death penalty, he could find no reasons justifying Stanley's reprieve. He strongly hinted that the Quakers should look to the legislature for change.

The press published the governor's letters and treated them as a call for abolition. Meanwhile Marvin Bovee—a Wisconsin farmer and America's leading opponent of capital punishment—arrived in Des Moines. Bovee gave a major speech in the hall of the House of Representatives, attended by many legislators, in which he urged the sacredness of human life: "If an individual kill his fellow man, shall the State of Iowa commit a greater outrage by deliberately killing him?"

Much of the press, led by the Des Moines newspapers, took up Bovee's arguments. Newspapers all over the state emphasized "the barbarism of the gallows" and the disgrace to Iowa of renewing hanging after twelve years without an execution.

Bovee lobbied furiously, stressing George Stanley's impending execution. Four days before the execution date, Governor Carpenter—at the request of the legislature—postponed Stanley's hanging for a month. The House then passed an abolition bill by a huge majority. But the Senate balked at this "sickly weakly sentimentalism." Supporters of the death penalty argued that it was essential as a deterrent, and that abolition would lead to lynch law. The two sides fervently exchanged quotations from the Old and New Testaments.

After two days of debate, the Senate voted to retain capital punishment. During the next nine days, Bovee lobbied to change the senators' minds. On April 20, 1872, the Senate by an overwhelming majority joined the House in voting for abolition. Iowa thus became the fourth state to abolish the death penalty. Stanley was taken to the Fort Madison prison, where he remained for thirty years.

The *Iowa State Register* credited Marvin Bovee's campaign with this victory: "Beginning, he was told there was no hope; that made no difference. Succeeding in half-way manner, he refused to accept the situation. His refusal ... led on to full success, thanks largely to his adhesion to *the magic of undiscouraged effort.*"

Efforts to restore the death penalty failed in the following two years. However, a dramatic lynching in Des Moines in December 1874 changed public opinion decisively in favor of capital punishment.

A bartender named Charles Howard was charged with a murder in Des Moines. His trial lasted three weeks and was vividly reported. After the jury had been out four days, it brought in a verdict of second degree murder.

During sentencing, Judge Hugh Maxwell called Howard "a fiend" and described lynch mobs as "our best citizens." Proclaiming, "I believe most firmly that capital punishment ought to be sustained," the judge sentenced Howard to life imprisonment. That night one hundred masked men stormed the Des Moines jail and hanged Howard from a lamppost in the courthouse yard.

Many Iowa newspapers blamed Howard's lynching on the abolition of capital punishment, declaring that Howard ought to have been legally hanged. However, a few newspapers pointed out that lynchings were common before abolition (in 1857 alone there had been nineteen lynchings), and that Howard was widely believed to be innocent. Furthermore, as Howard had only been convicted of second degree murder, he would not in any event have been sentenced to hang under the old law.

A few days later, there was an incorrect report of another lynching, and the myth of widespread mob executions sank into public consciousness. A major national financial crisis in September 1873 had led to an economic depression, which in turn had led to a major national crime wave. The increase in crime—especially murder—resulted in further calls in 1875 for restoration of the death penalty in Iowa.

In 1876, the Iowa legislature debated capital punishment at length. Petitions poured in on both sides of the issue. The restorers won the vote in the House, but could only get 25 votes in the Senate—one less than was required for a constitutional majority. Thus, the attempt to restore the death penalty failed—but only just.

The crime wave continued. In 1877, there were three convictions for murder in the first degree (compared to one in 1871), while second degree murders increased from three in 1871 to eleven in 1877. Criminal convictions overall more than doubled between 1871 and 1877.

Another widely reported lynching in late 1877 led to renewed press calls for the death penalty. That year several legislators were elected who had made campaign promises to restore capital punishment.

In 1878, the legislature again debated the issue. Those opposed to the death penalty urged that reenactment would be a retrograde step, "when this State has always been in the van of civilization." They emphasized that murders had increased just as much in states having the death penalty as in Iowa.

But the restorers won the day. Influenced by public concern over murder and lynching, the 1878 legislature voted by a large majority to restore the death penalty. Thus Iowa became the first jurisdiction in the United States and indeed the entire English-speaking world to restore capital punishment following its abolition.

Many states later imitated Iowa by abolishing capital punishment and restoring it not long afterwards. Maine abolished the death penalty in 1876 and restored it in 1883—and then re-abolished it in 1887. Between 1897 and 1920, Colorado, Washington, Oregon, Tennessee, Arizona, and Missouri all abolished and restored capital punishment within a few years. The reasons for the restorations, where they are known, were not unlike those in Iowa—specific murders, fear of a crime wave, or lynchings. The death penalty remained a part of the law of Iowa until it was again abolished in 1965.

The early history of the death penalty in Iowa is crammed with interest. Although it would last for only six years, the abolition of the death penalty in 1872 was achieved by a unique combination of an abolitionist governor, an anti-gallows press campaign spearheaded by the Des Moines newspapers, the petitions of Quakers, the pleas of Stanley's Catholic priests and, above all, Marvin Bovee's remarkable crusade.

Added to this was a legislature confronted by the prospect that George Stanley was about to hang. Four days before the scheduled execution, a leading member of the House wrote: "This brings home to every legislator the responsibility of saying whether a fellow being shall be killed by the State."

Faced with the actual decision of whether a man should live or die, the Iowa legislature overwhelmingly voted that he should live.

THE CHERRY SISTERS TAKE THEIR ACT
TO COURT

The Cherry sisters were legendary for being the worst performers in the history of American vaudeville. The sisters began performing in Iowa in 1893 and eventually moved to the national stage. Whether deliberately or by accident, their act was ludicrously bad, and audiences responded enthusiastically with jeers, tomatoes, and other projectiles.

But while the sisters could tolerate objects thrown from the audience, they could not tolerate criticism from the press. So when the *Des Moines Leader* reprinted a particularly nasty review of their act, the Cherrys took the newspaper to court. The case resulted in a classic Iowa Supreme Court decision on the law of libel—and the Cherry sisters passed from stage legend to legal legend.

The sisters were raised on a farm in Linn County. Ella was born in 1854, followed by Lizzie, Addie, Effie, and Jessie. After their father's death in 1888, "we five girls were left orphans to battle our way through life alone." The young women started a dairy business with six cows in Marion, Iowa.

Effie claimed that the idea of going on the stage was hers. In January 1893, Effie, Jesse, and Ella gave a concert in Marion before a crowd of curious onlookers. A member of the audience recalled: "[We] didn't throw things but [we] whistled and stumped and sang. Effie played the harmonica—there was absolutely no tune. One of them read an essay ... there was not a word heard. It was the audience you got the fun from."

Next the Cherrys took their act to Cedar Rapids. The *Cedar Rapids Gazette* review was damning: "Such unlimited gall as was exhibited last night at Greene's Opera House by the Cherry sisters is past understanding. ... Cigars, cigarettes, rubbers everything was thrown at them, yet they stood there, awkwardly bowing their acknowledgements and singing on."

The sisters filed an information for criminal libel against the city editor of the *Gazette,* but their lawyer persuaded them to withdraw the libel charge and instead hold a mock "trial" at Greene's Opera House. At this second performance, the "jury" in the audience sentenced the city

Condensed from "The Cherry Sisters: A Case of Libel," in *To Go Free: A Treasury of Iowa's Legal Heritage* (Iowa State University Press, 1995).

editor of the *Gazette* to work on the Cherrys' farm and to "submit himself to the choice of the said sisters ... in the holy bonds of matrimony."

The sisters' fame spread throughout Iowa. They performed in Davenport and Vinton, and then went on to Dubuque for a memorable appearance that would gain them national attention.

At the Cherrys' Dubuque performance, tin horns, cowbells, and roars from the audience drowned out the opening song. The sisters withdrew from the stage, then tried again. According to the *Dubuque Herald,* "a perfect fusilade of garden trash, decayed fruit, tin cans and other noxious missiles" showered the stage. The audience squirted the Cherrys with fire extinguishers and seltzer siphons, striking one sister full in the face. Down went the curtain.

The Cherrys tried yet again. More fruit, vegetables and seltzer greeted them. One sister came on with a shotgun, but was forced to retreat by a volley of turnips. Somebody threw a washboiler at the stage. Finally, the manager called an end.

Newspapers throughout Iowa reported the event. Within three months, the widely circulated *National Police Gazette* had printed a huge story on the sisters and the debacle at Dubuque. Thus the Cherrys became celebrities as far away as New York.

The sisters fled back to Marion, $150 the richer from their Dubuque performance. The experience had taken its toll, and Effie suffered a nervous reaction. But rested by a summer on their farm, Addie, Effie, and Jessie toured Iowa and Illinois during the next two winter seasons.

The newspapers and the Cherrys were always at war. For example, in the summer of 1895, the *Center Point Tribune* wrote that the Cherrys' arrival was timely, because "the vegetables are about the right size to toss on the stage very handily." The sisters went after the *Tribune*'s editor and "proceeded to give him a good flogging with whips." They were arrested and fined.

In La Porte in August 1895, Jessie Cherry showed that the sisters could also take on the audience. A newspaper reported: "The Cherry sisters' entertainment ended in a riot Saturday night. A gang threw onions, etc. on the stage, when one of the Sisters came down and struck Frank Fritz on the head with a club."

Then the famous impresario Oscar Hammerstein invited the Cherrys to perform in New York City. Hammerstein, in financial difficulties, is reported to have said: "I've tried the best now I'll try the worst."

The sisters' opening night at the city's Olympia Theater was relatively calm, but the following night they were pelted with vegetables. The *New York Times* wrote: "Never before did New Yorkers see anything ... like the Cherry sisters from ... Iowa. It is to be sincerely hoped that nothing like them will ever be seen again." The Cherrys stayed for four weeks, during which the price of vegetables in the vicinity of the Olympia Theater reportedly skyrocketed.

From New York City, the sisters went to Chicago, St. Louis, and Cincinnati. Next they toured in the east, from Brooklyn to Washington, D.C. This was the peak of their extraordinary career, and they were reputed to have earned considerable money.

The Cherrys were in constant legal battles. An unpublished biography reported: "The string of lawsuits growing out of the concert tours had been endless. Every season had produced its quota of arrests and counter arrests, actions for damages for property, actions for personal assault with and without weapons. They had seen Effie dragged by her hair down the aisle of a theater, Jessie belaboring a heckler with a cudgel, all three sisters combining to horsewhip an editor, rows, routs, and suits innumerable." The sisters' most famous legal battle lay ahead.

On February 9, 1898, Addie, Effie, and Jessie Cherry performed in the western Iowa town of Odebolt. The *Odebolt Chronicle* gave a vitriolic review. Under the heading "The Cherries Were Here," the report by editor William Hamilton began: "When the curtain went up on Wednesday evening of last week ... [t]he audience saw three creatures surpassing the witches in Macbeth in general hideousness."

The next passage was to be the subject of the great libel case:

> Effie is an old jade of 50 summers, Jessie a frisky filly of 40, and Addie, the flower of the family, a capering monstrosity of 35. Their long, skinny arms, equipped with talons at the extremities, swung mechanically, and anon were waved frantically at the suffering audience. The mouths of their rancid features opened like caverns, and sounds like the wailing of damned souls issued therefrom. They pranced around the stage with a motion that suggested a cross between the *danse du ventre* and a fox trot, strange creatures with painted faces and a hideous mein. Effie is spavined, Addie is knock-kneed and string-halt, and Jessie, the only one who showed her stockings, has legs without calves, as classic in their outlines as the curves of a broomhandle.

On February 23, the *Des Moines Leader* reprinted the infamous passage. All three sisters sued the *Leader* for libel, but the case was dismissed for technical legal reasons. Then Addie Cherry—whom the review had described as "knock-kneed and string-halt"—brought a separate suit against the *Leader* for libel, claiming $15,000 damages.

The case was tried in the Polk County District Court in April 1899, Judge C.A. Bishop presiding. The *Des Moines Daily News* reported that the courtroom was crowded with spectators, "anxious for a glimpse of the famous people." The Cherry sisters "were very talkative, and gave their attorneys a great deal of advice as to the manner to conduct the case."

Addie—who seriously understated her age as thirty-one—was the first witness. She testified that many people had mocked the sisters about the *Leader* review. On the streets of Des Moines, she heard: "There goes Effie, the *Leader* says she has got spavins, and Addie, she is knock-kneed and got string-halt." The review had made it difficult to obtain theatrical engagements, and had caused great distress and health problems.

During her cross-examination, Addie described a typical Cherry sisters performance:

> I recite essays ... I sing ... a kind of ballad composed by ourselves. I help the others sing it.
>
> "When the Cherry Sisters come to town, they are the cry both up and down, I want to see that modern show, and will ask Dad if I can't go."
>
> Then the chorus is Ta, ra, ra, ra, ra, Boom de ay, repeated four times. We beat the bass drum. The orchestra generally accompanies us. We kick a little with our feet.

The defendants' counsel asked Addie to show the jury how she kicked her feet, and she demonstrated. She strongly denied that spectators had ever thrown "cabbages at us, nor sticks, nor a dead cat, nor pieces of meat, nor old turnips."

Effie Cherry testified next—like Addie giving an optimistic view of her age. She complained that people on the streets repeated the *Leader*'s epithets, and even members of the Iowa legislature had drawn her attention to the review. She confirmed that Addie had indeed suffered a nervous reaction.

Jessie Cherry—who had shed a decade to proclaim her age as seventeen—was the third and final witness for the plaintiff. She testified about Addie's sleeplessness, and told how she had heard Addie described as "knock-kneed."

The sole defense witness was William Hamilton, the editor of the *Odebolt Chronicle* and the author of the original review. He testified:

> It was the most ridiculous performance I ever saw. There was no orchestra there, the pianist left after the thing was half over. She could not stand the racket ... When the curtain went up the audience shrieked, and indulged in catcalls, and from that time one could hardly hear very much to know what was going on to give a recital of it. ... The discord was something that grated on one's nerves.

Hamilton described the Cherrys' movements: "They went around the stage ... sort of a mincing gait, shaking their bodies and making little steps, that is what made me describe it as a cross between the *danse du ventre* and a fox trot."

When asked during cross-examination what he had meant in his review by "spavined," Hamilton said: "I mean a deformity of the limbs or legs, which was apparent. I could not see, but I would judge from the gait. The terms, string-halt and knock-kneed, was from the same standpoint, their appearance, walk, etc., on the stage." The defense rested.

The defendants then asked the judge to instruct the jury to find in the defendants' favor, because the article had been published without express malice and was "conditionally privileged." Judge Bishop agreed, and the jury duly entered a verdict for the *Leader.*

When Judge Bishop gave his ruling, Addie Cherry became very excited and, rising to her feet, announced that she wanted to say something about the case. Addie's attorney pushed her back into her chair, and the judge gave her a stern look.

Addie Cherry appealed her adverse ruling to the Iowa Supreme Court, which—on May 28, 1901—affirmed the judgment. The Court found that the review was "qualifiedly privileged," and gave broad scope to the right of comment on a public performance: "One who goes upon the stage ... may be freely criticised. He may be held up to ridicule, and entire freedom of expression is guarantied dramatic critics, provided they are not actuated by malice or evil purpose in what they write."

The Court affirmed the district court's ruling, concluding: "If there ever was a case justifying ridicule and sarcasm,—aye, even gross exaggeration,—it is the one now before us. [T]he performance given by the plaintiff and the company of which she was a member was not only childish, but ridiculous in the extreme. A dramatic critic should be allowed considerable license in such a case."

The case of *Cherry vs. Des Moines Leader* has since been regarded as having established important principles of libel law. One authority has described it as "[t]he case that is so often cited in judicial rulings on fair comment and criticism."

The Cherry sisters continued their tours until 1903, when Jessie Cherry suddenly died in Hot Springs, Arkansas, from typhoid and malaria. The other sisters retired from the stage, but over the years attempted periodic comebacks. However, their legendary days were behind them.

Addie and Effie both died in the 1940s, and on the death of the latter in August 1944, *The New York Times* published an obituary describing their act as "artistically the worst on any stage." But the *Times* concluded with what may have been the Cherry sisters' best review:

> Maybe the laugh was on their side. Maybe the Cherry sisters knew better than the public did what was really going on. Be this as it may, they left behind an imperishable memory. And they gave more pleasure to their audiences than did many a performer who was merely almost good.

A BRITISH SUFFRAGETTE CAMPAIGNS IN DES MOINES

Seventy-five years ago, the Nineteenth Amendment to the U.S. Constitution, whereby voting rights could not be denied "by the United States or by any State on account of sex," became the law of the land. In July 1919, Iowa had been the tenth state to ratify this amendment. For the supporters of woman suffrage in the state, the road had been long and arduous.

Des Moines Register, February 1, 1995.

One milestone had been reached in 1897. In that year, the convention of the National-American Woman Suffrage Association met in Des Moines. Some of the leading delegates, including Susan B. Anthony and Carrie Chapman Catt, were invited to speak to the Iowa Senate. But it seems that the first woman to address *both* houses of the Iowa legislature in a joint session was actually a foreigner—the English suffragette Sylvia Pankhurst.

Born in 1882, Sylvia Pankhurst was the second daughter of Emmeline Pankhurst, who founded the Women's Social and Political Union (the WSPU) in 1903. Emmeline and her eldest daughter, Christabel, were the moving force of the WSPU, which became increasingly militant in its efforts to obtain votes for women. (The militants came to be known as "suffragettes," as distinct from the non-militant "suffragists.")

Sylvia Pankhurst, an artist and writer, also threw herself into the cause of woman suffrage, and by the time she came to Iowa in 1911, had already been in prison twice. Subsequent to her visit, during 1913 and 1914, she was imprisoned eleven more times. The pattern of these last imprisonments was the same. She would go on hunger strike—and thirst strike and sleep strike—and the authorities would subject her to the agony of forced feeding. On release from prison, she would soon be re-arrested, and the cycle repeated.

In 1910, Sylvia Pankhurst wrote a history of her mother's movement called *The Suffragette,* and thereafter followed in Emmeline's footsteps to the United States for a lecture tour. Her purpose was to raise money for the WSPU and promote the cause of woman suffrage.

After a successful first lecture in New York on January 6, 1911, the twenty-eight-year-old Sylvia Pankhurst embarked on her travels. She had a personal friend in Boone, Iowa, named Rowena Stevens, who arranged that Pankhurst should lecture in that city on February 1st. Representative Goodykoontz of Boone introduced a joint resolution in the Iowa House: "That inasmuch as Miss Sylvia Pankhurst of England will be in the city of Des Moines tomorrow, February 1st, that she be invited to address the Joint Convention just after the Senatorial ballot is taken." The House and Senate unanimously agreed.

The English suffragette knew nothing of this invitation. Travelling by sleeper car from Kansas City, she alighted at the Union Station in Des Moines about 8:00 A.M. on February 1st with a terrible cold and a vast number of bundles. "I must hurry and take that Boone train," she said to a reporter. "You will help me, won't you?"

The reporter told Pankhurst she was to address the joint session at the Statehouse. "I never believe reporters," she said. "I must get that train to Boone."

However, members of the local suffragist committee convinced Pankhurst that she was, indeed, to speak to the legislature. She was whisked by cab to the Chamberlain Hotel, and a woman osteopath attended to her cold.

When, at noon, Sylvia Pankhurst walked down the aisle of a crowded House of Representatives, she was greeted by a burst of applause, started by woman suffragists and taken up by the male legislators. She began her speech nervously, but as she came to talk about the English suffrage movement, her confidence increased.

Pankhurst expressed her gratitude for the privilege of addressing the Iowa legislature, at a time when women's attempts to talk to English legislators resulted in their being imprisoned. She told how a procession of women had tried to present a petition to Parliament and was stopped by an army of mounted policemen. After a seven-hour struggle, she and many other women were arrested. She described the miseries of prison and how some of her friends had been force-fed by having tubes thrust down their throats.

As a result of their years of campaigning, Pankhurst was convinced Parliament soon would give women the vote. (It took longer than she thought. In 1918, eight and one-half million British women were enfranchised on an age and property qualification; in 1928, the vote was finally extended to women on the same basis as men.)

The English suffragette then turned to America. "Women here are taxed without representation ... which is unamerican. They are forced to stand trial in courts without a voice in the government and direction of those courts." Women were an increasing part of the work force and should be entitled to take part in shaping industrial and social legislation.

"Your women will press forward and demand the vote much as we have had to do in England," Pankhurst prophesied. "They are determined. They cannot be checked. Do not press them to militancy."

She declared that women's lives were too empty. "We give our women too little to do; all we ask of her is to see that the dinner is well cooked and the washing comes home properly from the laundry." Giving women political rights would not, however, break up the home. "Great ideas and great ideals never brought dissension into any home."

Pankhurst ended her speech with a prediction: "Your women in Iowa will be more grateful in time for the franchise than for any other boon that you can grant them."

On the motion of Senator W.S. Allen of Jefferson County, the legislators gave Sylvia Pankhurst a unanimous vote of thanks for her address. Lt. Governor Clarke asked "for a rising vote," and the entire Assembly stood for the speaker.

After a reception, the English suffragette went on to Boone with her friend, Rowena Stevens, and was able to have a short rest at her home. That evening, Pankhurst—whose cold had got worse—gave a two-hour speech at the Christian Church in Boone. Harriet B. Evans, president of the Iowa Woman Suffrage Association, and many other suffragists from all over the state were in the large audience. The *Boone News-Republican* observed: "She had created a most favorable impression for herself and her cause."

Sylvia Pankhurst's stay in Iowa was brief. Two days later, on February 3rd, she was speaking in Cincinnati, Ohio. She spent two more months travelling and lecturing the length and breadth of the United States before sailing back to England.

Many years later, Sylvia Pankhurst wrote in an autobiographical book, *The Suffragette Movement,* of her visit to Des Moines and her deep feeling of responsibility at having to address the Iowa legislature. She modestly summed up the episode:

"The women assured me I had helped them."

GOVERNOR HARDING PROCLAIMS WAR ON FOREIGN LANGUAGES

During World War I, many states restricted the public use of the German language. In Iowa—where about 41 percent of the population was either foreign-born or born of foreign parents—

Condensed from "Governor Harding's Proclamation and the School Language Law: 1918–1923," in *To Go Free: A Treasury of Iowa's Legal Heritage* (Iowa State University Press, 1995).

Governor William Harding sought to go much further. At the height of the war, he issued a proclamation that purported to ban the public use of all foreign languages, even those of America's allies.

The United States entered the war in April 1917. At a large "Loyalty Conference" in September, Harding pointed to the number of foreign settlements in America with their own languages and customs. "[T]he pot has not melted," he complained. "[T]here should be a strong sentiment created for the use of the American language in school, in pulpit and in press."

A major Americanization conference held at Washington, D.C., in April 1918 advocated that all preaching and teaching in German be prohibited. Soon afterwards, Iowa schools dropped the teaching of German; German textbooks were removed from schools and destroyed.

During April and May, signs went up in various Iowa towns, like the one at Le Mars:

> If you Are An American at Heart
> Speak OUR Language
> If you Don't Know It
> LEARN IT
> If you Don't Like It
> MOVE

On May 23, 1918, Harding issued his foreign-language proclamation. Henceforth, all teaching in schools, all conversation in public places, trains, and over telephone lines, and all public speeches and religious services should be in English.

Most Iowans appeared to support the proclamation. The *Council Bluffs Nonpareil,* which opposed Harding politically, on May 31 wrote: "The governor may have no law in support of his position but he does have public sentiment."

However, many foreign language speakers were openly angry. At Grand View College, a Danish pastor made a passionate speech challenging the constitutionality of the proclamation. He defiantly ended with a prayer in Danish, declaring: "I do not believe that any power on Earth has a right to dictate what language a man must speak to the living God."

The same day, Harding told the Chamber of Commerce in Des Moines: "[T]hose who insist upon praying in some other language ... are wasting their time for the good Lord up above is now listening for the voice in English."

A Danish pastor from Cedar Falls wrote to Harding that he was incensed the governor would thus "mock the thousands of praying men and women of foreign extraction ... within the state of Iowa." Harding replied: "I cannot see how any loyal American citizen able to speak English could desire to use another language in voicing his supplications to the Almighty."

Letters protesting against the proclamation poured into the governor's office, while the *Des Moines Register* and other newspapers printed critical editorials. Harding responded in a published letter that the proclamation was necessary because German propaganda had been spread in foreign languages. But he allowed that religious services conducted in English could be followed by a repetition of the sermon in a foreign language.

Disobedience to the proclamation resulted in a malicious incident in Mahaska County where, on June 13, a Dutch language church was burned down. That same day, the First Reformed Church at Pella voted to substitute English for Dutch at its services.

The main burden of the proclamation inevitably fell on German-speaking Iowans. On June 14, 1918, the chairman of the Scott County Defense Council summoned four Le Claire women, accused of speaking German over a rural telephone line. Mrs. Herman Lippold, the principal accused, stated: "I just asked my daughter 'How are you?' in German." Her daughter added that she only spoke German on the telephone when her mother failed to understand in English.

The chairman fined the women $225 and ordered them to sign pledge cards of membership in their local Defense Council. Mrs. Lippold, who wept openly during the hearing, exclaimed: "I'll never talk over the telephone again."

For the most part, Iowans obeyed the proclamation—even the Welsh language congregation at Williamsburg ceased holding services. Where the proclamation was disobeyed, some local patriotic associations took disciplinary action. A Sac County man was fined $25 (payable to the Red Cross) for repeatedly speaking German. Musicians of the Davenport Symphony Orchestra were ordered to stop using German at rehearsals. The Waverly Glee Club was forbidden to sing "The Blue Danube" in German.

Various clergymen received reprimands for using German during church services. The Jasper County Council of Defense ordered a minister to cease holding services in Dutch, and the Page County National Defense Council did the same to two Swedish-speaking pastors. The Lyon County Council of Defense stopped a preacher from conducting hymns in Norwegian.

The *Des Moines Register* repeatedly challenged the constitutionality of Harding's proclamation. Harding—himself a lawyer from Sioux City—attempted to defend its legality in a June 1918 speech before the Iowa State Bar Association. He argued that the constitutional freedoms of speech and religion did not guarantee the right to use languages other than English, particularly when their use created discord in wartime. However, in a widely circulated August 2 letter, Harding admitted his proclamation lacked legal teeth, writing that the "violation of a proclamation issued by an Executive does not carry a penalty."

Foreign language speakers did not challenge the proclamation in court; instead, they responded at the polls. In November 1918, Harding's share of the vote plummeted to 51.3 percent from 62.6 percent in 1916. Harding blamed the plunge primarily on those disgruntled by his proclamation.

With the Armistice on November 11, 1918, the wartime proclamation lapsed—but the English language question did not. During his inaugural address to the legislature in January 1919, Harding urged "that all schools use English as the medium of instruction in all branches."

In response, the legislature enacted a law, effective in July 1919, whereby English became the sole medium of instruction for secular subjects in public and private schools. The act permitted foreign languages to be taught as cultural studies above the eighth grade.

Two German Lutheran synods decided to test the constitutionality of the English language law in court. The test case concerned the Reverend August Bartels, a Lutheran minister and schoolmaster in Bremer County.

In January 1920, the president of Bartels' synod filed a "friendly" information with the justice of the peace court in Waverly, charging that Bartels had taught reading in German to pupils below the eighth grade at a Lutheran parochial school. Bartels was found guilty and fined $25. The district court upheld the conviction.

Bartels appealed to the Iowa Supreme Court, which, by a four-to-three majority, affirmed the conviction. The Court reasoned that there was "no inherent right ... to teach German to children of tender years that cannot lawfully be denied by the legislature when [it determines that] such right under existing conditions is inimical to the best interests of the state."

Bartels took his case to the United States Supreme Court. On June 4, 1923, the Court handed down separate decisions concerning similar statutes in Nebraska, Iowa, and Ohio. In *Meyer vs. Nebraska,* it ruled that the Nebraska statute violated the liberty interest guaranteed by the Fourteenth Amendment to the United States Constitution.

Justice McReynolds wrote for the majority:

> Mere knowledge of the German language cannot reasonably be re-
> garded as harmful. ... [The teacher's] right thus to teach and the right
> of parents to engage him to instruct their children, we think are
> within the liberty of the [Fourteenth] Amendment. ... The protection
> of the Constitution extends to all, to those who speak other lan-
> guages as well as to those born with English on the tongue.

Then the Court delivered its opinion in *Bartels vs. Iowa.* Based upon its ruling in *Meyer,* the Court reversed the judgment of the Iowa Supreme Court, holding that the Iowa statute was subject to the same constitutional objections as the Nebraska statute. The *[Iowa] Lutheran Herald* rejoiced: "[T]he highest tribunal of the country has again upheld the principle of religious and civil liberty all chauvinistic agitation to the contrary notwithstanding."

Before his famous court case, August Bartels had written: "We Germans are rapidly adopting the English language." This trend was conspicuous in the churches.

The German Lutheran Church Missouri Synod (Iowa District) in 1919 held 57 percent of its services in German. By 1929, the number had fallen to 41 percent. During 1931, the synod made English its official language. Over the next fifteen years, the number of its churches holding their services half in German and half in English declined dramatically, from sixty-five in 1930 to only ten in 1946.

Governor Harding would have been pleased.

"ENOUGH BLOOD AND HELL":
BONNIE AND CLYDE IN IOWA

Some day they'll go down together;
And they'll bury them side by side;
To few it'll be grief—
To the law a relief—
But it's death for Bonnie and Clyde.
—BONNIE PARKER, 1934

In the early 1930s, the Barrow gang passed into American folklore. The 1967 film, *Bonnie and Clyde,* with Warren Beatty and Faye Dunaway, enhanced their myth. But the junior member of the gang, W.D. Jones, stressed the horrible reality: "That Bonnie and Clyde movie made it all look sort of glamorous, but like I told them teenaged boys sitting near me at the drive-in showing: 'Take it from an old man who was there. It was hell.'" The gang's most hellish episode took place in July 1933 near the little town of Dexter, Iowa.

Twenty-four-year-old Clyde Barrow dominated the gang. The 5'7", 125-pound son of a Texas tenant farmer, Clyde began stealing cars as a seventeen-year-old in Dallas. He later progressed to armed robbery—his targets were small stores, gasoline stations, and sometimes banks. During 1932 and early 1933, Clyde murdered seven men, bringing him nationwide notoriety.

From August 1932, twenty-two-year-old Bonnie Parker—a 4'10", 85-pound former waitress from Dallas—was Clyde's constant companion as they drove stolen cars throughout the southwest. Obsessed by Clyde and his life of crime, Bonnie celebrated their lives in verse. Her best known poem, "The Story of Bonnie and Clyde," was widely published after her death.

W.D. Jones joined Clyde and Bonnie in December 1932. A seventeen-year-old petty criminal, Jones had known and hero-worshipped Clyde since their Dallas childhoods. On Christmas Day, Jones helped Clyde steal a car. Clyde murdered the owner and, as an accomplice, Jones became locked into the gang.

Clyde's elder brother, Buck, had received a five-year prison sentence for robbery in 1929. He escaped and, during 1931, married Blanche

---

"'Hell' in Dexfield Park," *The Iowan* (Spring 1994).

Caldwell, a tiny young woman whom his sister called "a splendid, gentle, good country girl." When Blanche discovered that Buck was an escaped convict, she got him to surrender. Later, she persuaded the Texas governor to pardon her husband. When the twenty-eight-year-old Buck—an even smaller man than Clyde—left prison in March 1933, he arranged a "family reunion" with his brother. Although Buck's plan made Blanche cry for two days, she went with him.

This strangely assorted quintet rented an apartment in Joplin, Missouri. Police spotted and surrounded them, but they shot their way out. Clyde killed two officers, while Blanche ran away screaming. Buck had held a gun, and thereafter he and Blanche also were locked into the gang.

In June 1933, Clyde had a car crash; the car caught fire and Bonnie was trapped in the flames. Clyde and Jones pulled her free, but she was shockingly burned. Jones recalled: "The hide on her right leg was gone from her hip down to her ankle. I could see the bone at places." It was months before she could walk again.

As Bonnie lay suffering, Buck and Jones robbed two Piggly-Wiggly grocery stores in Arkansas. While they were escaping, Buck killed a marshal. By mid-July, Bonnie was able to travel, but she had to be lifted in and out of the car. Needing funds, the gang drove northwards to Fort Dodge, Iowa, where the women were left outside the city. Buck drove, while Clyde and Jones robbed three gas stations of $150. The gang escaped to a tavern in Platte City, Missouri.

Their movements aroused the suspicion of local authorities, and at 11:00 P.M. the next night, officers raided the Barrows' cabins. The gang again shot their way out, wounding the sheriff. Even Blanche was reported to have fired. Buck was shot, the bullet passing through his skull, and the others dragged him into the car. As Clyde drove off, a volley of bullets shattered the car's rear windows. The glass cut Blanche's face and permanently blinded her in one eye.

A maimed gang re-entered Iowa on Thursday, July 20. Blood oozed from Buck's awful head wound; Blanche was half-blind; Bonnie was still crippled. A farmer at Caledonia, near Mount Ayr, watched Clyde, Blanche, and Jones burn bloody bandages and clothing. The gang bought food and gas in Caledonia and headed north.

Clyde decided to lie low until Buck's wound improved. He chose a spot next to Dexfield Park, a disused amusement park near Dexter, thirty miles from Des Moines. They drove up a side road and stopped in a small wooded area from which trees stretched down to the South Raccoon River.

Each day Clyde drove into Dexter to buy food at the Blohm Cafe. He got remedies and bandages from the Pohle and Stanley Drug Stores. When Mr. Stanley asked the purpose of all the gauze and bandages, Clyde pretended he was a veterinarian.

On Sunday, July 23, the gang drove to the nearby town of Perry, where Jones stole another car. During their absence, a farmer picking berries came upon their camp. Half-burned, bloody bandages made him suspicious, and he told the Dexter special deputy, John Love, what he had found. The latter, after watching the gang through binoculars, reported to the local county sheriff. Guessing they were the Barrow gang, the sheriff requested men with automatic guns from Des Moines.

That night, local armed men guarded Dexfield Park and the adjacent area. Later county officers arrived, and at midnight state officers, deputies, and police from Des Moines joined the posse. By the morning of Monday, July 24, fifty armed men surrounded the Barrows' camp on three sides. The posse left the side leading to the river unguarded.

At 6:00 A.M., Jones was roasting some leftover wieners on a small fire. Clyde and Bonnie were sitting on a car cushion, and Buck and Blanche were in the back of one of the cars. The posse was within fifty feet of the gang when Bonnie and Clyde saw them. The Barrows went for their automatic Browning rifles and automatic pistols. As they fired, the posse took refuge behind logs and trees and let loose a fusillade of bullets, badly wounding all the gang except Blanche. Only one of the posse, Rags Riley of Des Moines, was injured.

After a two-minute gun battle, the Barrows took to a car. Clyde drove onto a tree stump and got stuck. Jones tried to pry the car off with a rifle, but was unsuccessful. The posse's bullets had wrecked the other car, so the Barrows had to run. Jones carried the lame Bonnie. Blanche helped Buck, who was now wounded in the hip as well. The gang vanished into the woods.

Clyde realized that Buck could not keep up. Blanche would not leave him, so the others deserted them and made for the river. Jones waited with Bonnie, while Clyde went toward the road to steal a car. The editor of the *Dexter Sentinel* and another armed man were guarding the bridge. Clyde saw them and called: "Don't shoot." Thinking him a colleague, they held their fire. Clyde ducked behind a large tree, began shooting, and another gun battle raged. When his ammunition ran out, Clyde hastened back to Bonnie and Jones.

The two men half swam, half stumbled across the river, with Bonnie on Jones' back. They came out wet and bloody. Clyde's right leg and shoulder were wounded, and a bullet had grazed his head. Jones, bleeding profusely, had been hit six times. Bonnie had been shot in the chest and stomach. They made their way into a cornfield.

The farm belonged to Valley Fellers. He, his son, and a hired man were feeding the livestock when Clyde appeared, brandishing a pistol—unknown to them empty. Clyde threatened to shoot their dog. Then he whistled, and Jones emerged from the corn carrying Bonnie. Clyde ordered the Fellers to fetch their car.

Jones handed Bonnie over the fence to Valley Fellers, who remarked on her condition. Clyde said that he had given her a shot of morphine to deaden the pain. The Fellers carried Bonnie to the back seat of their Plymouth. The son showed Clyde—who usually stole Fords—how to operate the gear lever. Then Clyde and Jones got in and drove off.

After the trio had a flat tire, they stole another car in Polk City. They abandoned the Fellers' car, its seats covered in blood, and disappeared.

Meanwhile the Fellers reported that only three of the gang had escaped. Cautiously the posse searched the woods and, at about 8:00 A.M., some deputies found Buck and Blanche hiding behind a log. Buck held a pistol threateningly, so Dr. H.W. Keller, a Des Moines dentist, shot him in the shoulder.

Buck stiffened as if dead, and Blanche screamed. Two men caught her by her arms. Blanche struggled, and then shrieked to Buck lying on the ground: "Don't die, don't die!"

The men carried Buck into Dexfield Park, laid him down, and sent for a car. Buck asked for a cigarette, and Dr. Keller lit him one. Blanche, looking down at her wounded husband, cried: "Daddy, Daddy, are you all right?" Buck quietly answered, "Sure Baby, I'm all right."

Police drove the Barrows to a doctor in Dexter, where a thousand people thronged to glimpse the notorious gangsters. The doctor bandaged Blanche's blind eye and Buck's grievous wounds. Asked by police where he was wanted, Buck said: "Wherever I've been." The police drove Buck to the hospital in Perry, and Blanche to the Polk County jail in Des Moines.

At the site of the gun battle, branches had been shot off the trees and souvenir hunters dug bullets out of the wood. Spectators gaped at the Barrows' cars riddled with bullet holes. Among the gang's effects, the police found thirty-two automatic pistols, two revolvers, two automatic rifles ... and a Bible.

In the jailhouse, Blanche—still dressed in a thin, once-pink blouse, blood-stained khaki trousers, and leather riding boots—answered questions. She said of the shoot-out: "I figured it was the end." She denied using a gun: "There was plenty of hell but I didn't contribute to it."

Later Missouri authorities interviewed Blanche about the shoot-out at Platte City, and the next day removed her to the Platte City jail. Eventually Blanche pleaded guilty to assaulting the sheriff with intent to kill, and received a ten-year prison sentence, serving six years.

Meanwhile in the Perry hospital, Buck lay dying from the head wound received in Missouri. He admitted to the murder of the Arkansas marshal, and said to an Arkansas officer: "It was a good thing you got out of the way or you might have got yours."

Soon Buck's mother arrived from Texas. She sat by his bedside, while he called for Blanche and Clyde. On Saturday, July 29, Buck died. He was buried in Texas.

Police in Broken Bow, Nebraska, found the car that Clyde and Jones had stolen in Polk City, Iowa. The inside was covered in blood and strewn with empty medicine bottles, press photos of the Barrows, and a Des Moines newspaper dated the day of the Iowa shoot-out.

The fugitives drove through state after state. For W.D. Jones, Dexfield Park was the end. At the first opportunity—in Mississippi—he escaped from Clyde and Bonnie. As Jones put it: "I'd had enough blood and hell." He was arrested in Texas and received a fifteen-year sentence for murder, serving six years.

When they recovered, Clyde and Bonnie resumed their nomadic life—stealing and driving, forever driving. In early 1934, Clyde killed two or three more men, and Bonnie is said to have murdered a police officer. That year they returned to Iowa. The evidence is that on January 31 in Rockwell City, they stole a set of Iowa license plates numbered 13-1234. The next day, Clyde robbed $300 from a bank at nearby Knierim.

Apparently Clyde and Bonnie even came back to the Dexfield Park area. On April 16 in Stuart, near Dexter, a young woman waited outside a bank in a car—license plates number Iowa 13-1234—while two untidy men stole $1,500. Soon afterwards, they roared through Dexter at over 80 miles per hour. Then, on May 3, robbers escaped with $700 from a bank in Everly in northwest Iowa—their license number was Iowa 13-1234.

In Louisiana three weeks later, on May 23, 1934, Texas and local lawmen ambushed Clyde and Bonnie in their Ford and riddled them with bullets. Among the license plates in their car was Iowa number 13-1234.

Five members of the Barrow gang had come to Dexfield Park. Ultimately, the three principals were killed by law officers, and the two lesser members spent years in prison.

W.D. Jones was right. The gang's story was not glamorous. It was hell.

Postscript
A Brit Among the Hawkeyes

DEAR EDWARD,

In an earlier letter to you, I wrote that the most important thing about any place is the people, and how kind the people of Iowa are. I hope a glimmer of that attribute comes through as you read this book.

To complete the story, I think I should tell you about one particular episode that illustrates so much about my sojourn among the Hawkeyes.

Just before Christmas last year, I went to post some Christmas cards at the main Cedar Rapids post office, which serves 110,000 people. Eventually I got to the front of the queue, and the clerk told me that my dozen cards—all destined for England by air mail—cost sixty cents each. Having stamped them, I wished her a "Happy Christmas" and went on my way.

The next day I got a letter from her—the envelope was marked "Important!!" She explained that as my cards were a "non-standard" size (she drew the exact dimensions), each needed an additional eleven cents postage. She continued:

> I went ahead and put the additional postage on the letters you left today, but I wanted you to know before you mail any more.
>
> Sincerely,
> *Betty,* for the Post Office

At the busiest time of the entire year, Betty—out of kindness and out of her own money—was prepared to pay the extra postage on my Christmas cards.

Do you wonder that I like it here?

Your loving brother,
A Brit Among the Hawkeyes